GREEK MYTHOLOGY

ELIZABETH SPATHARI
ARCHAEOLOGIST

PAPADIMAS
EKDOTIKI

CONTENTS

INTRODUCTION

*M*ythology belongs to the intellectual creations of the Greek people. It is also a kind of poetry expressing, through its structure and content, the judgements of the Hellenes concerning life, its laws and paradoxes, man's destiny and the universe surrounding him.

Mythology consists of the myths created by the Greek intellect, when **REASON** had not found its role in the development of the mind and the phaenomena of the mysterious universe remained inexplicable.

Then, man attempted to turn the mysteries of an aenigmatic world into reality and created the **MYTH**. His resort to it was a way to interpret the questions torturing him, a way to overcome his fears before the unknown, an answer to everything his inner self was hiding.

What is the myth, though? It is a narration which combines real and imaginary events and refers to gods, heroes, of course, but also to social phaenomena, and is handed down from generation to generation by word of mouth.

The myth lies beyond human experience and, combined with imagination, explains man's environment.

Imagination is, mainly, what drives him from the early years to understand everything his reasoning is not able to explain, because man needs to see immortal beings surmount death and the infeasible become feasible.

To achieve this, he has always been aided by his "mytholigising conscience", which made up the myth for its fulfillment. This way the Greeks created the myths connected with their religious faith, and created gods who they enhanced with exquisite beauty. They created heroes, excellent figures of their past, and adorned them with accomplishments, which became an eternal focus of admiration and could be put up as emblems.

The Greek theology and heroic mythology did not remain mere folk narratives, like in many other peoples; they inspired poetry and the arts that offered topics exclusively from the world of the myths, about the gods and the heroes who consisted the main source of inspiration for painters, poets and, mainly, song makers. Every Greek region had its myths and saw that they are projected so as to symbolise glorious deeds of modern people.

The Greek myth owes its perpetuity to a crowd of epic, lyric and drama poets, who, through its content, made it an agent of the ideals of the Greek civilisation. In the myths they made up, there are depicted the characteristics of the Greek intellect, such as the joy of life, the love for beauty and a fighting spirit, which went beyond the limits of the Greek world and offered its ideals to the entire humanity.

Today, a time of triumph of the sciences and technology, a self-complacent time as far as the triumph of the human mind is concerned, but also a time when the human ideals have vanished and the individual as a human being has been ruined, the publication of the GREEK MYTHOLOGY may be considered utopic by certain people.

However, our aim is to offer the readers of today a Mythology simply written, accessible to the majority of people, which can be read by younger and older people alike. A Mythology whose purpose is to please its readers but also, along with the joy of life it will cause, it will remind them of the lines of the tragic poet

"There is plenty to admire but nothing is more wondrous than man"

Sophocles, Antigone, v. 334.

COSMOGONY

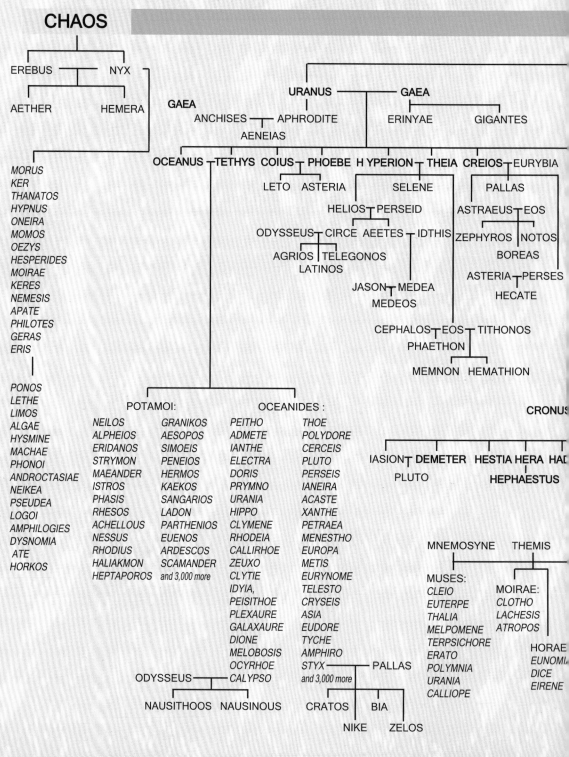

THEOGONY

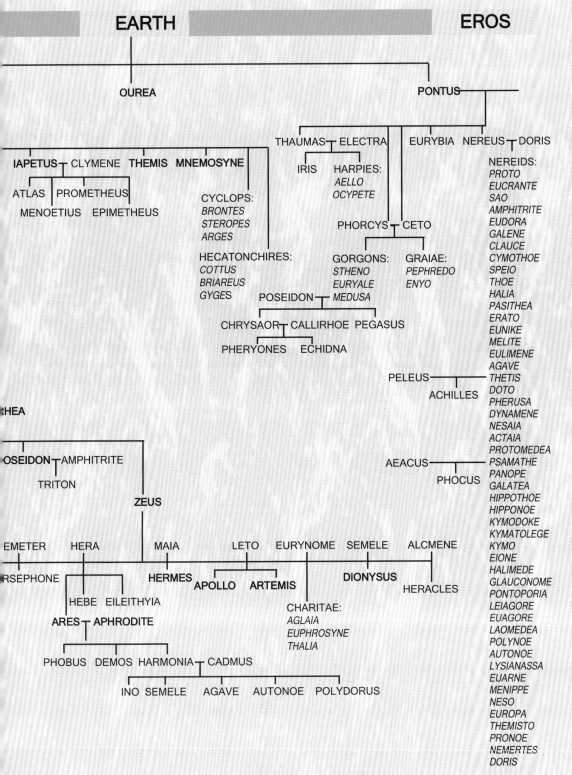

COSMOGONY
THEOGONY

C osmogony, the eternal question of origin, of "the beginning of beings", the creation of the changeable phenomena which are born and decayed, and, mainly, the human need to justify the precedents, the uncertain and the abstract, created the theogonic and the cosmogonic legends. In times when the human mind is still in childhood and "reason" takes a small place in a people's life, the legend becomes their intellectual creation, the expression of their inner worries and the inexplicable phenomenon of nature as well as their judgement on the laws and the paradox of life, and on fate and death. Thus, they philosophise through legends even before philosophy is born.

The meta-Mycenaean centuries fostered the admiration for the creation from which the Greek myth originates. It was then when people showed this inclination and the myths about gods and humans were created. This myth-making disposition ceased when reason wiped it out and when the deeds of gods and people mentioned in myths were considered to be another kind of very early history or even symbols or allegories. During the four centuries of the Hellenic thought through the myths, there evolved a peculiar "culture" which filled the life of the Hellenes and became an endless source of inspiration in art. The first mythical image of the universe is depicted in the poetic creations by Homer and Hesiod. In **Hesiod's Theogony**, creation began from **Chaos**, a shapeless blurred material which, however, defines that nothing begins from nothingness. After Chaos, there came the wide-bosomed **Gaea** (Earth), the ever-sure foundation of the immortals, a vast and flat surface with plains and waters. Later, Gaea put up **Uranus** (Sky) over her, a compact vaulted construction traversed by stars. From Chaos came forth **Erebus** (Darkness) and **Nyx** (Night); of Nyx were born **Aether (**Brightness) and **Hemera** (Day)**, Hypnos** (Sleep) and **Thanatos** (Death), who are brothers.

Athena from the pediment depicting the Gigantomachy (6th c. B.C.) Athens, the Acropolis Museum

The **Hellenic Theogony** arises from a female goddess, **Gaea**, who possesses a birth-giving power and bears **Uranus,** the **Ourea** (Mountains), **Thalassa** (Pontus - the Sea), the natural forces. From her union of love with Uranus were born a number of powerful beings, such as twelve **Titans** and **Titanides**, as well as Six Monsters: the three **Cyclops** and the three **Hecatonchires.** In the intellect of the Hellenes, the great work of creation, an incessant process in nature, initially appears in the form of a couple (i.e. Gaea with Uranus); that is to say, the fertilising element, with mother Earth conceiving, giving birth and nursing. The next divine dynasty consists of the children of a Titan, **Cronus**, three gods and three goddesses, the Cronides, who will be joined by the children (six sons and six daughters) of Zeus - to comprise **The Twelve Gods** of the Homeric deities. The first deity in the Greek mythology, Gaea, who never lost her power, is certain to have come in existence before the divine family of the Homeric epics. This is why both gods and heroes in Homer always swear by her name. This deity is the mother not only of the beings born from the earth but also of the people who owe their nutrition to her.

The cosmogonic poetry of Homer and Hesiod first pose the question of "the birth of everything". Examined genealogy-wise by poetry, this issue is examined from the perspective of rationale by philosophy. The Hellenes in Ionia first pose the question of the origin of the world and the myth passes the torch to word. This word, which is born at the far western edge of Asia, bears fruit in the west. Under the veil of myth, Asia is dissociated from Europe, where the intellectual works of the Hellenes are infused, resulting in becoming the continent of word, logic, science and technology.

The twin sons of Nyx, Hypnos and Thanatos, are removing dead Sarpedon from the battlefield; red-figured calyx- crater (appr. 510 B.C.) New York, Metropolitan Museum

THE TITANS – CRONUS

According to Hesiod's Theogony, **the Titans**, children of **Gaea** and **Uranus**, brothers of the Cyclops and the Hecatonchires, were twelve, equal in number with the Olympian gods. The six male Titans were **Oceanus, Coeus, Krios, Hyperion, Iapetus** and **Cronus,** the youngest. There also were six female Titanides: **Theia, Rhea, Themis, Mnemosene, Tethys** and **Phoebe.** More recent poets refer to a lot more names such as **Atlas, Prometheus, Apollo, Hero** and **Perses** as Titans.

Uranus was disgusted at the Titans, for they were violent and primitive beings of chaos, therefore, he imprisoned them deep down in the Earth. The Earth, however, who suffered from the burden in her bowels, decided to free them and avenge Uranus. She was assisted by their youngest son Cronus, who using a sickle (very sharp scythe) castrated him and threw his father's members away. From the blood of Uranus which splattered onto the Earth were born the **Giants,** the **Meliai Nymphs** and **Erinyes** (the Furies), cruel avengers on those having committed serious crimes. From the severed testicles of Uranus which fell into the sea was born honoured Aphrodite having with her Eros (Love) and Imerus (Desire).

Cronus took his father's throne, bound the Cyclops and the Hecatonchires whereas he freed his brothers, the Titans. The first born of them, **Oceanus,** and **Tethys** became a couple

Two Couretes are clashing their shields in an attempt to drown the crying of little Zeus, who is in Amalthea's arms; marble bas-relief of the era of Augustus. Paris, Louvre

and had three thousand sons, Potamoi (the rivers), and an equal number of daughters, the nymphs of the fountains and the lakes, the Oceanides.

Hyperion married **Theia** who gave birth to Helios (Sun), Selene (Moon) and Eos (Dawn). **Coeus** married **Phoebe** and had Asteria and Leto whom Zeus fell in love with and had Apollo and Artemis. **Crius** married **Eurybia**, daughter of Pontus, and had three sons: Astraeus, Pallas and Perses. **Astraeus** married **Eos** and had Boreas, Notos and Zephyrus, while **Pallas** and **Styx** sired Cratos (Strength), Bia (Force), Dynamis (Power), Zelos (Zeal) and Nike (Victory). **Perses** and Asteria gave birth to **Hecate**, an important goddess who preceded the Olympian gods. **Iapetus** married the Oceanid nymph **Clymene** and had Atlas, Menoetius, Prometheus and Epimetheus.

Finally, Cronus married Rhea and had three daughters, Hestia, Demeter and Hera, as well as three sons, Hades, Poseidon and Zeus.

When the abovementioned sons reached manhood, they ruled the world after they divided it; Zeus governed the sky, Poseidon was the master of the seas and Hades was responsible for the Under World.

Although Cronus had taken his father's throne, he could not feel at ease because his parents, Uranus and Gaea, had told him that he was to be overthrown by one of his offspring. This is why the moment he had a child he swallowed it and kept it within his body to ensure none of his children would rise against him. Then Gaea, heartbroken by the fact that she could not enjoy the children she birthed, asked for her parents' help who advised her to come up with a way to protect her son from his father. When she gave birth to her youngest son, **Zeus**, Rhea took him to Crete and hid him in "Mount Aigaion", (Goat Mountain). Before this, however, she swaddled a stone and tricked Cronus into swallowing it. Zeus was raised in a cave guarded by the **Couretes** who, when the baby was crying, clashed their shields so that his father did not hear him. He was nursed by the milk of **Amalthea**, a goat which Zeus, to honour later on, made a bright star in the sky, while he used its skin, the renowned **aegis**, to make a shield no enemy could attack. He was the only one to carry this shield while the goat's **horn** became a symbol of the abundance of goods.

In another version of the myth, Amalthea was a nymph who, along with Adrastea, Ida and other nymphs, raised Zeus. Once the son of Cronus had grown up, he fought his father and defeated him being superior to him in terms of strength and skills. He then made him vomit all his children he had swallowed, as well as the stone that had taken his place. He sent the stone to the Oracle of Delphi to remind both gods and humans of his power.

TITANOMACHY

At the war which started between **Zeus** and **Cronus** over the control of the Cosmos (world), Zeus' brothers stood by his side against their father whereas the latter had a lot of the Titans with him. Zeus released the **Cyclops** and the **Hecatonchires** (Hundred-hands) who were confined in Tartarus by Cronus, and recruited them with the promise that under his rule they would enjoy great benefits. Then, the Cyclops gave Zeus the thunder, the lightning and the thunderbolt, Poseidon the Trident, and Hades the "cynaean", a hood made of a dog's skin which made him invisible. Some of the Titans sided with Zeus, for example, the first born Oceanus and Prometheus, as well as Oceanid Styx with her children Cratos, Bia, Zelos and Dike (Justice). Along with them they were supported by Mother Gaea (Earth) who prophesised the Nike (Victory) of Zeus with the help of the Cyclops and, mainly, the Hecatonchires who were stronger and decided the outcome of the war.

The two armies had camped on the top of the mountains, the Titans on mount Orthrys whereas Zeus and his warriors took their place on mount Olympus. The war lasted ten years

Atlas is bringing the apples of the Hesperides to Heracles, who is holding the heaven's dome on his shoulders with Athena's help; metope from the temple of Zeus in Olympia (460 B.C.)
Olympia, Archaeological Museum

and only when the Cyclops and the Hecatonchires took part in it did Zeus gain the upper hand. The three Hecatonchires, having lifted huge rocks with their three hundred hands, threw them at the Titans and crushed them. The defeated were thrown beneath the earth, in Tartarus, where they were heavily chained, confined in a place surrounded by a bronze fence and a triple wall. The roots of the earth and the sea were located there. The Titans were doomed not to exit this dark place, as Poseidon had locked the gates which were guarded by indefatigable guards, the loyal to Zeus Hecatonchires.

The only Titan supporting Cronus who was severely punished by Zeus was **Atlas**, the commander of the Titanomachy.

After their defeat, he was exiled in the West, at the edge of the world near the garden of the Hesperides, condemned to hold the sky and the earth on his shoulders and back. From this place Atlas learned that the world is a big sphere, the sea is immense, as well as all the secrets of the sky and the earth. According to tradition, Atlas' children were the seven **Pleiades** who were transformed into stars (the star cluster Poulia) because they could not stand seeing their father suffering.

The gorgeous sisters **Pleiades, Alcyone, Merope, Sterope, Celaeno, Electra, Taygete** and **Maia**, were also called the **Atlantides** after their father's name, and were identified with the **Hesperides** after their mother's name, Hesperide, daughter of pious **Hesperus** (Evening) who the gods called with them and made him a bright star in the sky.

Tradition has it that the Pleiades consorted great gods and gave birth to gods and founders of tribes. For instance, Electra and Zeus had **Dardanus**, the first ancestor of the Trojans, Celaeno and Poseidon had **Lycus**, the first ancestor of the Arcades, Taygete gave birth to the son of Zeus **Lacedaemon**, and Maia's union of love with Zeus resulted in the birth of God **Hermes.**

GIGANTOMACHY

When Zeus, emerging the winner in Titanomachy, threw his father's supporters, the Titans, into Tartarus, Gaea was incensed because her children were severely punished and, in revenge, gave birth to the **Giants**. The Giants, oversized with an unbeatable power, had the figure of a human but with a frightful appearance, bearing serpents in the hair and their beards and their legs which ended in a dragon-like tail. Contrary to the Titans who were immortal, the Giants were mortal and, as it was said, the human race descended from them. According to the most renowned tradition, the Giants along with the Erinyes and the Meliai nymphs came from Gaea's body when the blood of Uranus splattered on it during his castration.

The Giants launched a sudden attack against the Olympian gods incited by their mother Gaea (Earth) or, in another version, taking the initiative themselves. All of a sudden, the gods received a rain of rocks and burning trees the Giants sent as they moved mountains, sank islands and rerouted rivers. The gods, with their leader Zeus holding the thunderbolts in his hands, wearing the aegis with the gorgonian and being supported by Nike and Styx, fought tirelessly to confront their enemies who also fought back bravely. The war between them lasted long and the leading part played Athena, Hera, Poseidon and Apollo. Athena, having been born in full armour during the Struggle from the head of Zeus, participated alongside her father, killed **Pallas**, a frightful Giant, flayed him and armoured her chest with his skin. The war was decided when there was heard the rumour that the Giants would banish if a mortal fought on the side of the Olympian gods. Zeus, then, sent Athena to bring Heracles

A representation of the Gigantomachy from the northern frieze of the Siphnian treasure (appr. 525 B.C.) Delphi, Archaeological Museum

as their ally. Meanwhile, Gaea set off in quest of an herb that would save the Giants, but Zeus ordered Helios, Selene and Dawn not to come out before he had found the herb himself and destroyed it. And so it happened. After that, the Giants fought without hope while the Olympians slew one after the other. Heracles shot his arrow at **Alcyoneus,** the leader of the Giants, who stood up again because he regained his power by stepping on the earth. Athena then advised Heracles to lift him in his arms and drag him outside his land to kill him. Eventually, Heracles slew him by hitting him with his club. It is said that he was buried under Vesuvius.

Enceladus aspired to marry Athena but she chased him to the Mediterranean Sea and buried him under Sicily by throwing the whole island upon his head.

The Giant **Polybotes** was pursued by Poseidon in the Aegean Sea and was crushed by a rock from the island of Kos he threw at him. This is how the island of Nisyros was formed, with the Giant being under it.

God Ares killed with his sword the Giant **Peloreus or Pelorus,** who threw mountain Pelion against Dionysus. **Ephialtes,** another frightful Giant, was slain by Apollo and Heracles who pierced him with their arrows. In a similar way, one after the other were killed a hundred Giants and, eventually, no one survived.

THE CREATION OF MAN ANTHROPOGONY

THE FIVE RACES

According to Hesiod, the human races were five and were created one after the extinction of the other by the gods.

The first human race the gods created was the **golden** one who could speak and lived in the era of Cronus.

People, back then, used to be blissful, enjoying the goods of the Earth who generously provided for them. There was neither misery and pain nor difficult old age for anyone. And, when this race was buried in the earth there derived good daemons, guards and saviours of the people.

The next race was the **silver** one. This race, however, was not perfect; it was not like the first one. The people were not wise and did not honour their gods. This is why Zeus, who ruled at the time, destroyed them and created a third race, the **bronze race**, which was frightful and horrible. This race brought along miserable works of Ares, wars and violence. Their weapons and their houses were made of bronze, and the people were cruel not even eating wheat; they only worked the bronze. They were subdued by their very hands and sank in freezing Hades.

This dark race was succeeded by a fourth one on the earth which was created by Cronid Zeus and was called **heroic**.

This was a divine race consisting of semi-gods and heroes who fought at the seven-gated Thebes or boarded ships and sailed to Troy for the sake of beautiful-haired Helen. They all settled at the ends of the earth and live forever without worries on the island of the Macars, in the deep Ocean.

The fifth race, last in the raw, was the **iron** one. It is the one during the existence of which there will never end the fatigue, the hardships and the worries subduing its people. It is the one the poet lives in, when good meets with evil. Zeus will also destroy this race, when there is no good relationship between the father and his children, the friend and his friend, the

Red-figured peliki with a
representation of the
Gigantomachy
(4th c. B.C.)
Athens, National
Archaeological Museum

companion and another companion and there is no honour to parents or respect for divine justice.

This myth of the **five races** of the human species, which starts with the best, the golden race, and reaches the worst one, neither has been made up by Hesiod nor is only Hellenic.

THE DOUBLE RACE

Plato records another myth concerning the human race. According to this myth, the first human race did not consist of only two sexes as we know, i.e. males and females. There was a third sex which was both male and female. These three sexes had a round body and all their members were double, in other words they had two faces, four legs and so on. It was then said that the males were born of Helios (Sun), the females of the Earth and the third was created by Selene (Moon) since she consists of the sun and the earth. These people had great strength as well as such arrogance that they desired to become gods.

To reduce their strength, Zeus decided to separate each of them in two. Thus, from each body were created two people, each one having half the original strength. This explains why, since then, people have been feeling incomplete and have been in the quest of love in order to unite with their other half.

EPIMETHEUS – PROMETHEUS

Many ancient authors mention a different myth concerning the creation of the human species from the **FIVE RACES** by Hesiod. In the era of the Titans there were no mortals on the earth, only immortal gods.

They decided to create mortal races, which they made of earth and fire. A little before they brought them to light, they called the sons of Titan Iapetus **Epimetheus** and **Prometheus**, and ordered them to adorn them and endow them with various talents.

Epimetheus, having in mind to carry out this mission on his own, asked Prometheus to let him attribute the traits himself and then have him check. Prometheus agreed and Epimetheus started with the animals, giving out strength to some and speed to others. He equipped all beings of the animal kingdom on the earth and in the sea with the right goods so as to live and perpetuate their species.

Carried away by his care for other beings, he left the humans short of any divine presents, bare and without attributes. As he was wondering what to do, Prometheus appeared to check the distribution of traits and found all the animals correctly armed and man left bare. He immediately decided to help him. He stole wisdom from goddess Athena and fire from Hephaestus and, after he had given them to the people, he taught them all the arts and sciences.

Certain authors, however, claim that Prometheus himself along with goddess Athena created man from clay and fire and shaped him in the figure of the gods.

According to another myth, when gods and humans gathered to define their rights, Prometheus deceived Zeus.

He slaughtered an ox and cut its skin in two halves. He wrapped the meat in one half and the bones with the fat in the other and presented Zeus with them to choose. Zeus chose the one with the bones and then Prometheus gave the other with the meat to the humans.

This is how the form of sacrifices to gods by humans was established; the humans would burn the fat and bones as an offering to the gods and would keep the meat to eat.

Prometheus paid his love and benefactions to humans very dearly.

Atlas carrying the burden of the earth on his back and chained Prometheus being attacked by the eagle; Laconic wide cup (550 B.C.). Rome, the Vatican Museum

Zeus was enraged and punished him severely. He expelled him in the East where he condemned him to tie himself on a stake at the top of Caucasus. There, every day, an eagle attacked him and ate his liver which was to be regenerated at night so that his torture would continue day after day. Prometheus had suffered from this pain for thirty years until Heracles, on Zeus' sufferance, released him by killing the eagle with his arrows.

Part of the northern frieze of the Siphnian treasure bearing a representation of a lion slewing a Giant (appr. 525 B.C.). Delphi, Archaeological Museum

PANDORA

Once Zeus found out that Prometheus had stolen the fire from the gods in order to give it to mankind, he was very angered and decided to punish them. He had Hephaestus mould a woman out of earth and water. Each goddess gave this woman a special gift. One gave her beauty; another gave her dexterity, while Athena taught her how to weave and Aphrodite offered her grace and lust. Hermes, however, infused her mind and heart with tricky and hollow words.

This woman was named **Pandora** (all-giving) by Zeus, because she was created with the gifts of all the gods. By order of Zeus, Hermes took Pandora to Epimetheus as a present to the humans from the gods. He fell in love with her, married her and introduced her to the people. However, among Pandora's gifts there was also curiosity which would make her cast lots of suffering upon the humans. A closed jar she was entrusted with and ordered never to open contained all the misfortunes in the world. Curious and disobedient Pandora opened it and filled the mankind with pain, diseases and death. Only hope remained in the jar because Pandora got scared and shut its lid rapidly.

Since then, all the misfortunes have tortured the mankind while hope has always remained last.

DEUCALION

THE FLOOD AND THE NEW HUMAN RACE

Another yet myth about the destruction of the human race is reported by the ancient authors.

Once, in the mists of time, the humans became so evil that Zeus decided to cause a horrible flood to destroy them. Prometheus, however, notified in advance his son **Deucalion,** who built an ark, provisioned it with all the necessities and locked himself in along with his wife **Pyrrha**, daughter of Epimetheus and Pandora.

For nine days the storm had been raging flooding the earth except for the top of certain mountains. Once the weather settled, the Ark landed on mount Parnassus or Orthrys or Athos or even on Etna, as different versions by authors narrating the myth have it. Upon stepping on dry land, **Deucalion** and **Pyrrha** offered sacrifices to Zeus thankful for their rescue since no other human being had survived. As well as thanking him, they begged the father of gods to repopulate the earth and Zeus, satisfied from their offerings, advised them to cover their faces and collect stones which, while walking, they were to throw over their shoulders without ever watching back to see the outcome.

The stones thrown by Deucalion were transformed into men while those thrown by Pyrrha became women. This way the earth was repopulated quickly and humankind survived.

Deucalion and **Pyrrha** also had their own children, some of whom became the founders of various tribes or renowned heroes. Their first born son **Hellene** is considered to be the patriarch of the Hellenes (the Greeks) and it is said that he was the son of Zeus. Another son of theirs was **Amphictyon,** and their daughters were **Protogeneia**, **Thyia**, **Melanthea** and **Pandora**, the granddaughter of the first gorgeous woman the gods presented to humankind.

THE TWELVE GODS OF THE HELLENES

T he ancient Greeks worshipped a group of twelve gods together, in a common cult, besides the special worship established for each one separately. This common cult of the twelve gods, according to the myth, must date back to the earliest years and had been designated by gods and heroes before the mortals adopted it.

As several local traditions have it, certain gods used to offer sacrifices to the "dodekatheon" (the twelve gods), for instance, Hermes in Olympia when he curved and roasted two of the fifty oxen he had stolen from Apollo, and divided them into twelve portions, one for each god. Moreover, when Heracles instituted the Olympic Games, he built close to the river Alpheios six altars, one for each pair of the twelve gods.

Deucalion offered sacrifices to the gods after his rescue from the flood, as it is narrated in Thessaly, whereas local myths in Byzantium have it that the Argonauts, passing through the land, built an altar in honour of the Twelve Gods.

In the area of Troad, it was said that Agamemnon first built a Sanctuary of the Twelve during the Trojan War. The people had great respect for the **Dodekatheon** and, when in difficulty or a very important case, they used to swear "**by the twelve gods**". When faced with an extremely difficult situation not even the gods did take a decision on their own. Zeus summoned the Twelve Gods who met and decided together. This is what happened when the two gods, Athena and Poseidon, had a contest in order to decide who would give his name to the city; and when Ares killed Alirrothios, a son of Poseidon who asked for the murderer to be brought to trial, it was the Twelve gods who decided to acquit Ares.

It was then, for the first time, that the first Athenian court in charge of murders sat atop **Areus Pagus,** which was named after the first accused. With the gods as judges, at the same place, the son of Agamemnon, Orestes, was tried for matricide and was found not guilty.

The **Dodekatheon** was initially worshipped as a group. The number, however, was very soon completed with the names of the main gods of the Pan-Hellenic cult. The most prevalent and best known list of the dodekatheon includes: Zeus, Hera, Athena, Poseidon, Demeter, Apollo, Artemis, Hermes, Ares, Aphrodite, Hephaestus and Hestia. However, there are several versions to the above list which replace Hermes with Pluto or Hades, Hestia with Dionysus and Demeter with Heracles.

The twelve gods were said to comprise six pairs of siblings or spouses, which were the following: Zeus - Hera, Poseidon - Demeter, Apollo - Artemis, Ares - Aphrodite, Hermes - Athena and Hephaestus - Hestia. In certain versions they are separated in six offspring of Cronus and six of Zeus with the male gods preceding the goddesses and thus the dodekatheon consists of four Triads: Zeus, Poseidon, Hades, Hera, Demeter, Hestia who were called the Cronids, and Hermes, Hephaestus, Apollo - Artemis, Aphrodite, Athena who were called the **Diogeneis** (born from Zeus).

The Twelve gods dwelled on Mount Olympus, between the sky and the earth. High up from the top, they could supervise and judge the mortals' acts, and thus support them or punish them. The people respected them and had deep faith in their fairness.

The Hellenes had created their gods to be good looking and strong warriors against any monstrous creature, as well as victors over the primordial more deficient and fiercer powers, demonstrating an upright will which always supported welfare.

The Olympian gods led a comfortable life in their palaces on Olympus and the arguments among them were always smoothed out with laughter, songs and dances. Being immortals meant that they were free from the anguish of death and their only commitment was their oath to the waters of **Styx**, the sacred river in the Under World, which Iris carried to Olympus in a golden cup. If a god, who swore to the golden cup, broke his oath, he was left without a breath for a year and then had to stay far away from the rest of the gods and their palaces for nine years.

King of all the gods of the Dodekatheon was Zeus while Hera was the first in the rank among the goddesses.

Apart from the principal gods of Olympus, there existed minor gods, gods of the earth, the sea, the sky and the Under World, who accompanied the Olympians and were honoured and respected by the mortals according to their attributes.

"The bas-relief of the gods"; marble dedicatory bas-relief (5th c. B.C.). Attica, the Brauron Museum

ZEUS OR DIAS

THE FATHER OF GODS AND HUMANS

In the Hellenic Pantheon, Zeus, the youngest Cronid in the cosmogonic evolution, is the supreme god. Homer calls him the father of gods and humans, while Aeschylus in his tragedy "Heliades" points out that Zeus is the air, the earth, and the sky and the lot, as well as that he stands above everything.

However, Zeus is not the creator of the Cosmos. Other primal, violent and revengeful powers precede which he will dominate on and destroy in order to create a new cosmos demonstrating ultimate moral values.

Zeus was the son of **Cronus** and **Rhea**. Since his father knew that one of his offspring was destined to overthrow him, he swallowed them (Hestia, Demeter, Hera, Hades and Poseidon) to escape the risk. In order to save her youngest child she was expecting, and being advised by her parents Gaia and Uranus, Rhea went to **Crete**, gave birth to Zeus and gave him over to the Nymphs to hide him in a cave in **Mount Aigaion,** close to **Lycton**, where Gaea undertook to raise him. Rhea gave Cronus a rock **wrapped in swaddling clothes to swallow instead of the infant Zeus.**

There are several versions to the myth regarding Zeus' birthplace and upbringing. The most common birthplace is **Crete**; however, the specific area differs according to the local traditions. In Apollodorus, Rhea delivers Zeus in a cave in mount **Dicte** and gives the infant to the **Couretes** and the nymphs **Adrastea and Ide**, daughters of **Melisseus**, who raised him with the milk of the goat **Amalthea**.

Callimachus in his Hymn to Zeus places Zeus' birth on **Mount Lycaeon** in **Arcadia**, where he is brought up by the Nymph **Neda** who rescues him in Crete in a cave of Mount Ida, the well known **Idaeon Andron. Dictaie Meliai,** the wives of the Corybands, are said to have raised him there. They are assisted by Adrastea and the goat **Amalthea** who feed him with not only her milk but with honey as well.

In the protection of the young god there participated the **Couretes** or **Corybands** or **Giants**, mythical armed figures, who used to clash their swords against their spears while dancing a war dance so that the father of young Zeus could not hear him screaming and crying.

The sacred baby's nurses vary depending on the traditions. In some versions they are animal-like, the main one being **Amalthea**, the renowned Aiga (goat) whose **horn** Zeus once broke and made it a **symbol of abundance**. When Amalthea died, Zeus wore its skin to be invincible. This is the famous Aigis which, in later years, he gave to his beloved daughter Athena who always had it on for protection.

When Zeus grew up, he struggled against numerous powers until he reached the point of being recognised as the dominant god of the lot. He fought with his father **Cronus**, defeated him and compelled him to disgorge his children he had swallowed. This way were freed the siblings of Zeus, Hestia, Demeter, Hera, Hades or Pluto and Poseidon, while the rock Rhea had tricked Cronus into thinking it was baby Zeus was set down at **Pytho** (Delphi) as a sign of eternal remembrance. Then Zeus also released the three Hecatonchires, **Vrontes, Steropes** and **Arges**, who, being grateful, gave him **thunder, lightning** and the **thunderbolt** with which he ruled the world.

Zeus also fought with the **Titans**, the siblings of Cronus, because they refused to recognize him as their leader. After he beat them he had to fight the sons of **Iapetus, Atlas, Menoeteus, Prometheus** and **Epimetheus**. Atlas was punished by having to forever hold the Cosmos on his back while Prometheus was chained on Mount Caucasus.

Next, along with the rest of the gods, he had to face the **Giants** who he also slew. A very hard time Zeus went through was when **Typhon**, the son of Gaia and Tartarus, attempted to destroy the world. Zeus struggled with determination but Typhon threw him unconscious onto a rock. He was rescued by Hermes and Aigipan, that is, Pan changed into an aiga (goat). They brought him round after they joined the nerves Typhon had taken out of his body. As soon as Zeus had recovered, he attacked his enemy all of a sudden from the sky, being in a chariot drawn by winged horses.

Their fight was horrible and bloody. Over Thrace, the wounded Typhon lost such a lot of blood (aema) that its mountain range was called Aemos. Finally, as he was rushing towards **Sicily** to save himself, Zeus dropped **Aetna** on him and buried him under it.

After all these hard struggles, victorious Zeus was acknowledged a leader and shared authorities with those who had helped him. He became the ruler of the sky, Poseidon of the sea and the waters in general and Hades became the ruler of the Under World.

Being the king of the gods, Zeus created the world from scratch, according to certain myths. One of them has it that Zeus married **Chthonie** that is, the earth, who he had dressed in a veil he had embellished with the whole world, the lands and the seas. After Prometheus' plan to help the people, Zeus created a new human race when he realised that the people had become arrogant and did not honour the gods. Thus he sent a dreadful flood on the earth which only **Deucalion and Pyrrha** did survive. They thanked him and then he allowed them to create new people with the rocks they threw behind them.

Bronze statuette of Zeus from Dodona (470 B.C.). Athens, National Archaeological Museum

From the known **five races** of human beings mentioned by Hesiod, Zeus destroyed the silver race when they showed signs of impiety as well as the bronze and the heroic ones he, himself, had created, with the exception of course of the heroes he had allowed to live on the **islands** of the **Macars**. It is said that even the iron race he was about to ravage because they had also evolved into evil people.

The ruler of the world, the first among the gods, became enraged when the other gods acted against his will, when they destroyed the harmony of the world with their actions. He, then, appeared as an avenger and exterminated every defector. This is what he did with **Phaethon** when he drove Helios' chariot or with the **Couretes** Hera had asked to kill **Epaphus**, the son of Zeus and Io. He also sent **Asclepius**, who brought the dead back to life, to Hades, thus upsetting the laws of nature concerning the mortals.

A guarantor for the order of the world, apart from an avenger he was also a protector and a fair god, and judged the actions of the gods and the mortals, the heroes and the kings of the earth, naming his descendants **diogeneis** (born of Zeus) and **diogetrepheis** (raised by Zeus). He was called **Poliouchos** or **Polieus** because he protected the states and cared for the defense of the cities at wartime and was worshipped along with his daughter, Athena, as **Promachus** (Defender) and **Soter** (Saviour). Moreover, he was given the epithet **Elefthereus**, because he freed those who were under his protection. His followers called him **Herceus** (ercos=fence) as he protected residences and their yards where there was located the altar of the god and the head of families offered sacrifices to him.

In addition, he used to bear the name **Ephestius**, since he guaranteed the family hearth, **Ctesius** as he cared for the possessions of every household and **Gamelius** because he cared for the goods of the institution of marriage.

Besides the families, Zeus protected the poor, the strangers and the refugees. This is why he was named **Icesius, Xenius and Phyxius Zeus.** Renowned for his being fair, the god protected anyone who turned to him asking him to see to

Ceramic complex of Zeus and Ganymedes from a corner ornament of a temple in Olympia (480-470 B.C.).
Olympia, Archaeological Museum

justice, and he always settled differences employing his faultless judgement.

Pre-eminently a god of the sky as his numerous epithets (**Uranius, Aitherius**) document, Zeus was responsible for all the weather phenomena. As he sent the winds, the clouds and rain, he was called **Evanemus, Nephelegeretes** and **Ombrius - Hyetius** respectively. As the dominator of the Thunder and the Thunderbolt, he also had the epithets **Cerauneus** and **Hypsibremetes**.

His abovementioned attributes are associated with his symbols: the **thunderbolt** and the **eagle**, which is the only bird flying the highest in the sky and darting towards the earth to catch its prey.

Zeus or Dias is a primeval god of the sky worshipped by the Indo- Europeans. These races brought him along when they moved towards the Balkan Peninsula. His worship arrived in Greece with the Hellenes-Achaeans in 2000 B.C. His name comes from the etymological root **din** which means **sky** and we see it in other Indo-European people, such as the Latins and the Hindu. The appeal to "**Zeus Pater**" (Father Zeus) corresponds to "Diespater" of the Latins (Jupiter of the Romans) and to "Dyaous Pitar" of the ancient Hindu.

As an almighty god ruling the entire world from his palace on mount Olympus, he was often called **Olympian**, being the father of gods and humans. Furthermore, as the dominator of the earth offering it fertility with his rain, he was worshipped as **Genethlius** (birth giver) and **Georgos** (farmer). Through the earth he connects to the Under World and receives the epithet **Chthonic, Plusius** and **Meilichius**. As Meilichius, Zeus was worshipped in the **Diassia** when they slew and burnt piglets being symbols of euphoria and productivity.

Gathering all these attributes, Zeus is the only Greek god who, as an almighty god, leads to monotheism.

The inner part of a red-figured wide cup bearing a representation of Zeus and Ganymedes (appr. 460 B.C.). Ferrara, Museo Archeologico di Spina

CONSORTS AND OFFSPRING OF ZEUS

THEOGONIC LEVEL	ANTHROPOGENIC LEVEL
DIONE → APHRODITE	CRETE → CAR - CARES
DEMETER → PERSEPHONE	IDA → COURETES - CRES
HERA → ARES-HEBE-EILITHYIA-HEPHAESTUS	EUROPA → MINOS-RHADAMANTHYS-SARPEDON
MAIA → HERMES	LAODAMEA → SARPEDON
SEMELE → DIONYSUS	PANDORA → GRAECUS
SELENE → ERSA	PYRRHA → HELLENE
ASTERIA → HECATE	FTHEA → ACHAEUS
LETO → APOLLO - ARTEMIS	EURYMEDUSA → MYRMEDON
METIS → ATHENA	THYIA → MAGNES - MACEDON
THEMIS → MOIRAE - HORAE	THRACE → BETHYNUS
EURYNOME → CHARITAE	ELECTRA → DARDANUS
MNEMOSYNE → MUSES - CORYBANDS	IODAMA → THEBE
IO → EPAPHUS	EURYNOME → ASSOPUS
ELECTRA → HARMONIA	ANTIOPE → AMPHION - ZETHUS
APHIANASSA → ENDYMION	MAIRA → LOCRUS
AEX or THYMBRIS → PAN	ISONOE → ORCHOMENUS
HELARA → TITYOS	IOCASTA → TROPHONIUS
HECATE or CARME → BRETOMARTES	ALCMENE → HERACLES
	NIOBE → ARGUS
	DANAE → PERSEUS
	SELENE → NEMEA
	TAYGETE → LAOCEDAEMON
	LEDA → HELEN - DIOSCURI
	CALLISTO → ARCAS
	SINTHYS → MEGARUS
	AEGINA → AEACUS

THE LOVE AFFAIRS OF ZEUS

The first wife of Zeus is said to have been **Chthonie,** whom he named Earth and, for her sake, he made the world adorning a veil she used to wear. Then, he became a couple with **Metis**, one of the daughters of Oceanus who had the wisdom of all the gods and the humans.

For fear that **Metis** would give birth to a son who was to overpower him, he swallowed her while already pregnant to a daughter who would later be born from her father's head, take the name Athena and become the goddess of Wisdom. Another tradition has it that his first wife was the Oceanid **Dione** and they had Aphrodite.

Nevertheless, according to the Dodekatheon, his lawful and eternal spouse was his sister Hera with whom he had **Ares**, the god of war, **Hephaestus**, the god of metalwork, **Hebe**, the goddess of youth, and **Eileithyia**, the goddess of childbirth and midwifery.

Exquisite and numerous are the myths concerning the extramarital love affairs of the god with goddesses and mortal women and the offspring he had are countless.

It is said that the principal god paired off with **Themis**, the goddess of law and moral order, and they had the **three Horae** (Hours), Eunomia, Dike and Eirine, deities who made time flow, as well as the **three Moirae** (Fates), Clotho (Spinner), Lachesis (Apportioner of

Lot) and Atrapos (Unturned) who determined the fate of every being.

With **Mnemosene** Zeus spent nine consecutive nights and she had the Nine **Muses**, patronesses of the Arts and the Letters. During the festivals held on Olympus, the Muses accompanied Apollo with divine songs while he played his guitar. The dance was led by the **three Charitae**, Euphrosyne, Thalia and Aglaea, also daughters of Zeus by the Oceanid **Eurynome**.

Except for the goddesses, there are countless mortals who paired off with Zeus. Goddess Demeter will unite with him and bring **Persephone** to the Cosmos while, by the mortal **Leto** he will have god **Apollo** and goddess **Artemis**, and by the mortal **Maia** he will have **god Hermes**. Among the mortals Zeus enjoyed their love was **Alcmene** who had **Heracles**, **Danae** the mother of **Perseus,** and **Aegina** the mother of **Aeacus**. In order to seduce them Zeus disguised himself employing various tricks; for instance, when alluring **Danae** he changed into golden rain or for the sake of **Leda**, the mother of the **Dioscuri, Clytemnestra** and **Helen of Troy**, he changed into a swan. To seduce **Europa**, the daughter of the king of Phoenice, he changed into a bull, went to the meadow she was playing with her girlfriends, enchanted her to the point she mounted the bull and abducted her fleeing to Crete where they made love. **Europa** gave birth to three distinguished sons, **Minos, Rhadamanthys** and **Sarpedon**, and gave her name to an entire Continent.

The abduction of Europa by Zeus guised in a bull; red-figured urn (appr. 400 B.C.).
London, British Museum

WORSHIP - FESTIVALS

The Hellenes never neglected to honour the dominator of the world Zeus in organised Sanctuaries holding festive performances and athletic contests. Two of the four pan-Hellenic festivals were dedicated to him: the splendid **Olympic Games - the Olympia** in Olympia and **the Nemea or Nemeia** at his sanctuary in Nemea.

The Olympia, the most important of all the pan-Hellenic Games, was held at the sanctuary of Zeus in Olympia in honour of the great god, Zeus. They were **penteteric** games, that is, they were held every four years in the eighth month by the calendar of the Heleans, July - August, during the first full moon after the summer solstice. After the 5th c. B.C., when the programme had gradually been enriched with 15 events, the Games lasted five days. Throughout the games and the time the athletes and the spectators needed to travel to and back from Olympia, there was the "**sacred truce**" in effect which did not allow any hostilities, execution of death penalties and settlement of legal disputes. All the free Greek citizens who had not committed a murder or sacrilege had the right to participate in the games. Barbarians and slaves could watch the games with the free citizens whereas women were not allowed to enter the athletic premises, with the exception of **Demeter's** priestess, **Chamyne**. The masters of the sanctuary and organisers of the Olympic Games were the **Heleans** for the longest period of their performance. Among them there were selected by throwing lots the **Hellanodikes**, noblemen who were responsible for the organisation of the games and the observance of the rules, whereas they could impose heavy fines in case they were violated by perjurer athletes. Two days before the beginning of the games, the procession of athletes and judges, accompanied by the noblemen of Helis, dignitary guests (**"theoroi"**) and the relatives of the athletes started from Helis and reached Olympia where they were welcomed by those who had come to watch the games.

The athletes took an official oath before the altar and the statue of **Orkeios Zeus**, the Bouleuterion. The prize for the victors was the **cotinus**, a plain wreath from the branches of a wild olive tree which grew next to the temple of Zeus. The foot races were held in the **stadium**, while the equestrian races in the **hippodrome**. In parallel to the competitions,

The Stadium at the Sanctuary of Zeus in Olympia.

philosophers and historians recited their works thus offering the young people the possibility of exercising both their body and their mind. Great poets such as Simonides, Bacchylides and Pindarus praised the glory of the Olympic Champions.

The Nemea was instituted in 573 B.C. and was held every two years in July or August, in turn with the other Pan-Hellenic Games. The programme resembled that of the Olympia and focused on athletic contests in particular. Obviously in commemoration of the tragic death of prince **Opheltes**, the athletes' prize was a **wreath of wild celery leaves**, the hellanodikes were dressed in black and, close to the temple of Zeus, there was a small wood with cypresses. Initially, the organisation of the games was in the hands of the neighbouring city of **Cleones**. At the end of 5th c. B.C., the sanctuary was destroyed and the games were transferred to **Argos** where they were held until 330 B.C. under the powerful state of the Argives. After the battle of Chaeronia in 338 B.C. and the domination of Philip B' of Macedonia, the games returned to Nemea, and a huge building plan, obviously included in the Pan-Hellenic politics of the Macedonians, changed the appearance of the sanctuary. It was then when the temple of Zeus was erected, a row of nine houses, according to the model of the treasuries in Olympia, the guesthouse, the bath, the accommodation of the priests and the hellanodikes and, of course, the changing rooms and the impressive **stadium** 400m southeast of the temple. It was 600 feet in length, and had a capacity of 30,000 spectators, a configured sphendone, a stone starting post with a starting line and a secret entrance.

A few years later, in 270 - 260 B.C., the games return to Argos where they will be held until the later antiquity with only two exceptions. The first also comprises the worst violation of the sacred truce in the ancient years. In 235 B.C., **Aratus the Sikyonian** announced **"alternative"** games in Nemea and blockaded Argos with his troops. The athletes who participated in the official games in Argos were captured and sold as slaves by Aratus.

For the last time the games were transferred from **Argos** to **Nemea** by the Roman conqueror **Mommius**, in 145 B.C., and continued to be held there for approximately half a century. Next, the sanctuary of Zeus was gradually abandoned. In the 2nd c. A. D., when the traveller Pausanius visited it, the roof of the temple of Zeus had already crumbled.

The temple of Zeus at the Sanctuary of the god in Nemea.

HERA

THE QUEEN OF THE OLYMPIAN GODS

Hera was the only one of the goddesses in the Olympic Pantheon who was particularly honoured by always finding herself beside Zeus as his lawful wife. She was the daughter of Cronus and Rhea and, thus also his sister, while her sisters were Hestia and Demeter, and Poseidon and Pluto were her brothers. Oceanus and Tethys raised her during the period when Cronus was in conflict with Zeus over the control of the cosmos. According to various local myths, Hera's birthplace was: On Samos near the river Imbrasus or Parthenius where, later, her major sanctuary, **Heraion**, was established and Admete, daughter of Eurystheus, the king of Argolis, was the first priestess of the goddess. Another birthplace of the goddess is considered to be **Argos,** where a more famous Heraion had been established in her honour. In Euboea it was said that a local nymph had been Hera's nurse, whereas in **Stymphalus**, Arcadia, it was believed that Temenus had raised her and had built a temple for her instituting her cult. He had decided on paying tributes to the goddess first the young girls as a **"parthenos"** (virgin) or "Paeda" (child) for the period before her marriage, then the married women as a "**teleian**" (matron) for the period when she was the wife of Zeus, and, finally, the widows as a **"chera"** (widowed or divorced) for the period when she had divorced her husband.

At a very young age and before her marriage, Hera had affairs with Zeus. According to a myth coming from the area of Nauplion, every year Hera bathed in the spring **Kanathos** and renewed her Virginity. In Hermione, there was a myth concerning the first union of the two gods. Zeus succeeded in uniting with her for the first time when he saw her going up Kokkyx, a mountain in the area which then was called Thornax. He caused torrential rain, took the form of a cuckoo and, shaking, he sat on the goddess' lap. She took pity on the scared bird and covered it under her robe. Then, Zeus took his real form and attempted to unite with her. Hera resisted because she was afraid of her parents but succumbed when Zeus promised to take her as his lawful wife. Since then the **cuckoo** has been the cult symbol of the goddess, especially of **teleia** (matron) Hera, i.e. the wedded one, and the mountain was named Kokkyx, while in the temple built on it, where she was worshipped as the patroness of marriage, the cuckoo was placed as a symbol on the sceptre in her statue. Of her marriage to Zeus Hera had **Ares**, the god of war, **Hebe** who was given Heracles as a husband, and **Eileithyia**, goddess of childbirth. Her own child was Hephaestus she had either with Zeus or on her own, without a man, when Zeus gave birth to **Athena** without recourse to her. Apart from her children, Hera raised **Thetis** as one of her own daughters, saw that she married well with Peleus and always protected her and her son Achilles. However, she also raised the Nemean

Hera in her attempt to seduce Zeus; metope from temple E in Selinous (appr. 460 B.C.).
Palermo, Museo Nazionale Archeologico

Lion, the Lernean Hydra and the Monster which guarded the Apples of the Hesperides, all beasts slain by Heracles. A myth has it that **Heracles** himself had nursed her breast without her knowing because it was a rule that no son of Zeus would deserve divine honours unless they had nursed with Hera's milk. When Heracles was born, Hermes took him and placed him close to Hera's breast without her taking any notice. Once the goddess realized who he was, Heracles had already had enough but, as she pulled herself away, a spurt of her milk smeared across the sky and this is the account of how the Galaxy was formed (Milky Way). Moreover, from the drops of milk that dropped on the ground there grew the white lilies.

Hera protected those who honoured her; nevertheless, she was terribly cruel and vengeful against those not paying tributes to her. With particular stubbornness she pursued the paramours and illegitimate offspring of her husband. She manically pursued **Leda**, the mother of Apollo and Artemis, **Io**, daughter of Inachus the founder of the Argives, **Semele**, the mother

Detail from the
Gigantomachy,
depicting Hera fighting.
Northern frieze of the
Siphnian treasure
(appr. 525 B.C.).
Delphi, Archaeological
Museum

of Dionysus, goddess **Aegina** and nymph **Callisto** in Arcadia whom she transformed into a Bear killed by Artemis. The one who underwent the greatest sufferings was **Heracles** who paid throughout his life for the love his father showed to him.

Hera was the most grandiose goddess of the Olympians and the rest of the gods respected her as did her husband despite his adulteries. However, when the goddess became angry, Olympus shook and the globe stirred the same way as when Zeus got angry. Being jealous, she watched closely his every step but yielded before her almighty husband although she never forgave his love affairs. Once, fed up with his infidelity, she decided to divorce him. So she left him and went to Euboea and she wouldn't return no matter how much Zeus begged her. Then, Zeus turned to **Kithaeron**, an elderly man renowned for his wisdom. He advised him to dress up a wooden statue as a bride and spread the word that he was about to get married. And so did Zeus. As soon as Hera heard of it, went to the place where the bride's coach was, rushed at her, tore up her veil and seeing the wooden statue laughed in pleasure, understanding her husband's trick and they reconciled. After that, there was constituted for the people in Kithaeron to celebrate the **Daedala** to commemorate the story with the wooden statue. (Daedala was the name for wooden statues).

WORSHIP - FESTIVALS

Hera's worship had spread all over Greece and the islands, especially the Peloponnese. The centre of her cult was in Argolid, mainly in Argos with the renowned magnificent **Heraion**, founded on the northern slope of mount Euboea, at a short distance from Argos. Temples dedicated to Hera stood in Tiryns, Corinth, Perachora, Epidaurus, Hermione, Sikyon, in the arcadic cities of Mantineia, Megalopolis and Stymphalus, in Olympia and in Sparta as well as on the islands of Paros, Delos, Kos, Astypalaia and Crete. Of particular significance was the Sanctuary of the goddess on **Samos**, where at the annual festival called the **Toneia** (the binding) her cult image was transferred to the beach, washed and offered a sweet. The people on Samos wore osier and laurel wraths and, out in the open-air, had sweet wine as in weddings, praising Hera for being the bride and the mistress of their island. There followed a wedding bath and the wedding banquet. Numerous are the epithets of the goddess in her cult, for instance, **Acraia, Alalcomeneis, Archegetes, Argeia, Inachis, Olympia, Urania, Tauropis, Telchinia.** Among them distinguished are the poetic and best known ones, such as **Boopis** (cow-eyed) which shows her association with the cow corresponding that of Zeus with the bull. She was also invoked Leucolenos, Kallistephanos, Olympiad, Basileia, Pelasgis and Chrysopeplos.

The Heraeon at the Sanctuary of Zeus, in Olympia.

ATHENA

THE GODDESS OF WISDOM

Goddess of Wisdom and warfare, of storm and meteorological phenomena, of agriculture and the arts **Athena**, daughter of Zeus and Metis, is the deity who combines bravery with prudence, and benefits the mortals more than any other Olympian god. Athena is the only goddess among the twelve gods who was born from the head of Zeus, father of all gods and humans.

According to the myth concerning the birth of the goddess, handed down by Hesiod and the Homeric hymns, when Zeus became the governor of the new order of the world, he mated with Oceanid Metis, goddess of prudence. Uranus and Gaia informed him that their mating would result in the birth of, first, a girl resembling him and then a more intelligent son than him who would displace him from his reign. Thus, he swallowed Metis and the fetus. This action of his gave him the name "profound". When time came, a new deity was born springing forth fully armed from the head of her father Zeus which was split open with an axe by Hephaestus or Prometheus. This kind of birth, as an adult daughter directly from a man, attributes the same values as his to her and allows her to always remain tightly bonded to him as an ideal assistant. She is the only one among his children who had the privilege to wear his terrible shield, the aegis, enter his arsenal and use his thunderbolt.

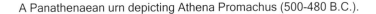

During the war of giants Athena fought next to her father and reinforced the Olympians with the assistance of Hercules she had asked along in order to defeat the Giants. On the frieze at the altar of Pergamus, Athena is portrayed routing giant Alcyoneus while a winged victory is about to crown her. According to the tradition, Athena killed Engelados crushing him under a big rock from which the island of Sicily came.

The goddess as a "**Promachus**" (Defender) as well as a "**Soteira**" (Saviour), protects all the great heroes during their fights and advises them on the approach they should employ in order to win while, very often, she replaces them in action so that she defeat the enemy and they be safe.

She will be the one to assist the hero of Mycenae **Perseus** to behead Medusa and, from then on, she will be bearing her

A Panathenaean urn depicting Athena Promachus (500-480 B.C.).

"Athena thinking", bas-relief (appr. 460 B.C.). Athens, the Acropolis Museum

horrifying "gorgonian" head on her shield as a deterrent. Athena will show Hercules the way to destroy the various beasts while he was performing his labours and she will supply him with the weapons in order to free his home country, Thebes. Moreover, she will advise **Bellerophon** on how to tame Pegasus and she will teach the Couretans how to dance a war dance, the pyrrhic.

During the Argonautic expedition she plays a leading part in building Argo, the ship which was to carry the Argonauts to Colchis so that Jason would achieve his goal. During the expedition of **The Seven against Thebes** she will accompany Tydeus, who was the delegate of the Argives, and advise him to be calm before Eteocles. She will help him win and heal his wounds; however, she will abandon him when he ends up in cannibalism. On the contrary, she will push his son, Diomedes, forward and make him known as a great hero of the Achaeans during the Trojan War.

During the **Trojan War**, the goddess, along with Hera, will support the Achaeans driven by her hatred towards Paris, who refused to give the apple of beauty to both of the goddesses preferring goddess Aphrodite. Although she is a warfare deity, she always fights with intelligence and prudence as the goddess of Wisdom contrary to her brother, the god of war **Ares,** who is known as a frivolous and furious warrior. She will frequently have to face him since her brother is an ally of the Trojans and fights with the enemy. Once she took him off away from the battlefield so that the Achaeans managed to beat the Trojans, whereas, during another battle, she injured him heavily by dropping a whole rock which hit him on the neck and paralysed his limbs. Furthermore, wearing her "helmet of Hades" which made her invisible, she helped Diomedes advising him on how to wound goddess Aphrodite and Ares who defended the Trojans.

Goddess Athena always supported the Atridaeans during hardship; however, she mainly helped, along with Apollo, their descendant Orestes to escape from the Erinyes who were after him being a matricide, and acquitted him with her vote at the court of Areios Pagus. Demonstrating special care, she sympathasises with

"Athena of Varvakeion", replica of the Gold and ivory Athena of the Parthenon (2nd or 3rd c. A.D.). Athens, National Archaeological Museum

Achilles whereas her relationship with Odysseus and his son Telemachus is outstanding mainly in Homer's Odyssey where she reaches the point of comparing her own divine intelligence to that of mortal Odysseus. "You, who in the world can compare to you in terms of knowledge and words, And I, myself, am praised among the gods for my willpowers and my skills…"

Finally, it was she who guided Epeius to construct the **"Trojan Horse"** and with this the Greeks gained entrance into Troy and occupied it.

Athena, being Metis' daughter, was very intelligent and ingenious not only as far as warfare is concerned but also in peace. She is **the goddess of Wisdom** and protects, besides the heroes, intellectual people as well.

Her advisory role towards everyone to do their best shows the superiority of the intellect to other powers. As **"Athena Ergane"**, she is the patroness of the craftsmen, who work with their brain and their hands. The goddess herself is unequalled as regards ceramics, carpentry and weaving. According to tradition, she was taught the crafts by the Cyclops and then passed them down to the people. Athena will weave the first fabrics and will dress the first woman, Pandora. At the same time, she will teach her the craft of the loom as she will do the Phaeasian women, a present which will make them incomparable at that craft.

A well known fable is that of Arachne, a young woman from Lydia who wove perfect tapestry and challenged the goddess to a competition. The goddess, however, became furious about not only the audacity of a mortal woman who dared boast that her craft compared to that of an immortal but also the fact that her tapestry displayed the gods' love affairs. This is why she turned her into the familiar insect, spider (Arachne), who spins eternally. Athena's association with the crafts, as brought out in the myth, attributes to her the same role as that of Hephaestus.

Bronze statue of goddess Athena by Euphranor (appr. 350 B.C.). Piraeus, Archaeological Museum

Red-figured vessel. Athena is guiding a giant as to where to place the rock he is carrying (440-430 B.C.). Paris, Louvre

This is why the two gods are frequently worshipped together, for instance, at the Hephaestion at the Agora of ancient Athens. Her oldest and initial attribute as the goddess of storm relates her to fire. Like Prometheus who first donated this divine gift to the people, Athena deserves the title of the agent of culture. Her works are not simply weapons and suits of armour or the construction of either the Argo for the Argonautic expedition or the boat for Danaos with the 50 daughters. They are gifts for the survival of the mortals such as the domestication of the horse, the planting of the first olive tree on the rock of the Acropolis of Athens, the medicine from the blood of Gorgo donated to Erichthonius or, according to others, to Asclepios in order to bring the dead back to life. Last but not least, the **flute** she had devised herself or the **dance, the "pyrrhic",** she first of all taught, not to mention the first statue of Pallas and the Trojan horse which elevated Athena into a goddess of culture.

Initially Athena was worshipped as the goddess of the **mountaintops** and as the **mistress of towers** (Akria and Epipyrgitis). As time passed, she was also worshipped as a **Poliouchos** (patroness). She was the patroness of Athens, the town named after her, to which she donated countless privileges and protected from misfortunes. According to the attic tradition, **Athena** had a fight with **Poseidon** for the possession of the town. They decided to offer a present. Whoever, after the judgement of the others of the twelve gods, would give the best present to the town, would gain its patronage. Poseidon struck a blow of his trident on the Acropolis rock and, immediately, water gushed forth. When Athena's turn came, she dropped a seed next to Poseidon's trident traces and the first olive tree in the world sprouted. The gods decided the goddess' present was a lot more precious, as there already was water, and assigned the victory to Athena who gave the city-state her name.

The Athenian traditions relate Athena directly to **Erechtheus**, one of the first kings who she raised and were worshipped together at her sacred temple, the Erechtheion.

It is said that the goddess had also raised **Erichthonius**, another previous king of the city, who was born from Hephaestus' semen impregnating the attic ground since the goddess herself refused to submit when he committed an indecent assault towards her. The goddess gave Erichthonius Gorgo's blood of which he would be able to produce medicine to cure the illnesses of the people as well as poisons to take lives. It is also believed that it was Athena who appointed **Ion,** the afterwards founder of the Ionians, king of the city. Ion was the son of Apollo and the Athenian princess Creusa. Moreover, she saw that Aethra meet Poseidon so that **Theseus,** the most important hero of Attica, be born.

Athena's name was often accompanied by the title **Pallas.** The word is of Greek origin, it means 'young girl' and relates to "pallax, pallakis" (maiden) or the modern Greek word palikari (daring man). It is said, according to the legend, that Athena had a beloved girlfriend who, unfortunately, she, accidentally, killed while playing and in memoriam she created the palladion.

The title **"Pallas Athenaie",** which corresponds to that of **Athena Parthenos** (Virgin Athena), characterises Athena as 'ever a virgin' a name deriving from her quality as a **Promachus** who, according to the ancient perceptions, depend their power on virginity. In Athens she was mainly worshipped as a Parthenos (virgin) and this is why her great temple was called **the Parthenon.**

Bronze statuette of Athena Promachus (480-470 B.C.).
Athens, National Archaeological Museum

WORSHIP - FESTIVALS

The main festivals in honour of the goddess Athena were **the Procharisteria, the Plynteria, the Kallynteria** and **the Arrhephoria** or **Arrhetophoria.** The Arrhetophoria is characterised by a ritual known nowadays as "speechless water" during which three women called Maria must carry water from a spring at night without speaking at all on the way.

In antiquity in Athens, there used to celebrate the Panathenaea which was directly associated with the "co-settlement" (synoecism) of various communities of Attica in a city by Theseus and expressed the political unity of all Athenian citizens. Tradition had it that the festival was inaugurated by the mythical king Erichthonius and was called **ATHENAEA**. It was reorganised in 566/5 B.C. by the tyrant of the town Peisistratus and was divided in the **Minor** and the **Great Panathenaea. The Great Panathenaea** was held every four years during the month of Hekatombaion (end of July) and, whereas it was a local celebration, it appealed tremendously to the entire Hellenic world of the times.

During the festive period, there were held athletic competitions, including all the Olympic games such as hippodromes, chariot races, stadion races, the pentathlon (long jump, discus throw, javelin throw, wrestling, stadion race), wrestling, pygme (boxing), pankration (full-contact fighting) and hoplitodromos (hoplite race). There also were certain local events such as the lampadedrome (torch-race), the horseback lampas, the anthippasia, the apobates race, and the evandria and rowing, in which only the citizens of Athens were allowed to take part, contrary to the Olympic Games in which foreigners were welcome. Moreover, there were held musical contests and poetic ones reciting the Homeric epics.

The organisation of the games as well as the final magnificent procession from Dipylon at Kerameikos up to the Parthenon on the Acropolis was entrusted to ten male priests and to the athlothetes. On the last day the magnificent procession, in which the whole Athenian citizen population participated, took place. They started from the Pompeion in the area of Kerameikos and from the Dipylon, the central gate at the city walls. The procession followed the Panathenaean Street, which crossed the Agora, towards the Parthenon on the Acropolis, with the aim to offer the goddess her newly-woven peplus. The procession was followed by the Athenians' sacred ship, the "Salaminian naus" which carried her peplus. The sculptor Phidias represented the magnificent procession in the frieze of the Parthenon, a unique offer of the Athenian state to the patroness as well as to humanity.

POSEIDON

THE GOD OF THE WATERS AND THE SEA

The Aquatic world, a defining factor for Hellenism, with its terrible, unbeatable powers but also with the unexpectable dangers for navigation, is governed by Poseidon, the son of Cronus and Rhea, brother of Zeus and Hades. According to the myth, the three Cronids, Zeus, Poseidon and Hades had the same rights concerning the division of the world and, in order to get their portion they drew lots. Zeus ruled the sky, Hades got the underworld and Poseidon became the ruler of the sea. The Earth and mount Olympus were not included in the lots so that all three gods enjoyed them.

Poseidon was the god of the water of every fountain and river and was worshipped as "Phytalmios", (the god of vegetation and the growth of plants). Initially, he must have been a chthonic god as his name denotes which compounds from "posis" (man - husband) and DA (a different version of GA-GH, the earth), in other words, the spouse of the earth according to an older version or, in a newer one, "the master of the waters, sharing the same etymology as **poto** (a drink), **posis** (drinking), **potamos** (river). On both occasions though, he is the god of the waters fertilising the earth. Later on, he would assume power over the sea too, and in the Iliad he appears as its only master.

His Third essential attribute is that of causing earthquakes. When he does not stir the sea with his trident, he strikes the rocks either to well up water or to cause earthquakes.

Poseidon owned two palaces. One was located on the top of mount Olympus, a magnificent work by Hephaestus, so that he is close to the rest of the Olympian gods. The second, a golden one, in the depths of the sea, is where he lives with his wife, Amphitrite.

In the Iliad, the god takes three steps which cause the mountains to shake and arrives from Olympus at his palace in the depths of the Aegean Sea. He harnesses his two horses, mounts his golden chariot and leads them over the waves so that his wheel axles stay dry. Full of joy the waters retrieve while the sea creatures and monsters start up at recognising their master.

This account by Homer, written in the 8th century BC and depicting the god's divine peaceful aspect that sheds elation everywhere, lasts throughout antiquity as documented in representations dated back even in the early Christian times. Many times, when travelling on his chariot, he is accompanied by his beloved wife Amphitrite, one of the 50 Nereids, the gorgeous daughters of Nereus.

Poseidon's other aspect, the fierce one, is described mainly in the Homeric Odyssey. From the top of the mountain the god watches Odysseus on his raft in the middle of the sea. He is the only god persecuting Odysseus because he had blinded his son Polyphemus. Bearing this in mind, filled with wrath, he grasps his trident, stirs the sea and, with a huge wave, smashes the raft of the king of Ithaca.

Poseidon had a bad fate in store for many of the Greeks returning home after the conquest of Troy.

Although he was on the side of the Hellenes during the Trojan War due to the Trojans' bad behaviour since they had not paid tributes to him being the founder of their city, he did not tolerate the fact that the victors destroyed Troy and assaulted its population. Therefore, he punished them causing them to struggle and drown in the rough seas.

For the ancient Greeks then Poseidon personified the two sides of the sea, the calm one and the rough one.

Being the unique master of the sea world, Poseidon was worshipped as **Enalios, Thalassios, Pelagios, Pontios, Vythios, Naumedon, Isthmios, and Porthmios.** At the same time, however, from his earliest aspect, he maintained the attributes of a chthonic deity throughout antiquity and, thus, he is credited with a series of geological phenomena. This is why he is ascribed the epithets **Gaeochos, Seisichthon** (who moves the earth and causes earthquakes) as well as **Asphalios** and **Themelios** since, being the one causing earthquakes he is also able to stop them, if he likes.

Like Zeus, Poseidon had affairs with both goddesses and mortal women.

According to tradition, the god was raised on the island of Rhodes where lived the **Telchines**, sons of the sea, skilful craftsmen and inventors, along with their sister **Halia**. Poseidon fell in love with her and they had six sons and one daughter named Rhodes, the island taking its name after her.

In another version, Rhodes was Aphrodite's daughter from her relationship with Poseidon. It was also said that he was the father of goddess

CONSORTS - THE FIERCE SONS & OTHER OFFSPRING OF POSEIDON

AETHRA →	THESEUS
HALIA →	*6 SONS & 1 DAUGHTER - RHODES
ALOPE →	HIPPOTHOON
AMYMONE →	NAUPLIUS (COLONIST)
AMPHITRITE →	TRITON (RHODE)
ARGIOPE →	CERCYON
ARETHOUSA →	ABAX
ASTYPALAEA →	AGAEUS
APHRODITE →	*ERYX - RHODES
EARTH →	ANTAEUS
DEMETER →	DESPOENA-*AREION (HORSE)
ELARA →	TITYOS
ELLI →	PAEON
EURYALE →	ORION
EURYCYDE →	ELEIOS (COLONIST)
EURYTE →	ALLERHOTHIUS
EUROPA →	EUPHEMUS
THOOSA →	*POLYPHEMUS
THRONIA →	ABDERUS (COLONIST)
IPHIMEDA →	*OTUS-EPHIALTES-ALOADAE
CERCYRA →	PHAEAX (COLONIST)
CLIETO →	ATLAS & 9 SONS
LIBYA →	AGENOR - VOLOS
LYSIANASSA →	BOUSIRIS
MEDUSA →	*PEGASUS-CHRYSAOR=GERYON
MELANTHO →	DELPHUS (COLONIST)
MALENIPPE→	AEOLUS-BOEOTUS (COLONIST)
MELIA →	*AMYCUS
MESTRA →	EURYPYALUS
MOLIONE →	*EURYTUS-CTEATUS (MOLIONS)
NAIS →	GLAUCUS
PERIBOEA →	NAUSITHRUS
PERO →	ASOPUS
PETANE →	EUANDNE
RHODE →	IALYSOS-CAMEIROS-LINDOS
TRITONES →	ATHENA
TYRO →	PELIAS - NELEUS
CHIONE →	EUMOLPUS
CHLORIS →	PERIKLYMENUS
CHRYSOGONE →	MINYAS
?	*DERCYNUS - IALEBION
?	MACHAON - PODALERIUS
?	*PROCRUSTE
?	PROTEUS
?	*SCERON
?	TAENARUS
?	CHIOS

*FIERCE SONS :
CYCLOPS - GIANTS - MONSTERS - VIOLENT DAEMONS

Athena from his relationship with Tritonis. He also mated with Demeter in the form of a stallion and she bore a horse **Arion** as well as his secret daughter, **Mistress**, or goddess **Despoina**. With Euryale, one of Minos' daughters, the god had the great giant **Orion** endowing him with the ability to walk on the waves. Several sea daemons like **Proteas, Triton** and **Glaucus** are considered to be Poseidon's offspring.

Among his sons is included the king of Athens **Aegeus**, a hero of the Aegaees race, the father of **Theseus** who also is thought to be the son of the sea ruling god. From the ancient times till today, Aegeus' figure has been considered to be Poseidon's personification as is the case with numerous other sea daemons.

The wide range of Poseidon's divinities either as the god of waters and the sea or as the god of geological phenomena has an impact on the characteristics and attributes of his numerous children. His inexhaustible powers and catastrophic attributes were expressed in a series of myths which present him as the father of Monsters and Fierce Creatures causing evil, raping, robbing and killing.

Apart from the six wild sons he had with Halia, Poseidon is considered to be the father of the Aloadae, **Otus and Ephialtes**, twin huge giants whose mother was Iphimedeia, daughter of Triops and wife of Aloeus. These two sons of his killed each other on Naxos, in their attempt to make a conquest of goddess Artemis.

A son of Poseidon from his union with the daughter of Orchomenus Elara was said to have been the furious giant **Tityos** who attempted to rape Leto and was slain by Zeus or her brother Apollo.

Chrysaor, the horrible son of Medusa and the father of three-bodied Geryon, was also sired by Poseidon as was **Pegasus**, the divine winged horse tamed by Bellerophon.

Another of Poseidon's fierce sons was **Sarpedon** who was killed by Hercules as well as Erycas, the king of the Aelymons in Sicily, from his union with Aphrodite.

A fierce son of his was also **Amycus** the king of the Bebryces, killed by Polydeuces when the Argonauts passed through his territory.

Attica was the field of activity for certain robbers - criminals who also were Poseidon's sons. **Procrustes** who was settled near Eleusis, the wrestler **Cercyon** and finally **Scyron** near Megara. All three of them were slain by **Theseus**, who also is considered to be Poseidon's son. Even the **Laestrygones**, as well as other fierce races were sired by the god.

Finally, Cyclop **Polyphemus** who was born from the union of Poseidon with Thoosa, the daughter of Phorcys, was his darling son and this is the reason why Odysseus suffered greatly on his way back to Ithaca because he had blinded him.

Poseidon's eventful personality is particularly associated with certain animals. According to a Thessalian tradition, he is the one who will bring the first **horse** to existence. His relation to this beautiful animal, known all over Greece, attributes the epithet **Hippios** to his cult.

Another animal, the **taurus** (bull), was closely associated with the god in a whole series of myths, such as the myth of the Minotaur or that of Hippolytus' death. This kind of Poseidon's relation to two wild animals reveals his violent and impetuous

Corinthian coin bearing
Pegasus.

Bronze statue of "Poseidon the Artemisian",
(appr. 460 B.C.).
Athens, National Archaeological Museum

Marble slab of the eastern frieze of the Parthenon depicting Poseidon, Apollo and Artemis watching the Panathenaea procession. Athens, the Acropolis Museum

qualities of the god, mainly during the early stage of his cult before his dominance over the seas. Since then, he has been connected with the dolphin which is considered to be sacred because it helped him in his attempt to take Amphitrite as his wife.

WORSHIP - FESTIVALS

As the master and ruler of the aquatic world and all the waters on the earth, thanks to his relevant attributes, Poseidon was worshipped at sanctuaries which were located either on peninsulas such as Sounion and Taenaron or in areas close to the coast such as the Corinth Isthmus. There, in the Isthmia area there was held **the Isthmia** in honour of the god, one of the most important Pan-Hellenic festivals.

The Isthmia as a Pan Hellenic festival was established in the 6th c. BC during the 49th Olympiad, in the year 582 BC or 579 BC. It was then when the performance of the athletic was instituted events according to the Olympic Games model.

Earlier in time, at the same place in the sanctuary, according to the local tradition, there were held funeral games in honour of a dead child, Melicertes - Palaemon.

Pausanias the traveler, who visited the Sanctuary, narrates the story of **Inos** who, being chased by her husband Athamas, threw herself into the sea with her son **Melicertes**. A dolphin carried the boy's dead body to Isthmus where the king of Corinth Sisyphus found it, built an altar there and later on organised funeral games in his honour. Then **Melicertes** was renamed **Palaemon** and the tributes paid to him lasted throughout antiquity at Isthmia. Plutarch, however, believes that the Athenian hero **Theseus** was the initiator of the Isthmian Games. He dedicated the Games to his divine father Poseidon.

These two myths concerning the Isthmian Games obviously represent on one hand the Corinthian side and on the other hand the Athenian side.

The performance of the Isthmian Games in the form of a Panhellenic festival took place every two years in spring (end of April) and the prize was a wrath of pine leaves in the early times while during the classical and Hellenistic era it was a dry branch of celery.

The programme of the athletic events in the Isthmian Games included nude and equestrian contests as well as 'amilla neon", in other words, oarsmanship.

Besides athletic events, there were also held music and reciting contests and also painting competitions.

Corinth was in charge of the supervision and organisation of the Games throughout antiquity. Only for the period after its defeat by the Romans in 146 BC and for a century after the reconstruction of the town were the Games not held in Isthmia. Sikyon acquired the presidency of the Isthmian games.

The temple of Poseidon in Sounion (appr. 440 B.C.).

DEMETER

THE FERTILE GODDESS OF AGRICULTURE

Demeter, the most ancient and respectful goddess of fertility and agriculture, grain farming in particular, was a daughter of Cronus and Rhea. Upon her birth, she was met with the same fate as her siblings Hestia, Hera, Hades and Poseidon. She was swallowed by her father and saw sunlight only when her youngest brother Zeus forced Cronus to bring all his brothers he had swallowed back to life. The Cronides settled on Olympus as assistants and supporters of all-powerful then Zeus. Golden-haired Demeter dazed the father of all gods and humans Zeus with her beauty and fell in love with her. From their union was born **Persephone** who Demeter loved tremendously and, thus, the goddess and her daughter became inseparable.

According to the Eleusinian tradition referring to the Homeric hymn about Demeter, the goddess ceased the fertility of the earth when god **Pluto** or **Hades**, with Zeus' consent but without her knowing anything, abducted Persephone while she was playing with the Oceanides far in the blossomed meadows, and took her to the Under World, the land of the dead, where he made her his queen. To abduct her, Pluto asked for the help of Zeus and Earth. She then created an exquisite scented flower, Narcissus. When innocent Persephone went close to pluck the flower, the earth opened and from its depths Pluto rode out on his chariot and took her. Her cry reverberated across the rocks and the mountains which sent Demeter the echo of her lament. The goddess began to look high and low for her but no one had witnessed the incident apart from Hecate and Helios (Sun).

She wandered the earth for nine days and nine nights asking if anyone knew who had abducted her daughter. On the tenth day, Hecate who had heard the daughter's cries, took pity on Demeter and led her to Helios since he had witnessed everything from high up in the sky. He revealed what had happened to her. The goddess, furious with Zeus' behaviour, left Olympus and began wandering showing no interest in the fruitfulness of the earth. Disguised as an old impoverished woman, she cried day in and day out and her tears prevented the earth from growing crops. This way she arrived in Eleusis and accepted to be accommodated by the king **Celeus** and his wife **Metaneira.**

She was offered food and water but she refused. Eventually, **Iambe,** who was a servant at the palace of Celeus, made her laugh with her jokes and accepted a drink, **"cyceon".** Disguised as a mortal, the goddess decided to nurse Celeus' little son, **Demophon,** who she decided to grant him immortality to pay back the hospitality they had offered her. She fed him ambrosia and baptized him in the fire of the hearth at the palace but her ritual was interrupted when his mother found out and she screamed in fright thinking her child was being burnt.

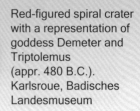

Red-figured spiral crater
with a representation of
goddess Demeter and
Triptolemus
(appr. 480 B.C.).
Karlsroue, Badisches
Landesmuseum

Then, the goddess revealed her divine identity whereas the citizens of Eleusis instituted her cult and founded her most important sanctuary. Demeter confined herself in it wailing for her daughter and nothing grew on earth any more. The earth's infertility made Zeus decide to intervene by asking his brother to send Persephone back. He agreed but before letting the girl leave the Under World gave her a pomegranate to eat, which meant that she had to return to the realm of the dead.

Finally, Zeus succeeded in persuading Demeter to let Persephone stay with her on the earth for 2/3 of the year and with her husband for 1/3. Demeter, then, taught the Eleusinians the **"Mysteries"** (secret rituals) of her worship and sent one of them, **Triptolemus**, to travel throughout Greece on her behalf and teach people agriculture and dedication to the earth so that they, civilised, could enjoy the earth's goods.

This wonderful myth signifies the phenomenon of fruitfulness and barren of nature during the year, which associates particularly with the great goddess of farming and fertility of the earth.

Marble dedicatory bas-relief depicting Demeter and her daughter Persephone (480-475 B.C.). Eleusis, Archaeological Museum

WORSHIP - FESTIVALS

Her name (De = Ge (earth) + Meter = Meter (Mother) is Greek and the Greeks believed that she protected especially cereal grains. Pro Hellenic elements have been added to her worship, of course, which attribute to her a character of a chthonic goddess of fertility. She is considered to be one of the predated goddesses of the Hellenic Pantheon although Homer rarely mentions her in his epics and never places her on Olympus. Demeter was worshipped mostly by peasants who always felt her presence, from the time they ploughed till harvest.

Several epithets given to her in various Greek cities express her prominent nature as a "fruitful". She is also referred to as **Sito, Imalys, and Megalartos.**

Her earliest sanctuaries were founded in rural remote areas such as mountainous Arcadia, where she was invoked **Deo.** It is said that in Arcadia Poseidon met her and wanted her. To avoid him she took the figure of a mare but he transformed into a stallion, united with her and they had the divine horse **Arion**.

In another version of the myth, their union gave birth to **Kore** or **Despoena**, a chthonic deity who was worshipped at a sanctuary in Lykosoura, Arcadia. A yet another allegoric myth mentions Demeter and **Pluto** who she gave birth to in Crete, after her union of love with Hero **Iasion** which happened in a field three times ploughed.

Pluto represents the earthly goods coming from the cultivation of the earth which Demeter taught farmers. The festivals held in honour of the goddess, who provided people with the gifts of the earth, corresponded to the main chores of the farming cycle.

The harvest festival was called **Thalyssia** and was held in the threshing floor. During this festival all gods were worshipped, Demeter in particular. Demeter and Kore (Persephone) as well as Dionysus were worshipped by women during **Aloa** in December, for the protection of their fields when the crops shot green. This is why the goddess was invoked **Chloe** (the green shoot).

Other festivals were the **Skirophoria**, the **Calamaea**, and the **Megalartia**.

The great festival, however, in honour of Demeter and Persephone was the **Thesmophoria** celebrated all over Greece at the beginning of autumn, the season of sowing. Only women took part in this festival. The magic rituals they engaged in aimed at ensuring not only a good harvest but also their own fertility. At the beginning of the summer during **Skira** or **Skirophoria**, they used to bury small pigs in big holes in the ground. During Thesmophoria, they unburied them in decay, mixed them with wheat and placed them on the altars beseeching the goddess to grant fruitfulness to their fields.

The inner part of a red-figured wide cup depicting Hades and Persephone (appr. 440 B.C.). London, British Museum

APOLLO
THE GOD OF LIGHT, PROPHESY AND THE ARTS

Apollo, one of the most important gods of the Greek Twelve Gods, was the son of **Zeus** and Titanid **Leto**, the daughter of Coeus and Phoebe, and the brother of Artemis. The ancient Greeks worshipped him as the **god of light** (**Phebus, Phaesembrotus, Lycegenes**), **harmony** and **tempo, prophesy** and **expiation.** He was considered to be the **patron** of **music** (**Musagetes**) and the **fine arts.**

Since the earliest times, his worship responded to the needs of life (**Agreus, Poemnius, Lycoctonus),** the works of the community and shipping (**Delphinius, Actius, Archegenes**), as well as of **medicine** (**Iatromantes, Acesius**), and the social and political institutions (**Genetor, Patrous**).

As we are informed by the Homeric and the Callimachean Hymns towards the god, when his mother Leto was pregnant by Zeus and about to give birth, she faced Hera who was enraged because of her husband's infidelity. In order to impede Leto's delivery, she commanded that no place accept and offer her shelter to have her baby. Leto wandered all over Greece, from Crete to Samothrace and from Ida in the Troad to the Cyclades and Carpathus, but no corner on the earth agreed to accommodate her. Finally, she reached **Delos**.

The myth has it that on this island there was once a Nymph, **Asteria**, Zeus had fallen in love with but, because she refused to make love with him, he changed her into a barren island. This barren island was not stable in the sea; it drifted with the wind. The seamen coming across it on their journeys used to call it **Ortygia**. When she reached Ortygia, Leto asked her to let her have her baby in her land and, in return, her about to be born son would honour her and make her important. Ortygia agreed but Leto, suffering from unbearable pain, could not deliver her baby because **Eilithyia**, the goddess of childbirth, was not there. She had been kept on Olympus by Hera, surrounded by a golden veil which prevented her from seeing and hearing, so that she did not help Leto to go into labour. Fortunately, other goddesses who supported Leto sent the messenger Iris to tell Eilithyia and bring her to the island without Hera taking any notice. Iris enticed her with a golden thread necklace and succeeded in taking her to the island. As soon as Eilithyia arrived at the island, Leto leaned onto a rock of mount Cynthus, put her arms around a palm tree that grew by the river Inopos and delivered first Artemis and then Apollo.

The island was filled with gold and took the name **Delos** which means a place visible to everybody. Its position became then stable, in the centre of a cluster of other islands which were called the Cyclades. The most glorious sanctuary of Apollo was established there.

Marble slab depicting the music contest between Apollo and Marsyas (appr. 320 B.C.).
Athens, National Archaeological Museum

Immediately after his birth and once Thetis put some nectar and ambrosia in his mouth, the young god freed himself from his swaddling clothes and stood upright so that he looked fearsome even to the gods. The first thing he did was to announce that he intended to live his life playing the guitar, travelling and informing the humans about his father's infallible will. Next, Apollo went to Olympus where he was welcomed by all the gods while Leto and Zeus felt proud of having such a son.

The god's first attention was to institute an **oracle** which would reveal his father's infallible will. He left Olympus and after having visited many places in Greece he reached the **plain** of **Lelaea** but he was not satisfied with the area. After wandering in the forests and mountains of Sterea Hellas, he arrived at the waters of **Telphusa**, below mount **Telphusio**. For the first time he had found a place he liked to build his oracle.

However, Nymph Telphusa made him change his mind when she showed him the plain of **Crisa** and a steep area at the foot of mount Parnassus. The god went there and decided to institute his oracle and build his temple at that particular area. Scanning the sea from high up the mountain, he saw a ship with Cretans onboard, heading for Pylos. He transformed into a **dolphin** and drove the ship in Itea bay, below Delphi.

The god revealed himself before the puzzled passengers of the ship, took them to the place he had chosen to build his temple and named them his first priests.

At the place where he had finally decided to establish his main oracle, the place where the rocks of mount Parnassus hung over the deep valley of Crisa, there was a sweet flowing spring, the lair of a huge dragoness. In the Homeric Hymn the dragoness is anonymous. Later on, she will be named **Delphis** or **Python**. Apollo slew this dragoness with an arrow and she, in agony, gave up her lethal ghost in the forest while the god boasted: "Now rot here upon the soil that feeds man. You at least shall live no more to be a fell bane to men - against cruel death neither Typhoeus shall avail you nor ill-famed Chimera, but here shall be the black earth and shining Hyperion make you rot".

The area where the she-dragon rotted was called **Pytho** (another name for Delphi) and Apollo was given the epithet **Pythian**, probably because "pythomai" means rot. Other authors such as Strabo interpret the names Pytho - Pythia etymologically coming from "pynthanomai" (seek to find out), an interpretation that associates the name of the area with its prophetic mission.

Ivory statuette of Lycian Apollo (3rd c. A.D.). Athens, the Ancient Agora Museum

To make amends for killing the monster, Apollo sentenced himself to a one year exile (eight years in other versions) in the Tempi valley.

There, he served king **Admetus,** who was aware of his divine origin and treated him with due respect. Apollo helped him to take **Alcestes**, the most beautiful daughter of Pelia, as his wife. The god knew that Admetus was to die young and asked the Moirae (Fates) to postpone his death provided that someone else would take his place. But when it came time for Admetus to die, no one accepted to sacrifice himself, not even his elderly parents.

Instead, only Alcestes volunteered. Fortunately, when Thanatus (god of death) was taking her, Heracles appeared and managed to rescue her and take her back safe and sound to her husband. Once Apollo's expiation was over, he returned to Delphi crowned with a laurel-leave wreath. To honour his return, the people of Delphi instituted the "**Septeria**" festival, held every nine years.

The rite of the **Septeria** was a representation of Python's slaughter by Apollo. Close to the god's sanctuary, they used to build a wooden hut symbolising the monster's lair. A procession, led by a child whose parents were alive, approached the hut holding firebrands in their hands. The child personifying Apollo shot an arrow at the hut. Then, they all set it on fire and while it burnt down they rushed away without looking back.

Next the **Daphnophoria** represented the ritual of Apollo's expiation. The child personifying Apollo at the Septeria set off with other peers to walk along the **Pythias path** the god had followed when going to Tempi. There, he offered a sacrifice to the god's altar and returned with his companion to Delphi holding laurel branches.

Of all the gods of Olympus, Apollo was the

Marble dedicatory bas-relief which depicts Apollo, Hermes and three Nymphs dancing (2nd c. B.C.).
Athens, National Archaeological Museum

principal god of **prophesy**. He was the first to teach the art of prophesy, as it is obvious in various relative myths which depict him as the father of many significant diviners (Melambus, Amphiaraus, Calchas, Teiresias, Mando, and Cassandra).

Being the god of **light** and **Helios** (the sun), he overwhelmed darkness and, through the light, was able to unveil the forthcoming events and reveal every secret to the people. There were many who associated him with **Lycauges** (dawn) that is, the first light of the day, and thus worshipped him under the name **Lyceus.** His oracles transferred by **Pythia** gave both the mortal ordinary people and the lords appropriate advice to do the right thing in their lives.

The Greek cities as well as other foreign countries received the god's oracles and made decisions according to the advice they were given by the Oracle of Delphi. The god consulted colonists, too. In this case he was called **Archegetes**. He would choose the leader of the colonists after an oracle, advised on the location of the new colony and the plan of the new city (**Themelios**=Founder).

According to the tradition, Apollo left his sacred oracle in the winter and travelled to the land of the **Hyperboreans** where the sun shone constantly and there was no darkness. During his absence, god **Dionysus** took his place, while, when springtime came, god Apollo returned bringing along light.

The inner part of an Attic white wide cup with Apollo making a libation (480-475 B.C.). Delphi, Archaeological Museum

ATTRIBUTES OF APOLLO   HIS CONSORTS AND OFFSPRING

ATTRIBUTES OF APOLLO	HIS CONSORTS AND OFFSPRING
MUSIC	THALIA → CORYBANDS CALLIOPE → ORPHEUS & HYMENAEUS PSAMATHE → LINUS
PROPHETIC	MANDO → MOPSUS CASSANDRA → TROILUS
MEDICAL	CORONIS → ASCLEPIUS CYRENE → ARISTAEUS
COLONIAL	DRYOPE → AMPHISSUS CORYCIA → LYCOROS THERO → CHAERON THYIA or MELAENA or CELAENO → DELPHUS ACALE → MILETUS - NAXOS - CODON FTHIA → DORUS CREUSA → ION ? → EPIDAURUS RHOYO → ANIUS PROCLEA → TENES

APOLLO'S CONSORTS AND SONS

Apollo had affairs with numerous beautiful women. He first fell in love with **Daphne** (Laurel), the daughter of the river Peneus. Daphne spent her time hunting in the woods. When he met her, the god desired her and wanted to have her so he started to chase her. She meant to remain a pure girl and tried to escape his chase but, in vain. She then begged her father to help her and he changed her into a laurel tree. Apollo, distraught by not having been able to enjoy her love, made her his emblem.

He used to always crown himself with her branches and leaves while, in the contests held in Delphi in his honour, the victors' prize was a laurel wreath. Moreover, Pythia, the priestess in Delphi, chewed laurel leaves before delivering her oracles. It is also said that both the first temple of Apollo in Delphi and his temple in Eretria (**Daphnephorus** Apollo) were made from laurel leaves.

Apollo attempted to seduce **Marpessa**, the daughter of the river **Euenus**, but he was unlucky as she was won by **Idas**, the twin son of Aphareus and Arene, the brother of Lygeus. The god then fought with his rival but, after the intervention of Zeus who asked Marpessa to choose between the two, she chose Idas on the grounds that the god would abandon her sometime.

Apollo also loved **Cassandra**, the daughter of Priam and Hecube in Troy, and in order to win her he taught her the art of prophesy. However, when Cassandra refused his love, the god, although he allowed her to exercise the art of prophesy, deprived her from the ability to convince with her prophesies. According to another myth, Apollo and Cassandra coupled and he fathered **Troilus**, a hero of the Trojans, who was killed at a very young age.

It is said that, in Colophone, the god fell in love with **Mando,** the daughter of diviner Teiresias, and they had a son, the great diviner **Mopsus** who established the oracle of **Clarus** in Ionia and of **Mallos** in Cilicia in cooperation with diviner **Amphilochus**.

Among the women Apollo loved were the Muse **Calliope** who gave birth to **Orpheus** and **Hymenaeus,** and her sister **Thalia** who gave birth to the **Corybands**, young warriors identified with the Couretes having a demonical strength in dancing.

The god also loved a very handsome young man, **Hyacinthus**, who, however, he accidentally killed while throwing the discus. The god did not also have any luck with his love for **Hymenaeus**, who other myths have it that he was his son.

In several poetic pieces such as Pindar's Odes, Apollo is considered to be the father of **Asclepius, Aristaeus, Linus** and other gods and heroes whose mission was to heal and protect the people from diseases and misfortunes cast on them.

Asclepius was born from his union of love with **Coronis** or **Arsinoe**, the daughter of **Phlegyas**, king of Thessaly. When Asclepius, being a doctor, cured the mortals, Hades complained to Zeus about the fact that the humans would become immortal and thus, Zeus struck him down with a lightning bolt. Then, Apollo in revenge killed the three Cyclops who fashioned the thunderbolts for Zeus. Zeus became so furious that he would have banished him to the Tartarus if Leto had not begged him not to. Instead, he sent him to serve a mortal, Admetus, king of Pherae, for one year (or eight years).

From Thessaly, he abducted beautiful **Cyrene**, the daughter of the king of the Lapiths Hypseus, carried her to Libya and from their union of love there was born **Aristaeus**, a benefactor to people since he taught them bee-keeping and saved them from epidemic diseases.

As we know through numerous myths, Apollo fathered a lot of sons who became local heroes, founders of tribes and colonists. Hence, his son **Epidaurus** became a renowned hero of Epidaurus, **Delphus**, whom he had by **Thyia**, the daughter of Castalius, became a hero of Delphi, **Chaeron**, whom the god had by **Thero**, was the founder of Chaeronia, and his son **Amphissus**, by **Dryope**, became the colonist of Amphissa.

On Minos' daughter **Acalle** he fathered three sons, **Cydon, Miletos** and **Naxos**, who founded the homonymous cities. On **Proclea**, Cycnus' wife, he fathered **Tenes**, who became the king of Tenedus and was killed by Achilles, an event that drove the god to cause his death later on by directing the arrow of Paris at the hero's weak heel (Achille's heel).

Head of a gold and ivory statue probably of Apollo (appr. 550 B.C.).
Delphi, Archaeological Museum

Apollo was known to be the father of **Dorus**, founder of the Doric race, as well as of **Ion**, founder of the Ionian race, who was born after his union of love with **Creusa**, the daughter of Erechtheus, and with the god's will he became the king of Athens.

THE GOD PROTECTOR AND AVENGER

Apollo always protected his beloved heroes and punished harshly those who were disrespectful. Using his bow and arrows, which accompanied him from the day he was born, aided the faithful and, frequently, killed or wounded his rivals.

With his arrows he took the life of **Tityos**, who attempted to rape Leto, of **Eurytus**, who dared challenge him in archery, as well as of the children of **Niobe**, when she boasted of her superiority to Leto because she had more children than her.

During the **Gigantomachy** he aimed straight at the eyes of **Ephialtes**, one of the most fearsome **Giants**, while he had the Giants **Aloadae** kill each other for his sister Artemis. It was for her that he also slew handsome **Orion** for fear that he would seduce her. When **Marsyas** challenged him to a music contest and after winning the competition, Apollo had him flayed alive, whereas **Midas** saw ears of a donkey grow on his head for having sided with Marsyas.

In the Trojan War Apollo fought by the side of the Trojans and did great damage to the Hellenes. However, he sent the plague to **Troy** because, although he had built its walls with Poseidon, king **Laomedon** refused to give him his reward according to their agreement. He also infected with the plague the Greek encampment, when **Agamemnon** insulted his priest **Chryses** by not sending back his daughter **Chryseis** he had captured.

Ruthless though he could become when the god angered, he was prodigious and propitious for his faithful who were granted with his favour. According to the myth, Apollo aided **Heracles** in freeing Thebes from its subjection to Orchomenus. He also protected **Admetus** by advising him to take **Alcestes** for a wife so that he escaped his early death. She accepted to replace him in Hades when time came for him to die. Furthermore, he saved the **Argonauts** from a wild storm in the Cretan sea. After the fall of the **Seven leaders** in Thebes, he assisted their descendants, mainly **Alcmaeon**, the son of **Amphiaraos**, advising him to avenge his father's death by conquering Thebes and killing his mother who had betrayed him and was the cause of his death.

In addition, well known is his support to **Orestes**, the son of Agamemnon and Clytemnestra, whom he ordered to slay his mother and her lover, Aigisthus, for having killed his father upon his return from Troy. Overwhelmed with guilt and relentlessly pursued by the **Erinyes** (the Furies), Orestes will turn to Apollo, who, in cooperation with goddess **Athena**, will protect him and free him from his guilt for having been a matricide. The god himself will plead before the court of the gods claiming that Orestes committed the crime under his order in order to maintain the paternal right.

Extracts from musical hymns to Apollo.
Delphi, Archaeological Museum

WORSHIP - FESTIVALS

Apollo's worship was broadly spread in every Greek region in the ancient years. It originated in the mainland of Asia Minor and spread all over metropolitan Greece where it integrated with numerous local deities such as Mycenaean **Paeona**, Lacons **Carnus** and **Hyacinth**, Boeotians **Ismenous** and **Ptoous**, whose attributes had to do with the bucolic life or the prevention of diseases and their cure. This mingling justifies the many-pleated cast of features of the god.

In metropolitan **Greece**, his worship was formed on the axis of the god's two greater sanctuaries, i.e. **Delphi** and **Delos** - cult sites of pan-Hellenic influence, although the first represented the Dorians and the second mainly the Ionians.

One of the most significant shrines of Apollo was at Didyma (**Didymaeus Apollo**), south of Miletus, on the SW coast of Asia Minor, which was also an oracle. At Didyma, there was held the **Didymia** festival with athletic and music contests to honour "the birthday of the god", the **Anoigmoi** festival for the opening of every oracular period, etc. Another similar cult site was in **Clarus** (**Clarius Apollo**), where the god was worshipped with mystic rites along with his sister Andaea, mother of gods, who was identified with **Hecate** or **Cybele**.

On Rhodes and other islands of the Dodecanese, Apollo was worshipped for being the patron of rural life as **Smintheus** (protector from rats) and as **Mylandius** (for the mill grinding grains). Moreover, in later years, the god identified with **Helios** (the Sun), which was represented by the renowned **Colossus of Rhodes**, in the port. On Samos, during every new harvest there was held a festival similar to the Athenian **Thargelia**.

In Athens the **Thargelia** was held in May (**Thargelion**). Then, there was offered the god the **Thargelus**, that is, the first-grains of the earth, and there took place the ceremonial procession

The Sanctuary of Apollo on Delos

of the "**eiresione**". The "eiresione" was a branch of olive tree bound with wool on which figs, bread rolls, olive and wine in containers were affixed, held by a boy whose parents were alive. Next, there followed the expiatory ritual of pursuing the **pharmacos** during which the Athenian citizens drove two men either of lower class or common criminals outside the city and treated them as **scape-goats**.

The first-fruits of the earth were also offered during the **Pyanepsia** festival in the month of Pyanepsion (i.e. after middle October).

In **Amyclae** in Laconia, there was held the **Hyacinthia** festival, with expiations at Hyacinthus' tomb, music contests and a ceremonial procession carrying a robe which was offered to god Apollo.

In Sparta, as well as in other Doric cities in Greece and Low Italy there was held the festival of **Carneia (Carneius Apollo)**, where the god was worshipped identified with the most ancient horned god **Carnus**. During the festival, **sciadia** (tents) were pitched symbolising shepherds' huts or encampments.

On the island of Delos, the birthplace of the god, the greatest Ionian cult site, Apollo was worshipped as **Delios** and there was held the **Delia**, with athletic and music competitions, similar to the **Pythia** in Delphi, the second great pan-Hellenic cult site of the Greeks. There

Head of the statue of Apollo from the western pediment of the temple of Zeus in Olympia (appr. 457 B.C.). Olympia, Archaeological Museum

the god was worshipped as **Daphnephorus** and Pythia used to chew laurel leaves in order to deliver the god's oracles at the most glorious oracular centre of the Greek world.

The **Pythia** festival included musical contests in honour of the god of music. It was initiated, according to tradition, immediately after the killing of Pytho by Apollo and, at first, it was held every eight years. Since 6th c. B.C., in 582 B.C., it was upgraded into pan-Hellenic games following the model of the Olympic Games, and was held every four years that is, the games became "pendederic". Then, equestrian and nude events were introduced, and the prize was a laurel wreath whose branches were cut from the Tempi valley by a "**paes amphithales**" (a boy whose both parents were alive).

The **Pythian Games** took place in the third year after the Olympic Games, in the month of Bucatius (end of August). According to the programme, they lasted from six to eight days and began with sacrifices to the god and other rituals. There followed the **musical** games with contests of guitar players, pipe players, dithyramb and drama. Then, there took place the **nude** games of adolescents and men and, finally, the **equestrian** games according to the model of the Olympic Games. The athletic games were held in a flat area at Chryseus plain. However, from the 5th c. B.C., when the Stadium was built, all the games took place there. Later on, the music and drama contests were held in the theatre, in the god's sacred shrine, next to his temple.

The temple of Apollo in Delphi.

ARTEMIS

THE HUNTRESS
GODDESS

The mistress of nature and protectress of new-born animals, goddess Artemis, the daughter of Zeus and Leto, Apollo's sister, identifies with the Achaean deity "**POTNIA THERON**" (mistress of wild animals), as well as Cybele, Rhea, Hecate and Selene.

She was born on the island of Delos on the same day as her brother Apollo, only she was first so that she could help with his delivery assuming the role of Eileithyia in aiding child-birth, which underlines her attribute as the protectress of child-birth (**ARTEMIS LOCHEIA**).

Since her early childhood she had her father's permission never to be confined by marriage. Goddess - virgin and, therefore, loveless, she supports innocent youngsters

Marble dedicatory bas-relief depicting Artemis seated on a rock, accepting offerings by her faithful (4th c. B.C.). Attica, the Brauron Museum

whereas she crushes those who violate the oaths of purity. Known is her liking towards Hippolytus, Theseus' son, who despised love affairs and hunted in the woods all day long like his beloved goddess.

Artemis spent her life on the high mountains hunting sometimes boars, sometimes deer and other wild animals always carrying her arrows on her back and her bow in her hands. This is why in the Homeric hymns she is called "pure agrotera", which means she who wanders in the fields "eocheaera" (shooting arrows) "chryselakatos" (with a golden bow).

When hunting, her companions were the Nymphs of the mountains while at dances, in which she played a leading part during the gods' feasts, she was accompanied by the Muses and the Charitae.

Whereas Artemis was protective and kind to all young people who were pure as well as unmarried girls, she became implacable with anyone who attempted to deceive or undermine her. She gave grave punishment even to those who lusted for her.

Actaeon, the son of Aristaeus and Autonome, daughter of Cadmus, who boasted that he saw her bathing naked in a pool, was punished severely. She turned him into a stag and let his fifty dogs tear him up into pieces.

She took revenge on **Niobe**, the wife of Amphion king of Thebe, by putting all her offsprings to death because she boasted about her seven children and considered herself, being the mother of fourteen children, to be superior to Leto who had only two. Artemis shot Niobe's seven daughters down with her arrows, and her brother, Apollo, shot her seven sons.

With her arrows she killed **Callisto**, her hunting in the forests companion, because she didn't keep her vow of chastity and had a love affair with Zeus. In addition, it is said that jealousy drove her to kill **Orion**, the son of Poseidon, in Ortygia because she had slept with Eos, the goddess of dawn. In some versions, the goddess punished him because he dared challenge her to a discus throwing contest or because he raped Opis, one of her followers.

Along with Apollo, she put **Tityos**, the son of Poseidon and **Helara**, to death because the moment he saw Leto he tried to rape her. She punished **Oenea**, the father of Meleager, by sending a wild boar to his country and, also, the Thessalian king **Admetos** by filling up his room with snakes because they both forgot to offer the sacrifices they had promised her.

During the Trojan War she supports the Trojans with her brother, Apollo, although she dislikes fighting. The one who Artemis cannot resist, though, is Hera, the wife of Zeus, who she calls "a female lioness" but only as far as women are concerned, and offends her by throwing her bow far away when they are engaged in a fight.

Goddess Artemis employs numerous tricks against the river **Alpheios** that fell in love with her, when his passion drove him to take her by surprise during a night-long feast. Along with her companions they painted their faces in clay so that the river, being unable to recognise her, left empty-handed.

A well known festival in honour of Artemis was held in Brauron in Attica, where the clothes of women who had died during puerperium were dedicated to her. In her temple there served little girls between five and ten years old, who were called "Arktoi" (bears).

Marble statue of a little girl dedicated to Artemis (4th c. B.C.). Attica, the Brauron Museum

HERMES

THE MOST INGENIOUS OF THE GODS

H ermes, who is a member of the Twelve Olympian gods, is of a genuine Greek origin and a very early god of **the air** and **the winds**. According to a pseudo-Homeric hymn to Hermes, he was the son of **Zeus** and one of the seven Pleiades, **Maia**, the daughter of Atlas and Pleione. Maia lived all alone in a cave of Mount Cyllene (modern Zerhia), in Arcadia. Zeus found her there and they slept together during a dark night when Hera was asleep and could not notice him leaving. As soon as Hermes was born, still being an infant, tricked his mother and left secretly to steal some cattle Apollo had in Pieria. On his way, he first met a tortoise. At once the idea of killing it and using its shell to make a musical instrument came to him. He added cattle skin to the shell and chords of lamb intestines which he strained tight on a piece of wood and, thus, he invented the first lyre in the world. He arrived in Pieria at night and stole 50 oxen which he took with him. In order not to be discovered, he had the oxen walk backwards and he wore sandals made from branches and leaves. On his way back, he encountered an elderly man, who he made swear not to tell anyone anything about seeing him. Shortly, he reached the outskirts of Pylos and on the banks of the river Alpheios he killed two of the oxen to eat and sacrifice to the gods while he concealed the rest in a cave. But he needed fire to cook the meat. Genius little Hermes made fire by rubbing a laurel twig on a thick log until sparks of fire sprang up. Therefore the god was the first one to invent fire. He, then, cut the animals in portions, one for each god, and offered his sacrifice without him eating any. He was very tired, though, and returned to his mother and their cave running as fast as the wind. Being aware of what he had been up to, Maia told him that Apollo was to punish him but the little god's response was a brave one saying that in such case he would destroy the god's oracle in Delphi stealing Apollo's treasure.

Apollo discovered that fifty oxen were missing but had to use his prophetic power to find out who the thief was. He rushed to the cave in Cyllene, found baby Hermes in his cradle and asked him angrily to bring back his oxen. However, Hermes as a new born god insisted on being innocent. As they could not solve the problem themselves, they climbed up to Mount Olympus and asked their father Zeus to decide who was right. Little Hermes charmed his great father with his eloquence and cunning wiles and made him laugh with his ingenuity, nevertheless, he ordered him to give Apollo his oxen back. Since then the two brothers had a close relationship. Hermes gave Apollo his lyre and he made another musical instrument for himself, the syringe, a multiple pipe.

Apollo, on the other hand, gave him the **kerykeion**, a golden wand, the symbol of wealth and goods, and proclaimed him a protector of shepherds and flocks. He also gave him permission to receive oracles by the Moirae and give them to humans. The young god was so glad with his brother's gifts that he swore to him that he would never rob him and, to make sure he would honour his oath, he would never visit him in his residence.

Once he grew up, Hermes became the **Messenger of the gods**. Before him the position was held by winged **Iris**, daughter of Thaumas and the Oceanid Electra. The ancient Greeks believed that after Hermes appearance the gods used Iris to deliver messages to women

Hermes by Praxiteles
(appr. 330 B.C.).
Olympia, Archaeological Museum

and Hermes to men or, in another version, Iris being a companion to Hera she was also her personal messenger while Hermes served Zeus (**Zeus' Agent**). The God used to wear winged sandals and he often bore the winged cap on his head, **petassus**. Holding in his hand the "kerykeion" so that he was recognised as the official messenger of the gods by everyone, he delivered their orders fast, as fast as the wind. Thanks to his versatility and inventive intelligence, he carried out every difficult mission. As the god of the wind, Hermes had the ability to travel and reach every place. Hence, he became the patron of travellers (**Hegemonios - Enodios**) while, at the same time, he was responsible for the security of residences and cities securing the gates in the walls and the houses. For this attribute he was worshipped as **Thyraeus** or **Propylaeus** or **Pylaeus Hermes** (of the Gate Way). Hermes, the associated with any kind of journey god, was honoured with wayside markers. The most important ones were called **Hermae Hills**, that is to say, piles of stones in the centre of which there used to place a column symbolising the god himself. At the crossroads, there used to place the **Hermean columns** as signposts marking distances and roads. They were topped by a bust of Hermes bearing a wreath. Statues of the god were in most of the marketplaces (agora) of the ancient Greek cities, which proves the fact that Hermes was also the god of **Commerse** and was worshipped as **Agoraeus** (of the market). In addition, he is considered to be the deviser of the measures, the weights and the scales. He was especially honoured by the merchants as **Kerdoous** (of profit) **Hermes** in order to sell their goods and earn even the random finding called **hermaion**.

Every single attribute of god Hermes derives from the fact that he is the god of the wind and all phenomena associated with the wind. Tradition has it that he was the first to observe the stars in the sky and understand the changes of the weather and the alternating seasons. As the god of the wind, the winged god could reach any place in a split second and, as the wind whirls and changes everything, he also changes the fate of the humans. Flying everywhere, Hermes managed to exceed the boundaries of the earth and reach the Under World. Being a traveller, the god also becomes a **psychopompos** or **Psychagogus** (conductor of the soul) who guides the dead to Hades. On the last day of the **Anthesteria**, a festival dedicated to god Dionysus, people used to honour the dead offering sacrifices to **Chthonian Hermes**. Moreover, as a tireless runner and a dynamic warrior, he constituted a raw model for adolescents practising in Gymnasiums and arenas. His statues decorated athletic facilities where he was worshipped as **Agonios** or **Enagonios** Hermes (of an athletic competition), mainly during the posterior antiquity. Due to the fact that in the premises of gymnasiums there taught scholars of the time, Hermes was also given the epithet **Logios** (scholar), as the patron of orators, philosophers and literary men. It is not without a reason that the Greek word **hermeneia** (interpretation) derives from his name.

The god is the interpreter of Speech and things. He himself is an orator and negotiates the orders of Zeus towards the mortals or the immortals. As the god of the wind he also gives tone to speech so that everyone's words can be understood by everyone.

Marble tomb vase with two handles depicting Hermes psycho pomp; detail (appr. 420 B.C.).
Athens, National Archaeological Museum

Furthermore, when **Pandora**, the first woman, is created, he gives her a human voice. He makes such a perfect and long speech before the Argives that he attracts the audience's interest in an effort to cover Zeus' extramarital love affairs while his speech persuades Hades to allow Persephone to return to her mother Demeter.

His attribute as the god of the wind makes him the messenger of the gods and mainly the only god responsible for their **communication** with the mortals. In a split second he brings Zeus' orders to Agamemnon and Aegisthus in **Mycenae**, and simultaneously he does the same to Paris and his father Priam in **Troy**, as well as to Prometheus in **Caucasus**, while he arrives at the island of Calypso on the other side of the Cosmos.

Hermes was especially loved not only by the immortal gods but also by the mortals. He offered his help generously to everyone. On several occasions he helped his father with his love affairs and saved his children from Hera's wrath. He also helped Apollo's children and released Ares from the fetters the Aloadae giants had him under. He always got on well with goddess Hera and particularly loved the heroes such as Heracles and Perseus. He greatly cared for **Odysseus** who was his grandson from his son **Autolycus**, and protected him during the Trojan War and on his way back home to Ithaca.

The god, like his father Zeus, often fell in love with beautiful young girls and nymphs of the forests. Of the goddesses, his greatest passion was **Aphrodite**, who he tried to make her fall for him telling her beautiful things and, eventually, she did. From their relationship was born beautiful **Peitho**, who, like her father, had the charisma to persuade, mainly the in love ones, with her words, as well as the exceptionally handsome **Hermaphroditus**. A nymph, however, **Salmacis**, fell madly in love with him and asked the gods to unite their bodies forever. Since then, **Hermaphroditus** (intersex), having become both a man and a woman, lost his masculine power.

Hermes' relationship with a nymph of Arcadia, Orsinoae, resulted in the birth of **Pan**, a peculiar being having hair on his face and body and goat-like legs, tail, horns and ears. His mother was frightened and abandoned him but Hermes took him along on Olympus where the gods welcomed him as he was a cheerful baby and smiled at everyone. Pan, however, is considered to be the son of several other deities or mortals. He was a chthonic god, patron of fertility, the soul of nature, companion and patron of shepherds and hunters. He belonged to the retinue of Dionysus as a great dancer, a wine lover and a skilful pipe player.

From Hermes' love affairs with various other Nymphs there were born many offspring such as **Myrtilos**, a stableman of the king of Pissa, Oenomaus, the king of Corinth **Vounos**, the king of Sikyon, **Polyvos, Autolycus, the grandfather** of ingenious Odysseus, **Abderus** who gave his name to the city of Abdera, **Aethalides**, who was the messenger of the Argonauts, as well as the hero of the Trojan War **Eudoros**.

Hermes was worshipped all over Greece and its settlements; however, his main site of worship was Cyllene in Arcadia. In many places he was honoured with festivals, the **Hermaia**. In Athens, on the Third day of the Anthesteria festival, which was dedicated to the dead, the faithful used to offer sacrifices solely to Hermes.

Marble statuette of Pan (2nd c. B.C.).
Athens, National Archaeological Museum

ARES

THE GOD OF WAR

Ares is a member of the Olympian gods, the son of Zeus and Hera. His first homeland is considered to be Thrace, the land of a warlike people, where he was first and foremost worshipped along with Dionysus and Artemis. His cult began there and then spread to the south up to Boeotia and Thebes. As a warfare god he is liked neither by gods nor by humans.

Homer in his epics characterises him as a capricious, stormy, man-corrupting and bloodlust warrior. He fights violently, brutally and frivolously contrary to his sister Athena who, also being a goddess of war, combined strategic warfare with wisdom.

During the Trojan War, Ares sides with the Trojans with his sister **Eris** (Discord) and two of his children, **Deimos** (Terror) and **Phobos** (Fear) who represented the fright and rout at the sight of the enemy. His father himself dislikes his impulsive and choleric character resembling his mother's Hera as it is cited in the Iliad: "no other god do I fight like you, for you are always in quest for arguments, pains and wars". Although his two sons, **Ascalaphus** and **Ialmenus** have sided with Agamemnon, Ares fights viciously against the Achaeans. However, whenever he has to face Athena, who belongs to the opposite side, he is defeated and seriously wounded by the goddess, by Argive Diomedes and, on another occasion, by Heracles, all of whom were guided by her.

Being a fierce beast which finds pleasure in slaughter and bloodshed, contrary to the rest of the Olympian gods, Ares always finds himself confronting many different heroes, both mortals and immortals. The risks and his destructive predisposition to everyone drive him to defeat and ridicule quite often. All the gods are pleased and laugh at him when he is overpowered.

According to tradition, the **Aloadae** giants, Otus and Ephialtes, captured him and put him in a bronze urn where he remained for thirteen months until Hermes released him. After the incident of his confinement he did not appear before the immortals, because he knew only well that they would laugh at him, and hid on the island of Naxos. Moreover, there is an account in the Odyssey according to which, after committing adultery with his beloved goddess **Aphrodite**, he was snared in a metallic net fashioned by Hephaestus, being the cheated upon spouse, so as he, too, to become a ridicule before the eyes of all the gods.

Beautiful Aphrodite became the wife of Hephaestus forced by Hera. She adored the violent but handsome god of war. Together they had four children, **Deimos** and **Phobos,** who were fierce like their father and accompanied him to fights and battles, and **Harmonia** and **Eros** who resembled their mother. Harmonia was created by the sexual intercourse of two opposite elements therefore she is considered to be the synthesis of the hard and the soft or the fierce and the peaceful, as well as the symbol of balance and order through the union of two opposite forces.

Ares is also thought to be the father of a number of bloodthirsty and violent kings. His son was **Oenomaos** king of Pisa in Eleia who was born from the god's union of love with Harpis. Another son of his was **Diomedes** king of Thrace, who bred carnivorous horses. His offspring was **Cycnus** who slew anyone travelling towards Tempi. Both of them were killed by Heracles, who also destroyed the **Stymphalian Birds** bred by Ares thus causing the god's wrath. (See the labours of Heracles). Ares and Chryse had a son **Phlegyas** whom Apollo killed with his arrows when he attempted to burn his temple down. Another son of his is thought to be the dragon ravaging Thebes which was slain by Cadmus making the god furious.

Ares' daughter was **Penthesileia**, queen of the Amazons, as well as **Alcippe** who was created from his union with **Agraulo,** daughter of Cecrops, king of Athens. Tradition has it that Alirrothios, son of Poseidon, attempted to rape Alcippe and was killed by Ares in the act. Poseidon then demanded that Ares be brought to trial before the gods who were acknowledged as a supreme court for murder cases for the first time. Ares was brought to trial and was acquitted on a rocky hill beside the Acropolis of Athens which was named **Areos Pagus,** that is, the rock of Ares, and has been established as the supreme Athenian court since then.

Due to his attributes as the god of warfare, Ares was worshipped less than the rest of the gods. The most archaic worshipping centre in honour of the god is believed to be **Thebes** where he was considered to be the father of Harmonia, wife of Cadmus, as well as of the dragon from the teeth of which grew the **Sparti**, the ancestors of the Thebans.

Traveller Pausanias, in his work, accounts temples in honour of Ares in various regions of the Peloponnese such as in Hermione and Troezen, on the way from Argos to Mantineia, in Tenea, Geronthes in Laconia and in Sparta. During Classical times, in Sparta as well as in Mycenae he was identified with **Enyalius**, a most ancient warlike god of caran descent whose believers used to sacrifice dogs, being powerful animals, and dedicated their armoury after their victories.

In Athens, there was a temple in the Ancient Agora which had been transferred from Acharnes during the Roman occupation and was similar to the temple of Hephaestus and Athena, the well known Hephaesteum, on the hill of Agoraeus Colonos in the Agora of Athens. The two temples had been built in classical times, in 5th c. B.C.

Ares confronting the Giants; from the northern frieze of the Siphnian treasury (appr. 525 B.C.). Delphi, Archaeological Museum

APHRODITE

THE GODDESS OF BEAUTY AND LOVE

The goddess of beauty and love was born, as mentioned in Theogony by Hesiod, arising from the sea foam (aphros). When Cronus cut off Uranus' genitals and threw them in the sea, there was formed foam which, floating, reached Cyprus and took the figure of a woman. There she was welcomed by Horae, who dressed her up like a queen with a golden crown and jewellery and led her to the gods. This is how a gorgeous goddess was born and was named **Aphrodite** because she rose from the sea foam (aphros). She was also given the names **Anadyomene** because she arose from the waves, **Cypris the Cyprogeneia** (the Lady of Cyprus) when she first set foot on the sea-washed Cyprus and **Cytherea** because her white foam floated past Cythera before reaching Cyprus.

The cult of the goddess dates back in antiquity, is lost in the depths of centuries, originates in the East and identifies with that of Astarte. According to another tradition referring to Homer and the epic poets, Aphrodite is the daughter of **Zeus and Dione.** In Classical times Aphrodite was believed to have been born from a sea shell. Aphrodite's relation to the sea is documented by her epithets **Pontia** (of the sea), **Limenia** (of the harbour), **Pelagia** (of the open sea), **Thalassia** (of the sea) and **Galenaea** (of the calm sea). Patroness of the seamen, she offered them a good voyage. Seamen were grateful to her as **Limenia** for reaching their destination safely. In addition, as **Akraia,** she had temples situated upon hills near the coast especially close to capes so that she "forever watches the bright open sea in its infinity".

Her cult had spread over several of the Aegean islands such as Lesbos, Lemnos, Samos, Rhodes, Melos, Naxos, Paros and Crete, as well as the Asia Minor coast and, of course, lots of the towns on Cyprus and the mainland in Greece. Cosmogonic powers spring from the goddess. Foam born and sea arising Aphrodite was the earth, the life which springs from the ocean, the watery vastness that gives birth and empowers and ensures continuity of existence. Her mating with Poseidon, the chthonic god but at the same time the master of the waters, depicts the life-giving coexistence of the Earth and the Sea.

Aphrodite, the most beautiful female being in the world, was the goddess who inspired love to all the mortals as well as immortal gods. And she was the one who excited this passion and charmed all living creations on earth. No one could resist or elude any of her desires and this is why everyone honoured and respected her being aware of the fact that the goddess, who generously offered her love, could become an avenger for those despising her or acting against her wishes.

The goddess took part in the Trojan War supporting the Trojans. According to the myth,

Red-figured peliki depicting the birth of Aphrodite (370-360 B.C.). Thessaloniki, Archaeological Museum

she was the moral perpetrator of this war as she initiated it when, after being awarded the title of the most beautiful goddess by Paris, she chose gorgeous Helen as the most beautiful mortal woman, made her fall in love with him and follow him in Troy. Naturally therefore she sided with the Trojans and opposed the Hellenes inventing excuses in order to punish them. Aphrodite made Diomedes pay dearly for wounding her during a fight of theirs on the battlefield. She had his wife fall in love with Cometes, his close friend and comrade-in-arms.

She punished the two sisters Clytaemnestra and Beautiful Helen (Helen of Troy) by making them engage in love affairs and, thus, ridicule their husbands, because their father Tyndareos did not worship her. For the same reason she caused the Lemnian women to emit a disgusting odour so that no man approached them. Their miasma ended when, after her husband, Hephaestus, wholeheartedly begged her, she decided to send the Argonauts to Lemnos to pair off with them. She even took revenge on Eos, the goddess of dawn, causing her to always changing lovers because she slept with Ares who was her darling god.

Her biggest victim was Hippolitus who, being an innocent youngster, scorned the love for Aphrodite and worshipped Artemis. In revenge, she caused Faedra, his father's wife and thus his stepmother, to fall madly in love with him. Eventually he rejected her passion and had a horrible death.

Aphrodite targeted her arrows not only at the mortals but also the immortals. She liked to have fun mainly with her father's Zeus love affairs. There came a time though that he decided to punish her in the same way: he made her fall in passionate love with Anchisis, a

The statue of "Aphrodite of Melos" (2nd c. B.C.). Paris, the Louvre

handsome young man of the Dardanus of the Troy family. Aphrodite seduced him with her exquisite beauty and slept with him. From them Aeneas was born who, later on, took part in the Trojan War siding with the Trojans.

Another of Aphrodite's great lovers was mortal handsome **Adonis**. When he was a baby she left him with Persephone to raise him for her, but when he grew into a handsome young man, Persephone refused to return him. Zeus decreed that Adonis spent half a year on Earth and the rest in Hades. Unfortunately, during his stay on earth, he got killed by a wild boar and of his lost blood the first roses ever grew while of Aphrodite's tears a new flower sprung up, the anemone. Adonis became the symbol of nature's bloom and withering. Aphrodite became

Marble complex of Aphrodite and Eros on a Dolphin (3rd c. B.C.).
Thassos, Archaeological Museum

the protectress of the life cycle. She was given the name **Gennetyllis (Genetrix)** as well as **Antheia** since through love and lust she acted as a generative force and this attribute of hers had an effect on the fruits of the earth and the flowers and the plants and all the living creatures.

In the world of the gods Aphrodite became the wife of Hephaestus following Hera's suggestion. However, her dearest lover was the god of war, **Ares**. From their mating four children were born: **Harmonia, Deimos, Phobus** and **Eros.** Always attending her along with the Charitae and the Horae, the little winged god targeted his arrows mercilessly, causing happiness, joy but also pain to the mortals and the immortals.

Aphrodite was often depicted armed and was also worshipped as **"Panoplos"** (Fully armed) since she associated with the war caused by love. In addition, she was given the epithet **"Pandemos"** because she represented not only innocent love but also sexual attraction to the point that she associated with even prostitution.

In ancient Corinth, at her sanctuary on the Acrocorinth, there worked a large number of courtesans who also took part in the celebrations held in her honour. One of them, the well-known for her beauty Phryne, inspired the famous sculptor Praxiteles to create one of her most beautiful statues.

Marble complex of Aphrodite, Pan and Eros (appr. 100 B.C.). Athens, National Archaeological Museum

Marble bas-relief with a representation of the birth of Aphrodite (appr. 465 B.C.). Rome, Museo Nazionale Romano

HEPHAESTUS
THE MASTER CRAFTSMAN OF THE GODS

Hephaestus, the god of earthly fire and the fire of the volcanoes, was also a member of the Olympian Twelve Gods. There are two myths concerning his birth. According to the first one, he was a son of Zeus and Hera, and grew up with the rest of the gods on Olympus. Once, during one of his parents' quarrels, he tried to stop them siding with his mother. His enraged father cast him off Olympus onto the island of Lemnos, where he was taken care of by its people, the **Sintians**, since he was injured on one leg which left him crippled.

Another myth has it that Hera gave birth to Hephaestus alone, without a man, because Zeus had also fathered Athena on his own. Hephaestus was born sickly and limping so Hera, feeling ashamed, cast him into the sea. However, he was rescued by two sea deities, Nereid **Thetis** and Oceanid **Eurynome**, who raised him secretly in the cave of Nereus. When Hephaestus grew up, he decided to return to Olympus and avenge his mother. Having become a great craftsman working with metal, he made her a throne on which, when she sat extremely pleased, she was trapped in invisible nets. After a lot of attempts, either politely or strictly, on the part of the gods to persuade Hephaestus to release her, god Dionysus made him drunk and managed to take him to Olympus on the back of a mule accompanied by the Satyrs and the Nymphs. Hephaestus demanded and was granted the permission to become equal to the Olympian gods and take as a bride Aphrodite. Before Aphrodite, though, Hephaestus had married Charis, whereas Hesiod mentions Aglaia, the youngest of the three Charitae.

Only in the Odyssey is Aphrodite first introduced as his wife. After making Zeus swear to him that he would satisfy all of his desires, he released his mother and from then on he became her loyal companion. He was also devoted to Zeus, as we are informed in the Gigantomachy. Apart from his renowned throne Hephaestus forged, as described in the **Odyssey**, he made an excellent metal net in which he ensnared his unfaithful wife Aphrodite in the arms of his lover, god Ares.

In all justice, therefore, Homer attributes to him the epithet **Chalkeas** (coppersmith) since of all the gods he was the most skilful and the most inventive as a metal craftsman. In Lemnos, he had organised his workshop when he was very young, while, in another version, when he was appointed a guard of the tamed Typhon who he had crashed under Etna in Sicily, it is said that he had organized another workshop on the neck of his father's enemy. On Olympus, he had yet another workshop in which he created the most significant metal works in the world.

Numerous extraordinary objects playing an important role in certain myths are considered to be the works of Hephaestus **(Hephaestioteucta)**.

As a great architect and builder he had constructed the dwellings of the gods on Olympus and the bed for god Helios so that he has a rest on it at Night as he is carried from West to East before he begins his journey in heaven in the morning. Moreover, he had fashioned the arrows of Apollo and Artemis, the sceptre of Zeus, Ariadne's wreath, Harmonia's necklace, Demeter's scythe and Perseus' scythe with which he decapitated Medusa, Heracles' golden weapons and Achilles' armour with his famous shield adorned with exquisite depictions, as described in the Iliad by Homer.

Hephaestus was not only a mere constructor of metal object but also a great inventor of machinery and living creatures. He, himself, using earth and water moulded **Pandora**, the first woman, and gave her beauty and a human voice. He had also constructed two golden girls to support him since his legs were weak. He used copper to create a giant, **Talos**, who guarded Crete roaming continually the island, a valuable gift to Minos. He also infused life to a golden hound - guard of Zeus, the golden and silver hounds-guards at the palace of the king of the Phaeacians Alcinous and to two bulls which belonged to the king of Colchis Aeetes. For him, because he was a son of Helios, to whom he was grateful since he had helped him during the Gigantomachy, Hephaestus had made exquisite works such as four fountains which poured milk, wine, aroma and water, either cold or warm depending on the season of the year.

Due to his craftsmanship, the god was closely bonded with the goddess of wisdom **Athena**. He was the one who, during his birth, split Zeus' head open with his axe and the fully armed goddess sprang out. Later, he fell in love with her and attempted to unite with her but with no success. From his sperm, however, which fell on the Athenian ground, was born **Erichthonius**, a subsequent king of Athens.

According to other versions, **Erichthonius** was born after his intercourse with **Atthis**, daughter of

Red-figured peliki; drunken Hephaestus is tottering and a satyr is supporting him (435-430 B.C.).
Munich, Staatliche Antikensammlungen

Cranaus, as well as **Cecrops**, another very early king of the city.

According to other local traditions, Hephaestus fell in love with **Cabeiro**, the daughter of Proteus, and he fathered the **Cabeiroi** who aided him in his workshop in Lemnos. Hephaestus was a generous and lovable god. He liked to offer gifts to the mortals and the immortals, and sympathised with the miserable ones seeing to their well being. It was with great reluctance that he followed Zeus' orders to rivet **Prometheus** on mount Caucasus; Prometheus identifies with the god as far as several of his attributes are concerned.

He sympathised with handsome giant **Orion** who was blinded by Oenopion in Chios and helped him meet Helios to ask for his eyesight back. For his travel, he gave him **Cedalion**, his instructor and assistant in working with metal in Lemnos, as an aid. When **Pelops** threw Myrtilus into the Myrtoan Sea and in his quest for expiation reached the edge of the Ocean, Hephaestus took charge of his expiation. In addition, when Lemnos was left without men because of the rage of Aphrodite, the god, who loved the island a lot, persuaded his wife to forgive the women and send them the Argonauts so that a new generation is created.

During the Trojan War, Hephaestus sided with the Hellenes. Feeling grateful to Thetis who had rescued him when he fell from Olympus into the sea, he forged her son's Achilles armour and when the river Scamander rushed to drown the hero who was slaying the Trojans, Hephaestus accepted Hera's plea and filled the river banks with huge fires and burnt everything in the plain.

The **cult** of Hephaestus was located in Lemnos and the northwest Asia Minor, and was transferred to **Athens** at the end of the 6th c. B.C. when Lemnos became an Athenian dominion. During the 5th c. B.C. at the Athenian agora on the hill of Agoraeus Colonos, there was constructed his luxurious temple in which he was worshipped along with goddess **Athena Ergana**. His cult was combined with that of other similar to him gods such as Prometheus and Athena. In Athens there were held the Hephaesteia and the Chalkeia in his honour, festivals with torch-races, during which **Athena Hephaesteia** was worshipped as well.

The temple of Hephaestus in the Ancient Agora of Athens.

HESTIA

THE HOME GODDESS

T he goddess Hestia belongs to the Twelve Gods cycle and makes a couple with Hephaestus. Other versions of the myth give her seat to Dionyssus. The goddess represents **virginity** and **chastity**. She protects the family hearth or the "sacred fire" in the altars. According to Hesiod, she is considered to be the first born daughter of Cronus and Rhea, sister of Zeus, Poseidon and Hades, Hera and Demeter.

In the Homeric Hymn to Aphrodite, Apollo and Poseidon sought for her hand in marriage but Hestia refused and swore to retain her virginity forever (aeiparthene).

Then Zeus ordered to bestow honours on her in every temple as well as respect by everyone. As her cult shows, the fact that Hestia had the first place in the divine hierarchy is documented. The so-called by the ancients "aph' hestias" (starting with Hestia) means that when sacrifices were offered, she was invoked first and the first libation in feasts was made to her honour. At the pan-hellenic sanctuaries at Olympia and Delphi, the goddess' altar constitutes the public Hestia (Hearth) of the Hellenes.

Every Greek city had its public hearth with an ever-burning flame, always paying tribute to the goddess. At the prytaneum there was her altar where the 'fire of the town' burned incessantly. Only in this type of cult does Hestia identify with the Roman deity Vesta. The meaning, that is, was the centre of the household, the community or the town, of Greece, of the earth and eventually the earth itself as the fixed centre of the Universe.

Detail from the outside of a red-figured wide cup depicting Hestia (appr. 520 B.C.). Tarcinia, Museo Nazionale Archeologico

DIONYSUS
THE GOD OF GRAPEVINES AND WINE

One of the major gods of the Greek Pantheon, god Dionysus incorporated three initially self-existent deities of a different origin. The most ancient one associates with the Under World and stands out under the name **Zagreus**, i.e. "the great Hunter". The second deity presents himself as a god of fertility and vegetation, **patron of tree growing**, of vines and wine; the third one represents **ecstatic worship**.

Zeus saw Semele, the gorgeous daughter of Cadmus, king of Thebes, from the sky and fell in love with her. He came down to the earth and during the night visited her in her chambers and they spent the night together. However, the vigilant eye of his wife Hera saw what had happened and decided to avenge. She knew that Zeus had promised Semele to grant her any favour she might ask him for. So, Hera told her to ask him to reveal himself before her in all his glory, as he had done on their wedding day. When Semele asked Zeus for this favour, he tried to dissuade her but in vain. Since he had given her his word, he had to present himself on his chariot, amidst thunder and lightning. Semele's chamber as well as the whole palace was set on fire and Semele was burnt to death in the flames. Zeus, though, rescued the fetus she was carrying by sewing it into his thigh so that Hera did not see it. When time came, Zeus cut the stitches, released the fully-grown baby and brought him to daylight.

This is how **pyrigenes** (born in the fire)**, merorraphes** (sewn into the thigh)**, dimetor** (from two mothers) and **dyssotokos** (of double birth) god **Dionysus** was born.

Being fully aware of Hera's hostile disposition against all of his illegal offspring, Zeus tried to rear the infant secretly and gave him to Ino, Semele's sister, and her husband Athamas to raise him as a girl along with their own children. Hera, though, was not deceived. She infused such mania to the couple that they both killed their children. Zeus turned Dionysus into a little kid and gave him to Hermes to take him to the Nymphs who lived in Nyssa, a distant mountain in Asia. Dionysus was raised there; nevertheless Hera went on pursuing him. She struck him with madness and made him wander in Egypt and Syria. Rhea, however, cured him in Phrygia, taught him the religious rites, which later on took his name, and specified his outfit, the **nevris** (pelt from a young deer), which was also worn by the Maenads as his companions. The God travelled everywhere in order to make the rituals in his honour and the cultivation of grapevines known, accompanied by the Nysaees nymphs who had raised him, the Maenads, the Satyrs and the Seilenes as well as Pan. Some people adored him, some others, though, sent him away, and therefore the god treated them accordingly later on.

In Aetolia, **Oeneus**, the king of the land, welcomed him in a friendly way and Dionysus, in return, gave him the first vine to plant. In Attica, where he claimed to have been the first to grow grapevines, **Icarius**, after whom the Municipality of Ikaria is named, welcomed him and the god taught him how to make wine. Icarius paid the god's wondrous gift with his death. He was so excited with the wine that he offered it to some shepherds. The wine muddled them and after they drank enormous amounts, drunk as they were, they killed him and buried him secretly. However, his loyal dog, Maira, found the place he had been buried and showed it to his daughter Herigone, who hung herself in her despair.

Apart from those who adored god Dionysus, there were certain people who did not accept him as a god and abstained from any religious rituals in his honour. They considered him to be a strange mortal of suspicious behaviour who seduced women and drew them on to the mountains to take part in orgies during the rituals of his worship. Their disrespect, though, was not let go by the god.

The daughters of Proetus, king of Tiryns, went mad when they denied him and so did the three **daughters of king Minys** in Orchomenus, who did not participate in the festivities for Dionysus, instead they stayed home and wove. They were struck by such mania that they killed the child of one of them, took to the mountains and, at last, transformed into birds. In

The bronze spiral crater of Derveni
depicting Dionysus and Ariadne
(330-310 B.C.).
Thessaloniki, Archaeological Museum

a similar way the daughters of the **Municipality of Eleutheres**, in Attica were driven to madness, whereas **Lycurgus**, king of the Hedones in Thrace, was slain by his own horses because he was against the god. So it happened to **Pentheus**, who was torn into pieces by his own mother, **Agave**, and the women in Thebes, as Euripides narrates in Bacches.

After the worship of Dionysus had been established in many regions, especially in those where grapevines were cultivated, the god went up to Olympus along with his mother Semele who, she too, became immortal and was renamed Thyone or Dione.

According to a myth associating Dionysus with **Naxos**, a vine producing island too, the god met there **Ariadne**, daughter of Minos, who had followed Theseus after he had killed the Minotaur. When they arrived in Dia (Naxos), Theseus, regretfully, had to give her over to Dionysus obeying to the order of goddess Athena. The God had seen her sleeping on the beach; he fell in love with her and took her for his wife. They had two children together, **Oenopion** and **Staphylus**.

Dionysus on a panther, mosaic floor (appr. 320 B.C.). Pella, Archaeological Museum

This myth of the god's union of love with Ariadne or Ariagne or Aridela, which has several versions, symbolised the fertility of the earth, as Ariadne is believed to have been the Minoan goddess of vegetation.

Another interesting myth concerning Dionysus is first mentioned in the Homeric Hymn to the god, not to mention other authors. Once, Dionysus was standing on some rocks scanning the sea on his own. There sailed past a ship with **Tyrrhenian** pirates onboard who spotted him, mistook him for a wealthy prince and kidnapped him in order to ask for ransom. Only the steersman did realise he was an Olympian god. Dionysus did not object to the pirates even when they attempted to bind him, besides, the ropes broke loose on their own. Suddenly, as they sailed, the ship filled with wine, the sails turned into grapes, ivy sprang up around the mast whereas flowers grew in the rowlocks. The god himself turned into a lion and slew the chief pirate. The rest of the pirates, frightened by the event as well as by a huge bear which appeared onboard from nowhere, leapt into the sea and were turned into dolphins. Finally, the god was left alone with the steersman who was against the pirates' plans and this is why he survived.

Dionysus, being the son of Zeus, according to other myths, was confronted by the **Titans** who pursued him since he had been a child. They captured him, slew him and, after cutting him into pieces, they ate him. They even offered Apollo some of their meal but he took the pieces and buried them under the Tripod in the Delphi Oracle where Pythia prophesised. What he did is the reason why Dionysus is co-worshipped at Delphi, Apollo's place. Concerning Dionysus' slaughter, it was said that the Titans acted in accordance with Hera's will. Others said that in his attempt to escape, the god turned into a calf and in this form he was captured and slain. Afterwards, Zeus turned the Titans into ash from which came the humans on the earth. It is, moreover, mythologised that Dionysus came back to life again because Demeter, who is also believed to be his mother, or Rhea assembled his pieces. In addition, it is said that Athena saved Dionysus' heart and gave it to Zeus who swallowed it or gave it to Semele who gave birth to the god again.

During the **Gigantomachy**, Dionysus along with Hephaestus and the Satyrs on braying donkeys gave the Giants a scare with the noise and made them run away. Dionysus touched them with his "thyrsos" (a staff) until he exterminated all of them. Changed into a lion, he mangled gigantic Eurypus or Roetus.

Once Dionysus reached the Peloponnese, he had to face **Perseus** who dominated Argolis. In the battle there took part the god with his wife Ariadne and the Maenads, whereas Perseus had Hera in the form of Melambus by his side. When Perseus turned Ariadne into stone by showing her the head of Medusa, Dionysus wanted to destroy Argos.

After Hermes' intervention, Hera's favourite city was saved and the opponents reconciled. It is also narrated that Perseus won and dropped Dionysus dead in the water of Lerna. Dionysus was popular with all mortals and immortals but for Hera. He came to terms with her, though, when he

Bronze head of Dionysus crowned with ivy
(2nd c. B.C.).
Athens, National Archaeological Museum

managed to persuade Hephaestus with his wine and his kindness to go up on Olympus and reconcile with his mother. Then, she agreed on Dionysus becoming a member of the family of the Olympian gods. Zeus, in particular, appointed him an heir to his throne and made him king of the gods.

WORSHIP - FESTIVALS

Dionysus' cult started in the rural regions and then spread all over Greece and the Greek settlements. The god was especially worshipped in Thrace, Boeotia, mount Parnassus and Attica. The Greek Dionysus is the god of wine and, in general, of fertility and vegetation except for grains which are protected by Demeter. His valuable gifts were grapevines and wine. The Hellenes worshipped him as a god of joy, liberator and saviour. His religion is characterised by **ecstasy** which helps people free their emotions by drinking wine and dancing wildly. Thus, the god is called **Lyssios** because he freed people from hardships and worries.

The god's **orgies** (the word does not have the modern degraded meaning; instead, it means **sacred works**) included religious rites on mount Parnassus every two years, at the beginning of December. Only women organised in "thiasoi" (the ecstatic retinues of Dionysus) participated in them. They were called the **Maenads or Bacchae or Thyiads** who went into a religious hysteria: holding a lit **davlos** (torch) and a **thyrsus**, a long stick wrapped in ivy and vine leaves and tipped by a pine cone, the emblem of the god, ran frantically up to the mountain top in the winter dark and cold, dancing in frenzy to pipe music until they dropped exhausted onto the ground. In their desire to communicate with the god, whichever wild animal they came across on the wooded slopes of Parnassus they tore it up to pieces and ate its raw flesh believing in the god's reincarnation to an animal.

In suchlike rites, the women honoured the god in the regions all over Greece up to Macedonia, which borders Thrace, and in Asia Minor, too. In later years during the archaic period, Dionysus was officially accepted at Delphi, where he spent the winters when Apollo left for the Hyperboreans.

In Athens, the worship of Dionysus spread from Eleutherae in Boeotia during the 6th c. B.C. In the city of Athena Pallas were laid the foundations for the creation of the theatre, and the **drama** in particular, having its origins in the dithyramb. The **dithyramb** was a hymn to Dionysus chanted by a group of dancing men. This hymn evolved through a series of changes and enrichment with chorale songs, imitating moves, speech and dialogue. Thespis, from the municipality of Ikaria, for the first time in the middle of 6th c. B.C., introduced the first actor, a person outside the chorus who conversed with it. During the 5th c. B.C. there was constructed the first theatre building near the temple of god Dionysus, at the south foot of the Acropolis rock, whereas the drama reaches its peak demonstrating three types: tragedy, comedy and satiric drama. Performances were always held during the festivals in honour of the god, the **Great Dionysia** and the **Lenaea**.

The **Great Dionysia** was held in honour of Dionysus in the month of Elapheboliona (March -

The inside of a black-figured wide cup depicting Dionysus sailing in the company of dolphins (appr. 540-520 B.C.). Munich, Staatliche Antikensammlungen

April), in commemoration of the introduction of the worship of **Dionysus Eleutherios** (Liberator) in Athens. In a long procession, in which the citizens participated, the faithful, holding torches, carried the god's statue from his temple outside the walls of the city and brought it back in the evening. During the procession they carried images of phalli. At the god's sanctuary they used to offer sacrifices and the contest of dithyramb began. The rest of the festival was dedicated to drama performances during which five comedies by five poets were presented on one day, while on the rest three days three tragedy poets competed with three tragedies and a satiric drama each.

The **Lenaea** was held in the month of Gamelion (January - February) in order to thank the god for the wine production. On the days of the festival there were held drama performances which two tragic poets presenting two tragedies each and five comedy playwrights with a comedy each competed in.

The **Anthesteria** was also dedicated to Dionysus. They were held in the month of Anthesterion (February - March) and included a citizens' wine-drinking competition and feasting. At the same time, they offered the god wreaths and the god's wedding ceremony with the wife of the "archon - basileus" (lord - sovereign) was held, during which all the citizens communed with Dionysus so that they ensured a rich harvest. The last day was devoted to the dead, and the faithful offered the god and Chthonic Hermes seeds in pots. Another festival dedicated to Dionysus was the **Minor Dionysia** which was held in the month of Poseidaeon (December - January) and was connected with the most ancient traditions concerning the god.

The theatre of Dionysus on the south slope of the Acropolis rock of Athens, as it is today.

HADES OR PLUTO

THE GOD OF THE DEAD

Hades was the son of **Cronus** and **Rhea** and the brother of Zeus and Poseidon. After the fall of Cronus, his three sons shared the authority of the world by drawing lots. Zeus ruled the sky, Poseidon the sea and Hades the crowded kingdom of the dead located in the Under World.

The main attribute of Hades was the fact that he was **invisible** as is denoted by his name which bears the privative prefix **a** and *idein* (see) as well as by his epithet **Aidoneus**. The ancients believed that Hades became invisible wearing the **cynen**, that is, a magic hood which hid the god not only from the mortals but also from the other gods.

The god's relationship with the death of the mortals gave him a lot of epithets which prove that everyone considered him to be fearsome and unconquerable. In many regions in Greece, it was believed that there existed various gods of the Under World, all of which were merciless such as **Catachthonius Zeus** or **Zagreus** (the Great Hunter) or **Melanippus** (Black Rider), who pursues people on horseback like the Modern Greek **Charos**. Some people called Hades **Admetus**, i.e. merciless, or **Neleus**, i.e. unconquerable. Because the death of every mortal is inevitable, many people used "euphemistic" names, for instance, **Clymenus** was called the king of the Under World in Hermione or **Eurupylus** and his palace **eurupylus do** that is, a big dwelling with wide gates so that the crowds of mortals leaving life every day could enter easily.

One of his most common and comforting names was **Pluto**, in other words the wealth giver to the people, because the vegetation and the crops of the earth come from its depths and can be considered as a gift from the god of the Under World. By this name a lot of people honoured him and had numerous sanctuaries in the Greek cities as the god of fruitfulness and wealth, whereas by the name **Hades** he was a hateful god.

The goddess of the dead and life-giving earth was Pluto's wife, Persephone, the beloved daughter of goddess Demeter. After the god had abducted her and the agreement he had made with her mother, Persephone spent four months a year with her spouse while she spent the rest eight months with her mother in the upper world. During this period, the earth got green and gave her fruits, whereas in the summer months, when the Kore (Girl) went down to the kingdom of Hades, the sun burnt the earth which remained dry.

The Under World, where the souls of the dead gathered, was also called the Hades. It was a large area under the earth, very far away from the world of the living. This is where the deceased entered but there was no way out for anyone. Its gate was guarded by **Cerberus**, a mythical hound, which welcomed those arriving at the gate, but tore into pieces those who tried to leave the domain. Cerberus was taken alive to the Upper World by Heracles while carrying out his last labour.

According to certain myths, the realm of the Dead was visited by renown for their bravery heroes such as **Heracles**, **Theseus** and **Odysseus**, who were able to descend to the Hades through some mouths that were said to be found on the earth and led to it, for instance, one on mount Taenaron, and come back to earth again alive.

In the Under World there flowed three rivers: **Acheron**, in the waters of which there took place the introduction of the deceased to the beyond, since their souls had to cross it on the **acation** (small boat) initially ferried by **Hermes Psychopomp** and later by **Charon**; **Styx**, the horrible river upon which even the gods took unbreakable oaths, and lastly, **Cocytos**, the river of lament.

In many regions, Charon ferried the souls of the deceased to the Under World crossing Lake **Acherusia**, not the river Acheron. Once the dead reached the Hades, they presented themselves before **Minos**, **Rhadamanthys** and **Aeacus**, the three judges who judged the actions of the dead while living with justice. Minos, whose laws were familiar to people for thousands of years, judged ambiguous cases, Rhadamanthys, who settled people's disputes always in a fair way, judged the souls of the Asians, and Aeacus, the wise and fair king of Aegina, judged the souls of the Europeans.

In the realm of Hades there was no special place for the virtuous or the corrupt ones. Therefore, the big sinners underwent their punishment before the eyes of all the dead. **Sisyphus**, king of Corinth, because he had shown disrespect towards Zeus and the gods of the Under World, had to push a huge rock all day long until he reached the top of a hill from where the rock rolled back down and he had to push it up again. King **Tantalus**, who dared not only reveal divine secrets to the mortals but also slew his son to offer him as a meal to the gods in order to test their intelligence, was convicted to eternal hunger and thirst. Thus, whenever he went close to water to drink, the water receded or whenever he tried to pick the fruits from a tree, the wind blew suddenly and drifted them away.

Pluto and Persephone seated in their thrones in the Under World. A Locrian Painting (470-460 B.C.). Region, Calabria, Museo Nazionale

OTHER DEITIES

F or the ancient Greeks there was a crowd of other divine figures having different attributes, who lived either in mythical places or in heaven or even on the earth and in the depths of the sea.

CELESTIAL DEITIES

A member of the **Celestial deities** was **Helios** (the Sun), the son of Titan **Hyperion** and Titanid **Theia**. The Hellenes believed that he was a huge eye in the sky that watched every form of life on the earth from up there. They also imagined him as a face framed by lush golden hair and crowned by the shining aureole of his rays. His name denotes someone who radiates and warms or burns. On a daily basis, Helios crosses the sky on his chariot, driven by two winged horses, following his incessant path over lands and seas, while in the evening a golden cup carries him asleep to the starting point of his run.

His starting point is located on the one side of primordial **Oceanus**, which washes circularly the entire globe, he leaves behind **Aea**, his homeland, the red sea and the land of

the **Ethiops**, rises towards the centre of the celestial dome, over all the places of the world and then, he goes down to the other edge of Oceanus in **Erytheia**, the west land of the Ethiops (the black faces of the westerners) where are the god's sacred herds of deep red oxen.

It was also said that Helios had two palaces, one in the East and the other in the West, from where he started in the morning and ended in the evening.

Helios had a lot of spouses and a lot of children: a myth has it that he united in love with **Selene** and had the **Horae,** who represented the seasons of the year.

By the Oceanid **Perse** or **Perseis** he had **Aeetes**, the father of **Medea**, and **Circe**, **Pasiphae** and **Rhodes** who gave him seven wise children.

By **Neaera**, the mother of the **Heliades maidens** who guarded his herds, as well as by **Clymene**, the wife of Merops, king of the Ethiops, he had numerous daughters and

Marble head of Helios (2nd c. B.C.). Rhodes, Archaeological Museum

sons respectively. It is said that by the latter he had **Phaethon** (in other versions he was the son of Eos) who, in order to make sure that his father recognised him, he asked him to drive his chariot.

Helios had to satisfy his desire but the horses reacted and escaped causing such catastrophe on the Earth that Zeus was forced to strike unfortunate and inept Phaethon with his thunderbolt.

The sisters of Helios were **Selene**, whose name means light (bright - shining) and **Eos** - the **rose-fingered** in Homer - who was the personification of dawn, which brings the first light of the day and announces the trip of Helios. Her incomparable glow and freshness caused plenty of young men to fall in love with her.

According to a tradition, once god Ares slept with her and jealous Aphrodite cast a curse on her to fall in love with every attractive young man she came across. And so it happened. Eos made love with **Astraeus** and gave birth to the winds **Zephyrus, Borheus** and **Notus, Eosphorus** that is, the Morning Star, and the stars in the sky.

From her union of love with handsome **Tethonus** she had **Hematheon** and **Memnon** who was killed by Achilles during the Trojan War. By **Cephalus**, the son of Hermes, he had **Phaethon** who was so good-looking that Aphrodite fell in love with him.

Despite the numerous, good-looking lovers, Eos could not find happiness. Thus, it is said that when she loved **Tethonus**, she begged Zeus to make him immortal. However, she forgot to ask the gods to grant him eternal youth. **Tethonus** lived with her, grew old and shrank so much that only his voice could be heard. Then Eos, to free him from eternal old age, changed him into a **cicada**.

Selene, the third child of Hyperion and Theia, offered the humans the moonlight. It is said that her beauty caused Zeus to fall in love with her and from their union there was born **Pandia**, the mother of the Athenian king Pandion.

According to other myths though, from Selene's affair with Helios the three **Horae** were born. The favourite lover, however, of the **"supreme sweet-glowing goddess, the queen of the Sky"** was good-looking **Endymeon**, who had asked Zeus for eternal youth and eternal sleep. Selene would visit him in a cave of mount Latmo close to Miletos and from their affair she had 50 daughters representing the 50 weeks of the lunar year.

Selene (the Moon) is rising; from the inside part of a red-figured wide cup by the painter of Brygus (appr. 485 B.C.). Berlin, Staatliche Museen

It was believed that Eos was the mother of **Erse** (according to some she was the daughter of Cecrops) who symbolised the coolness of the night, as well as the **Nemean Lion.**

Selene's figure is covered by other deities who connected with the night such as Hecate, Artemis, Persephone, Cybele and Isis. Similarly, **Helios** is set apart by the like gods of the light and the day such as **Apollo**, **Prometheus** and **Zeus**.

For the ancient Greeks, the divine messenger **Iris** was the personification of the **rainbow**, connecting the earth with the sky with its multi-coloured line, which they also thought to be the line of her path as she ran swiftly in the sky to deliver divine messages.

Iris was the daughter of **Thaumas,** son of Pontus, and **Electra**, daughter of Oceanus, and her sisters were the **Harpyae,** who were some sort of storm, while her husband was **Zephyrus**.

The **Harpyae, Aello, Ocypetes, Celaeno, Podarge, Ocythaee** and others, dashed like a storm and carried away everything on their way, ravaging people's goods. One of their victims was the king of Thrace, diviner **Pheneas**, who they left without food for days and nights. The blind diviner was about to die, but he was rescued by the **Argonauts** who wanted to consult him and sent the sons of Boreus **Zete** and **Calae** to kill them on condition he showed them the way to Colchis.

In the ancient Greek myths, apart from the Harpyae, who symbolised the disastrous winds, there also were the **Anemoi** (Winds) who had the figure of a man and beneficent attributes. These were **Boreas**, **Notus**, **Eurus** and **Zephyrus,** sons of **Io** and **Astraeus,** except for Eurus.

Boreas (north wind) was thought of as the king of Thrace, since he blew from its northern mountains. He was depicted as a horse having wings on his shoulders.

According to the popular Athenian myth, Boreas abducted the daughter of Erechtheus **Oreithyia** from the banks of the river Ilyssus, took her to Thrace and made her the mother of the **Boreadae, Zete** and **Calae**, of **Cleopatra**, who married Pheneus, and of **Chione**, who paired off with Poseidon and gave birth to **Eumolpus**.

In certain myths such as the epics, the relationship of these beneficent winds with the **horse** is mentioned. It is said that Boreas fell in love with the mares of Erichthonius in Troy and fathered twelve exquisite horses which could gallop in the air.

Zephyrus is the personification of the west wind. The myths have it that he had fathered **Hyacinthus**, who Apollo fell in love with but killed accidentally, when his arrow or discus

Black-figured representation of Iris from a ceramic utensil (500 B.C.).
Eleusis, Archaeological Museum

missed the target due to a gust from the wind Zephyrus. This wind of the west fathered the renowned stallions of Achilles, **Balias** and **Xanthus** who had a human voice. From the union of the wind with **Flora** there were born the spring flowers.

Notus and Eurus were the personifications of the south and southeast winds respectively.

The **stars** in the sky also had a human figure. The **Pleiades** (modern day cluster of Poulia) were the seven daughters of Atlas and Oceanid Pleione, who changed into stars because they could not bear their father's anguish carrying the weight of the whole world on his back.

The **Yades**, also stars in the sky, are associated with the constellation of Taurus. They were the Nymphs who nursed god Dionysus in Nyssa. According to the myth, they had a brother, **Hya**, who died bitten by a snake and they wept from their grief. Zeus changed them into stars to free them from their pain.

The winged wind Zephyrus abducting young Hyacinth; from the inside of a red-figured wide cup (appr. 490 B.C.). Boston, Museum of Fine Arts

HECATE

A great goddess, preceding the twelve gods of Olympus, was **Hecate**, the daughter of Perses (son of Titan Creus) and Asteria. She was worshipped particularly by the lower classes and was associated with the attributes of Selene and Artemis. She was thought of as the patroness of night travellers, unguarded places and witches. Closely related to witchcraft and witch activities, especially during the night, she was believed to have control over the criminals and the ghosts who harm the people.

People always turned to her for support. This is why in every Greek household there was a small shrine in her honour, where an oil lamp was alight all night. In addition, her shrines were found in passageways or rough roads where travellers offered her grains or sweets seeking her favour.

In Hesiod' "Theogony" there is preserved a text by one of her followers which refers to Hecate as the most beloved to Zeus goddess. He honoured her in a special way by making her all-powerful, so that she could help the king to judge in a fair manner, the warrior win the battles, the athlete win the games, the seaman avoid dangers, the fisherman enjoy a rich fish catch and the herdsman breed his herds.

EARTH DEITIES

Members of the deities on the earth, apart from **Gaea** herself and **Rhea**, are the goat-legged **Pan**, **Priapus** and a deity coming from Phrygia, **Cybele**. She was a goddess of nature like so many others in the world of the Hellenic myths, widely known in Greece and Rome. She was worshipped as a **Great Mother**, the **Mother of Gods**, **Idaea Goddess**, and also bore the epithets **Dindymene** and **Berecynthia**. She was identified with Rhea, Gaea and Demeter. Tradition particularly accounts the passion of the goddess for **Attis**, a handsome man from Lydia, her priest, who was killed by a wild boar sent by Zeus having been upset when he saw the tributes the Lydians paid to him because he was the priest of the great goddess. Cybele mourned the dead Attis with laments which became the core of her worship.

According to the Athenian tradition, when a wandering priest of Cybele initiated the Athenian women into the orgiastic cult of the goddess, their husbands were annoyed and dropped him into a chasm. The goddess punished them by sending the plague which did not end until after, directed by the Delphi Oracle, they dedicated a statue to him at the **Metroon** in their Agora.

The centre of Cybele's worship was the Phrygian city **Pessinous**, on mount Dindymo after which she was called Dindymene. The cult of the great goddess of nature passed from A. Minor to Thrace and then to the mainland in Greece and Attica where they preferred to honour her by the name **Great Goddess**. In Athens she was worshipped at the Metroon of the Agora, where, initially, since 6th c. B.C. there was her temple.

Cybele was also worshipped in Piraeus where orgies took place, as well as all over **Attica** such as in Kephissia, Ramnous, Oropus, Marathon and Anagyrous (modern Bari) where in a cave there is the figure of the goddess sitting on a throne carved on the walls. She was also worshipped in the rest of Greece and, indeed, in Epidaurus has been found an epigraph praising the goddess, attributed to the Argive poetess Telesilla.

PAN

Pan, the cheerful companion of Cybele and Dionysus, was also worshipped as the patron of fertility, especially that of herdsmen and hunters.

According to the most popular myths, Pan either did not have parents or was the son of **Arcas**, or of a goat-shepherd, **Cranthes**, and a goat, or of Aether and nymph Oenoe, or of Uranus and Gaea, or of Cronus and Rhea, or even of Zeus and Callisto or of Hermes and Nymph Arsinoe.

In the Homeric Hymn to **Pan** is reported that when his mother saw she had given birth to a son that looked like a monster, she was

Small temple with a statuette of Cybele (400 B.C.). Athens, National Archaeological Museum

Philip, Olympiad and Alexander or Dionysus, Ariadne and Pan; ivory affixed jewel from the Tomb of the Prince in Vergina (4th c. B.C.). Vergina, the Royal Tombs

frightened and abandoned him. Hermes, however, liked him, took him along to Olympus where he presented him to all the gods and they welcomed him and loved him, but Dionysus loved him most of all.

Another myth has it that Pan was the brother of Arcas and had been raised with Zeus in Ide, Crete. Therefore, being his friend from an early age, he stood by him during the Titanomachy or the Gigantomachy, screaming fiercely during the battle which scattered them in panic. It is said that he acted alike during the Marathon battle in 490 B.C. and drove the Persians away. This is why the Athenians honoured him and spread his worship while they made up the myth having it that Pan had **Crotus** with one of the Nymphs.

A myth presenting Pan as the inventor of the pan flute that is, the **syrinx**, has it that **Syrinx** was a nymph who the goat-legged god chased and, to avoid being raped, changed into a reed from which Pan fashioned his flute. Playing this flute, he contested god Apollo, aspiring to prove that he was a superior musician than the god. However, the god won as of the three judges only **Midas** liked Pan and gave him his vote. Apollo avenged not only Pan for

Marble head of goddess Tyche (1st c. A.D.). Corinth, Archaeological Museum

his conceit but also Midas, by turning his ears into a donkey's.

Apart from Syrinx, Pan pursued numerous women to have a relationship with, such as **Peuce** (Pitys) who turned into a pine tree to escape him and since then the god adorns himself with her branches. The same thing happened with **Echo,** who pretended not to hear his call and then was torn to pieces by herdsmen after Pan had sent them mania. There was nothing left from the Nymph but the echo of her voice. In another version, Pan managed to seduce her and they had **Hiygga**, who Hera, being her rival, changed into a wagtail. In another myth, though, it is said that Echo died from her unbearable grief when she did not win Narcissus she was in love with. However, his greatest success was when he achieved to seduce **Selene**. The goddess used to play by jumping on the backs of her sheep; thus, Pan took the opportunity to unite with her dressed in a sheepskin.

According to a myth popular with the people of Phygalia in Arcadia until Pausanius' era (2nd c. A.D.), this goat-legged bucolic god has a connection with goddess **Demeter**. When the goddess had disappeared in her anger after her daughter was abducted or due to her being raped by Poseidon, it was Pan who discovered her hiding in a cave outside Phygalia, and told Zeus who sent the Moirae to persuade her to return to the gods and the humans.

From the crowd of divine figures surrounding the Olympian gods, some are excluded in the Greek mythology.

Hebe, the symbol of youth and the joy of life, was the daughter of Zeus and Hera and lived with her parents on Olympus, aiding her mother and offering the gods the nectar. During the gods' festivals she accompanied the Charitae, Harmonia and the Horae in the dances and the music by the Muses. When Heracles went up to Olympus, Hebe became his wife, earning him eternal youth.

Another beloved to the mortals goddess was **Tyche**, who offered the people wealth and abundance. She is depicted usually holding the **horn of Amaltheia**, little god Pluto (Wealth) or a bunch of wheat, a symbol of the abundance of the earth. Governor of the destiny of the cities, she is depicted wearing their walls as a tiara. Her other symbols are the **rudder** and the **scales**.

In numerous cities there were temples of the goddess, mainly during the roman era, while the most renowned was the **Tychaeon**, a splendid building in Alexandria dedicated to her. The goddess was particularly associated with the Moirae (Fates) who were responsible for the course of life of every mortal.

THEMIS

The daughter of Uranus and Gaea, the Titanid goddess, is the personification of the sense of law and righteousness. She dwelled on Olympus, beside Zeus as his **deputy**, since her attributes are closely associated with the ruler god, governor of the Universe, from whom justice emanates.

Marble statue of Themis from Ramnous (3rd c. B.C.). Athens, Archaeological Museum

In myths, Themis, sister of **Mnemosyne,** is mentioned as the second wife of Zeus after **Metis**. She and the great god had the **Moirae** (the Fates) and the **Horae** (the Hours). The patroness of the weak ones, offering hospitality to them, the keeper of moral order and every institution, she also had the charisma to foresee the future. The Delphi Oracle was her own before she gave it to her sister **Phoebe**, who in turn gave it to her grandson Apollo.

The worship of Themis was widespread all over Greece, mainly in Attica, Boeotia, Thessaly as well as Olympia and Delphi where, in the Sanctuary of the Earth there was an altar dedicated to the goddess, which establishes her nature.

NEMESIS

Nemesis is the personification of meting out justice and law keeping; she is the avenging power, that is, the spirit of divine retribution. Hesiod in **"Theogony"** considers her to be the daughter of **Nyx** (the Night), sister of the **Moirae**, the **Hesperides** and **Eris**. He also believes that if Nemesis abandons the earth along with Aedos (Decency), the humans will have no chance of survival.

According to other myths, the goddess was the daughter of Oceanus or Dike (Justice) and she was depicted as a strict punisher of arrogance and disrespect towards the gods, which the ancient Greeks thought of as **hubris** (insult). In case a mortal committed **hubris** they suffered the consequences of Nemesis.

GROUP DEITIES

A considerable category of divine figures is that of the grouped deities who appear **collectively**, such as the Muses, the Nymphs, the Horae, the Charitae, the Moirae, the Sirens, the Gorgons, the Seilenes, the Satyrs, the Couretes, the Anemoi and lots of others.

Mosaic floor representing the Nine Muses with their Emblems; from Cos (Roman era). Rhodes, the Palace of the Great Magister

Satyrs at a wine-press; black-figured urn by the painter of Amases (6th c. B.C.). Würzburg, Martin von Wagner Museum

Marble tomb statue of a Siren holding a lyre and a plectrum; from Athens (330-320 B.C.). Athens, National Archaeological Museum

Three Nymphs are accompanying Hermes and Pan, while three donors are approaching them on the right; marble dedicatory bas-relief from the cave of the Nymphs in Pendeli (4th c. B.C.). Athens, National Archaeological Museum

NYMPHS

The Nymphs are female deities of the nature, daughters of Zeus, born from the waters in the sky which fell onto the earth, collected underground and welled out as springs. They were considered to be young, beautiful maidens dwelling in forests, mountains, rivers and, in general, close to waters and vegetation. They liked music and dancing and had the power to inspire the mortals poetic and prophetic qualities. According to the area they lived in, they are classified as follows: **Alseids, Napaeae** and **Dryads**, dwelling in forests and groves, **Hamadryads**, nymphs of the trees, **Horestiads** or **Oreads**, dwelling in mountains and related to the Muses of the mountains, **Leimoniads**, nymphs of the meadows, **Naiads** and **Hydryads**, living by the rivers and waters in general.

There also existed local Nymphs, such as the **Acheloadae**, named after their father, the river **Achelous** or the **Nyssiads** from mount Nyssa. Moreover, there were bigger groups of Nymphs which consisted of smaller ones, for instance, in the Hamadryads belonged the **Meliae** or **Meliad nymphs**.

The nymphs accompanied the gods of vegetation and fertility, **Pan** and **Dionysus** in particular, fell in love with mortal young men and gave birth to local heroes while, quite often, they engaged in raising gods and heroes (infant **courae** = nurses). In myths, they are closely associated with **Nymphegetes or Musegetes Apollo, Artemis, Aphrodite, Chthonic Hermes** and the **Satyrs**.

The worship of the Nymphs was widespread in Greece from antiquity. Their cult sites are considered to be caves which are called **Nymphaea** or **Andra**. The Nymphs survived in the folklore tradition of the Hellenes where they are met as the **Nereids**.

THE NEREIDS – THE OCEANIDS

In this divinity family are classified the **Nereids** and the **Oceanids**. The Nereids (Nymphs of the seas) were daughters of Nereus and the Oceanid Doris. They are commonly reported to be fifty, but Homer and Hesiod list one hundred of them. Some Nereids play a major role in the Greek myths. For example, **Thetis**, the wife of Peleus and mother of Achilles, **Amphitrite**, the consort of the god of the sea Poseidon, **Galatea**, the sweetheart of Cyclop Polyphemus and mother of Galates, and **Calypso**. The Nereids dwelled in a silvery cave in the depths of the sea from where they hurried everywhere to help the gods and the mortals, especially seamen.

Oceanids were called the Nymphs of the deep and rough sea. They were the daughters of Oceanus and Tethys. In Hesiod's "Theogony" they are reported to be three thousand in number. Their most known names are those of the continents, such as **Asia**, **Europa**, **Libya** and **Africa**.

Golden medal; a Nereid on an aquatic monster (250 B.C.).
Thessaloniki, Archaeological Museum

SEA DAEMONS

Long before Poseidon became the Master of the Seas, in the conscience of the ancient Hellenes and the Pre-Hellenes there dominated several other spirits of the water, males such as **Nereus, Triton, Phorcys, Proteus, Palaemon,** and **Glaucus**, and females such as **Thetis, Leucothea, Cleto, Scylla** and **Charybdes**.

All the above spirits belonged to the world of the pre-Olympian religion and had common

The Three-bodied Daemon, from the limestone pediment of the archaic temple of Athena on the Acropolis of Athens (appr. 570 B.C.).
Athens, the Acropolis Museum

characteristics which combined people's faith with fairy tale fantasy, and magic with the theory of cosmogony. The main common characteristics among all the ancient spirits of the water are the following: they knew the depths and the secrets of the sea; they could forecast the weather and foretell the future and had the magic power to transform into animals, plants and the elements of nature such as wind, water and fire. All these sea spirits particularly appealed and caused awe to ordinary fishermen and seamen.

As they lacked scientific knowledge at the time, seamen, employing entreaties, cunning artifices, magic deeds and even violence, tried to make these spirits reveal their wisdom and prophetic skills when they did not volunteer.

It was essential that they could foretell the weather and the sea conditions in other seas and other countries not only to avoid dangers and potential hazards during their voyages but also to learn the whereabouts of their companions who had been away for a long time.

Mosaic floor with a Tritonid and Eros (2nd c. B.C.). Delos, Archaeological Museum

THE HEROES

In every people's mythology, apart from their gods, a distinguished place is saved for their heroes whose accomplishments adorn their tales, their traditions, their poetry and their literature.

In his quest to touch whatever his powers do not allow him to realise, man created figures that achieve the impossible and adorned them with supernatural and superhuman talents. These special **mortals,** who were endowed with beauty, physical strength and special attributes were called **heroes** by the Hellenes, a term Homeric poetry gave us.

The word **hero** which nowadays mainly denotes the fearless warrior, the brave one in every struggle, the *pallikari* (stout-hearted man) of later Greek poetry used to bear a broader meaning in antiquity. It expressed the honour and the respect due to someone called a hero exactly like the words in other languages which relate to the Greek one, the Latin **herus,** the German **herr** and the English **sire** which literally mean "**kyrios**" (mister).

In the Homeric epics, heroes are characterised not only the brave warriors, the kings and the noblemen but also those who distinguish themselves for something like **Odysseus** for his intelligence, **Demodicus** for his craft as a chanter or **Mulios** for his craft as a herald. In myths, the heroes were usually of divine descent and were brought to life from the union of a god or a goddess with a mortal man or woman respectively. According to their contribution to humanity they became gods or semi-gods who, as they are presented by Hesiod, live eternally in the land of the Macars in great happiness, away from sufferings.

In the Greek mythology, there dominate the myths referring to the life and the accomplishments of heroes. Every region in the Greek world had created its own heroic figures and accounted their numerous adventures and "**labours**". At first, these labours were in the people's minds who narrated them orally until they made them fairy tales and tradition. These local tales were once collected in Ionia and comprised a wondrous treasure becoming the first source of topics for the epic poets who either praised each of the heroes' deeds separately or placed the heroes in a Pan-Hellenic accomplishment, a war or an expedition.

Initially, the heroes in the tales had a mostly passive role as superior powers such as gods directed their actions while they provided them with magic devices and countless pieces of advice in order to succeed in performing their feat. In addition, the heroes were assisted by certain animals so that they could overcome the difficulties they encountered.

First the poets in Ionia received the legacy of the tales and oral narrations of the Greek people in the first three centuries of the historic times (10th-7th c. B.C.). They organised this legacy reshaping it from a fairy tale in tradition and enriching it with heroes demonstrating intellect, a heart, strength, beauty and mainly initiative. The Homeric hero acts as a responsible individual. He accepts, and gladly so, the protection from divine powers, only this protection does not make him independent but an individual free to decide upon his actions.

Moreover, Homer frees his heroes from witchcraft. He narrates the myths having taken out any magic elements in them. For instance, in the myth on Meleager, in earlier narrations, the hero's death depended on a half-burnt log whereas in the Homeric narration the reasons for his death are either the maternal curse or the hero's will to die for a cause. The Greek hero accomplishes his feats with his natural strength without having any magic powers. He uses this strength in the service of the common welfare because he is interested in the struggle of ordinary people. Heracles and Theseus saved the people from many wild beasts, while Prometheus was tormented for years chained on Caucasus because he had helped them.

What particularly characterises the Greek heroic world is the fact that the heroes' attributes are purely human. Bravery, self-sacrifice, pride, loyalty to friendship and family bonds, humanity in general are the main traits of each of the hero in the Greek myths.

These "**beneficent**" heroes who with bravery destroyed mischievous elements thus helping their country, such as **Heracles** and **Theseus**, or even offered their country social institutions, such as **Phoroneus** or Theseus, as well as various devices contributing to the people improving their lives and becoming civilised, such as **Prometheus**, **Palamedes** or **Asclepius**, were frequently supported and guided by the gods themselves such as goddess Athena who supported Odysseus, Jason, Heracles or Achilles and his mother Thetis. However, it is they who decided on what to do.

Nevertheless, there also existed "**Hubrist**" heroes who forgot that they were mortals and, dominated by arrogance (the **hubris** of the Ancient Greeks), they believed that they were gods or ignored them like Ceaneus, the king of the Lapiths, or Salmoneus, or Actaeus. The gods then became avengers and the punishment for all those was so severe that drove to their death or their destruction.

Grateful for everything their heroes had offered them, the ancient Greeks worshipped them and this **hero-worship** they had developed concerned not only the mythical heroes but the heroes of the historic times as well.

Complex of Centaur and Lapith; detail from the western pediment of the temple of Zeus in Olympia (470-456 B.C.). Olympia, Archaeological Museum

HERACLES

Heracles, the fearless and indomitable hero in the Greek mythology, constitutes the richest in context figure in the Greek myth. The most representative image of the hero, who constantly "struggles", appears in the early prehistory almost simultaneously with the birth of the first heroic myths. His works place him beyond the frame of a local hero and, throughout the centuries he becomes a Panhellenic and, eventually, a paneuropean hero. In the early myths, Heracles was the "strong man", the "brave one" of the Greek tradition, who fights imaginary, supernatural beings by performing wondrous feats. The myths about him are older than the Homeric epics and date back in the era of the Achaean Mycenaeans. As time passes, Heracles turns into a human being, becomes the avenger for any injustice who always struggles for the benefit of society, and evolves in a cultural agent aiming at the salvation of humanity. During his long-lasting course, from a simply dynamic figure he develops in an ethical one and becomes civilised. From a hero in the Achaean-Mycenaean myths he transforms in a mainly "Doric hero". From being a mortal, achieving the impossible, he becomes immortal and finds his place on Olympus along with the gods who compensate him for a life full of adventure and hardships through all of which he manages to emerge the winner.

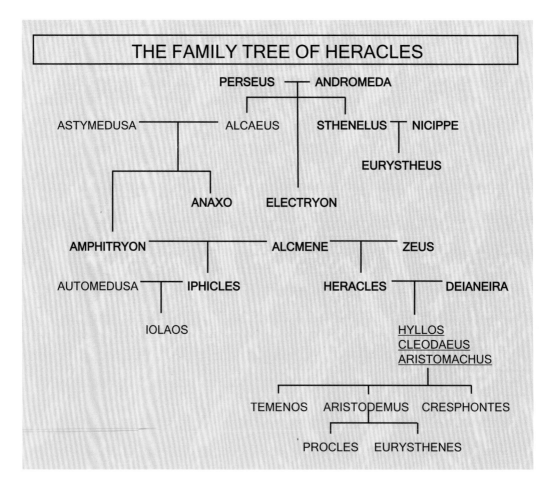

THE FAMILY TREE OF HERACLES

THE MYTH

Heracles, the most popular of all the heroes of the ancient Greeks, was a "DIOGENES" that is, his father was Zeus, while his mother was the mortal Alcmene, the wife of Amphitryon and the daughter of Electryon, king of Mycenae of the Perseus House.

During the rule of Electryon, Perseus' son, the **Taphians**, descendants of Mestor's brother, arrived from the Echinads islands in order to claim their home land back. Electryon refused to recognise their right to his land. During the subsequent battle, his nine sons were killed whereas the invaders returned home safely. Electryon had to trust his throne to his only daughter, Alcmene, as well as his wife's brother, Amphitryon, as he went to pursue the Taphians. However, before he set off, he was accidentally killed by Amphitryon. Then, his younger brother, Sthenelus took over and drove Amphitryon out of Mycenae. Alcmene followed him and promised to become his wife on condition that he avenged the death of her nine brothers. Amphitryon and his companions found refuge in Thebes, where Alcmene stayed while he started his expedition leading an army the king of Thebes Creon had helped him recruit. Alcmene's beauty made Zeus fall in love with her and want to have the bravest man among the mortals with her, a man who would save people from their sufferings. When Amphitryon returned after winning the war, he also slept with her. After a few months,

The inner part of a red-figured wide cup, which depicts Heracles with his bow and arrow travelling in the ocean in the golden pot of Helios (5th c. B.C.). Rome, Musei Vaticani

Alcmene gave birth to her twin sons: Heracles, the son of Zeus, and Iphicles, the son of Amphitryon.

According to Homer's narrations in the Iliad, shortly before Heracles was to be born, Zeus stated that this descendant of Perseus who would be born first was to become the king of Mycenae or Tirynth. Hera, however, who was dead jealous of Zeus, stopped Alcmene's labour so that Eurystheus, the son of Nicippe and Sthenelus, the grandson of Perseus, be born first. This way Eurystheus became the king of Mycenae and Heracles had to serve him for many years.

Hera was not satisfied with the fact that Heracles would not become the king of Mycenae and tried to eliminate him employing various methods. Thus, on an evening the twins were lying in their cribs, she sent them two serpents to kill them. While Iphicles was scared, Heracles grabbed the serpents on the neck, killed them and threw them at the feet of Amphitryon and Alcmene. Then, they all realised that he was the son of Zeus, as he was endowed with such power.

When Heracles grew up, he went to be educated with the best tutors of his time. Linus, a son of Apollo, was one of those who paid dearly Heracles' violent and irritable temperament. During a music lesson, Heracles became furious with his tutor's criticism, hit him on the head with a stool and Linus dropped dead. He was not, however, accused of murder because, according to a law by Rhadamanthys, he had not been the one to start the fight.

After that, Amphitryon sent him to tend his cattle in the countryside.

He was eighteen years old when Heracles carried out his first labour. On mount Cithaeron there had appeared a lion preying upon the area and slaying the cattle of Amphitryon and Thespius, the king of Thespiae. For fifty days Heracles was after the lion before he caught it. During all these days, he stayed at Thespius' palace and he spent each and every night with all but one of Thespius 50 daughters. Heracles had 50 children, though, as one of them gave birth to twins.

After Heracles had killed the lion he left the area immediately.

Following his abovementioned first accomplishment, he organised an expedition against the Minyeans at Orchomenus in order to free the Thebans from the tribute they had to pay to them. He won the war and forced them to pay double the amount to Thebes. As a reward he married Megara, the daughter of the king of Thebes.

During the battles between the Thebans and the Minyeans, his mortal father Amphitryon was killed and, therefore, his mother Alcmene married Aeacus later on.

Despite his successes, Heracles always had to face envious Hera who pursued him mercilessly. As a new trial he sent him rabies and, in his madness, he killed all his children he had with Megara. When he came to his senses and realised the crime he had

Head of Heracles; detail from the pediment of the temple of Zeus in Olympia (470-456 B.C.). Olympia, Archaeological Museum committed, Heracles fled to Apollo's Sanctuary at Delphi to require advice on how to expiate the crime. Apollo directed him to travel to Argolis and serve the king Eurystheus. Heracles was required to carry out twelve labours in twelve years. If he managed to carry them out successfully he would expiate the murder of his children.

Heracles struggled to carry out the tasks successfully and accomplished the tasks within the deadline.

His assistants to his accomplishments were certain very close friends of his, such as Iolaus, Abderus and Hylas.

His weapons were the club he had made himself, the bow - a gift by god Apollo, a golden armory - a piece of work by Hephaestus, a sword - a present by Hermes, and Poseidon's fast horses.

THE TWELVE LABOURS OF HERACLES AND HIS EXPIATION

The twelve labours constitute the first group of the most popular feats Heracles accomplished while serving Eurystheus for twelve years. The ancient sources do not agree on the reasons for Heracles' mandatory service and subjugation to someone inferior to him, Eurystheus.

Homer acknowledges the fact to Hera's desire to avenge and degrade Zeus for his infidelity. Another version adds that, eventually, Heracles accepts such a fate after Hermes and Athena promise to grant him immortality.

The immortality reward after carrying out the labours is documented by Zeus' order upon Heracles' refusal to serve Eurystheus and the direction given by the Oracle at Delphi when he asked it.

There also exists a different justification for this mandatory offer on the part of Heracles to Eurystheus, according to which he goes back to his father homeland Argolis in order to expiate the crime burdening his House and to re-establish his family bonds. In this aspect, his commitment is considered to be a process of expiating the murder either his father or he himself had committed when he killed his wife Megara and his children.

Besides, the myth mentions Heracle's expiation by Thespius after the murders he had committed. The notion of expiation after a crime is closely associated with the Delphic religion. God Apollo himself accepts to undergo the punishment of expiation after the murder of Dragoness Pytho.

Most modern research attempts to attribute Hera's enmity and the competition between

Red-figured urn depicting Heracles and Apollo fighting for the domination over the Sanctuary of Delphi (appr. 420 B.C.).
Berlin, Staatliche Museen

Golden head of Heracles with a lion head embodied in a necklace; from Derveni (tomb Z, 4th c. B.C.). Thessaloniki, Archaeological Museum

Heracles and Eurystheus to the conflict between the Achaeans and the Doreans. This version, however, does not justify his subjugation to Eurystheus as far as carrying out the labours is concerned. Expiation justifies better the works and the feats of the hero. Certain labours leading the hero to immortality and eternal youth constitute part of this process. The destruction of the Lernaean Hydra, the expedition to the Hades, Heracles' fight with Cerberus, the herding of the cattle of Geryon, the release of Alcestes at Parerga are in close connection with the hero's course to immortality.

The twelve labours of Heracles have already been anthologised in a set of their own. They were depicted as early as the 5th c. BC on the friezes of the temple of Zeus in Olympia. Moreover, in Sophocles' reference to certain of the labours of Heracles one can see that he is aware of the "twelve labours". What we are not aware of is whether there was a defined order of the labours at the time, an order followed in their presentation in groups of six on the frieze of the narthex and the opisthodomos of the temple of Zeus in Olympia.

THE DEEDS OF THE HERO

The labours of Heracles as well as his adventures were anthologised, since the ancient years already, in three big sets, according to their content and the reasons for their performance:

THE LABOURS or THE ERGA

1st	THE NEMEAN LION	ARGOLIS - CORINTHIA
2nd	THE LERNAEAN HYDRA	ARGOLIS - LERNA
3rd	THE ERYMANHIUS BOAR	ARCADIA - LAMBEIA
4th	THE "CERYNITIS" HIND	ARGOLIS - ACHAEA - CERYNEIA
5th	THE STYMPHALIAN BIRDS	ARCADIA
6th	THE STABLES OF AUGEAS	ELIS
7th	THE CRETAN BULL	CRETE
8th	THE MARES OF DIOMEDES	THRACE
9th	THE BELT OF HIPPOLYTE	EUXEINOS PONTOS - THEMISKYRA
10th	THE CATTLE OF GERYON	ERYTHEIA - WEST
11th	CERBERUS	THE UNDERWORLD
12th	THE APPLES OF THE HESPERIDES	WEST - BEYOND THE OCEAN

THE PARERGA

THE EXTERMINATION OF THE CENTAURS	PHOLOE
THE SLAY OF CENTAUR EURYTION	OLENOS
THE RELEASE OF ALCESTES FROM HADES	PHERAE
THE SIEGE OF PAROS	PAROS
THE RELEASE OF HESIONE	TROY
THE SLAY OF MYGDON	MYSIA
THE SLAY OF SARPEDON	AENUS
THE SUBJUCATION OF THE THRACIANS TO THASOS	THASOS
THE FIGHT WITH THE SONS OF PROTEUS	
THE SLAY OF IALEBION AND DERCYNUS	LIGYSTINE
THE EXTERMINATION OF SCYLLA	SICILY
THE FIGHT WITH ERYCAS	SICILY
THE CLASH WITH THE LAESTRYGONES	
THE SLAY OF CRIMINAL CACUS	ITALY
THE RELEASE OF THESEUS FROM HADES	
THE DUEL WITH CYCNUS	
THE FIGHT WITH NEREUS	
THE FIGHT WITH ANTAEUS	LIBYA
THE SLAY OF BUSSIRIS	EGYPT
THE SLAY OF HEMATHION	ETHIOPIA
THE RELEASE OF PROMETHEUS	CAUCASUS
THE SLAY OF LYCAON	MACEDONIA
THE SLAY OF ALCYONEUS	

THE DEEDS (EXPEDITIONS)

TO TROY	LAOMEDON
TO KOS	EURYPYLUS
TO ELIS	AUGEUS
TO PYLOS	NELEUS
TO SPARTA	THE HIPPOCOONS
TO THESSALY	THE DRYOPES - THE LAPITHS

OTHER ACCOMPLISHMENTS

THE STRANGLE OF THE SERPENTS	THEBES
THE CITHAERONIAN LION	CITHAERON
THE DEFEAT OF ERGINUS	ORCHOMENUS
THE GIGANTOMACHY	
THE EXTERMINATION OF THE BOREADAE	TINOS
THE FIGHT WITH ACHELOUS	AETOLIA
THE SLAY OF NESSUS	EURYTANIA
THE FIGHT WITH APOLLO	PHENEOS
THE FIGHT WITH THE CERCOPES	EPHESUS
THE SLAY OF SYLEUS	LYDIA
THE SLAY OF LITYERSE	PHRYGIA
THE SIEGE OF OECHALIA	OECHALIA

This way all his heroic accomplishments and the wondrous deeds of the "strong" man, which give him superhuman dimensions, are classified, while the first adventures in his life, before he started his feats in the service of Eurystheus, as well as his last ones (the marriage to Deianeira and the Apotheosis of the hero) have not been anthologised yet.

The twelve Labours of Heracles constitute the first group of the accomplishments he achieved during his mandatory service to Eurystheus - king of Argolis - obeying his orders.

The Parerga are closely connected with the "labours" of Heracles, as they took place at the same time and area as the predefined twelve labours, however, they differ in that they are chance events and of the hero's own initiative, bearing a superhuman and tale-like character.

The Deeds, as independent events, include feats he accomplished during expeditions and wars organised by the hero himself, who fights with an army, not on his own. What characterises the Deeds is the fact that their heroic element does not go beyond the human nature. They are small epics which belong to the heroic world and constitute newer work compared to the "Labours" and the "Parerga".

Heracles is fighting neck to neck with the Nemean lion (appr. 510 B.C.). Brescia, Museo Civico

THE NEMEAN LION

In the Peloponnese, in the area of Nemea, near the mountains Tretos and Apesas, there was the cave where lived the lion Echidna had given birth to from Orthos, her son from Typhon.

This invulnerable beast roamed the valley of Nemea and slew animals and people. It is said that the gods had sent it to punish the people of Bendida because they neglected to offer their sacrifices to them.

There was a second version regarding the origin of the beast, according to which Selene gave birth to and nursed it and, fulfilling Hera's desire, she threw it from the mountain of Nemea. The first of the labours of Heracles, commanded by Eurystheus, was to destroy the lion of Nemea. Heracles set off for Nemea armed with all his weapons, bow, arrows and sword. On his way, he encountered Molorchus, a king or a herdsman, whose son and cattle had been slain by the lion.

When Heracles told him about the purpose of his mission, the herdsman was so glad that he offered to kill his only ram left in order to honour him. Heracles did not accept the offer and suggested the sacrifice should take place a month later, either to honour Zeus Soter if he returned safe and sound, or to honour him as a hero in case the lion had torn him to pieces.

Heracles continued his way in search for the monster. He spotted it at a distance and shot his arrow but without success. His arrows could not penetrate its skin. From a closer distance he tried to pierce the beast with his sword or smash his club onto it so as to destroy it. Eventually, the man fought the beast with his bare hands.

After some time, Heracles managed to wrap his big hands round its neck and strangle the creature to death, he being unharmed. Then, carrying it on his shoulders, returned to Cleones where he met Molorchus and sacrificed a ram in honour of Zeus Soter. Tradition has it that, in memoriam of this victory of his, Heracles established the performance of athletic games at Nemea. The hero, carrying the beast on his shoulders, continued his way to Mycenae and Eurystheus who, upon seeing him was filled with fright and awe. Eurystheus realised that Hercules possessed imperishable power and that he was in great danger, therefore he ordered the hero not to ever again enter the walls of the city and demonstrate the trophies of his feat outside the castle.

Heracles kept the lion's pelt and would use it ever since as a defense weapon, wearing the beast's head as a helmet and making the pelt into an armour. It is also considered that he had it on for ritual reasons, perhaps for exhortation.

The first labour of Heracles - the lion slaying - has become a common tale topic for the eastern, mainly, populations, conveying the characteristics of a brave and strong man.

THE LERNAEAN HYDRA

The second labour Eurystheus assigned Heracles was remarkably more difficult than the first one. This time he had to exterminate a terrifying beast, a serpent-like monster, the Lernaean Hydra. Born to Typhon and Echidna, along with other monsters of the world, it appeared on earth sent by Hera, who wished it became the cause of Heracle's death.

The beast with the serpent-like body and the nine or fifty heads lived in the area of Argos, near Lake Lerna, and had its lair on a hill where the lake of Amymone was. The Hydra had a huge body and her nine heads sent out fire while her nostrils gave off poisonous fumes. Every time it emerged from its cave, it burnt everything on its path. No one was able to slay the beast because, in fact, it was immortal, since one of its heads, the central one, was immortal, whereas when one of the rest of its heads was severed, two more would grow in its place.

Slabs from the bas-relief pediment which decorated the front of the stage at the theatre in Delphi depicting various labours of Heracles (appr. 67 A.D.). Delphi, Archaeological Museum

Heracles journeyed to Lake Lerna along with Iolaos who was driving his chariot. He reached the lake but the monster was hiding in its lair. Then, Athena, always supporting the hero, gave him the idea of shooting flaming arrows into the monster's lair thus forcing it to come out. The Hydra attacked Heracles, wrapped its nine necks around his leg while trying to kill him with its deadly venomous breath. The hero started to cut off her heads but before long he realised that this was ineffective since the heads multiplied. To make things even more difficult, Hera sent a giant crab (cancer) which grabbed Heracles' other leg with its pincers. Being cornered, he asked his friend Iolaos for help. Heracles got rid of the cancer easily, smashing it with the very foot that had been bitten. It is said that Hera set the cancer constellation in the sky later on.

Apart from power, the struggle to slay the Hydra demanded also wisdom. Heracles sent Iolaos to put a clump of trees on fire and make burning firebrands. This way, after cutting off each head, Iolaos cauterised the open wound with the flaming torch preventing them from growing again. When he cut off its immortal head, though, he buried it deep in the ground and placed a heavy rock on top to prevent it from surfacing and uniting with the Hydra's body. Heracles skinned the hideous beast and dipped his arrows in its poisoned gall making them deadly. The hero returned to Eurystheus in Mycenae and announced the extermination of the monster. But when the king found out about Iolaos' help, he declared that this feat could not count in the labours set for him as he would not have completed it on his own.

There are two basic elements apparent in the myth of the Lernaean Hydra:

A) The struggle with a serpent associated with some spring waters. There is almost always an evil dragon preventing people from taking water from the spring and this drives them to kill it.

B) The serpent which causes destruction in the area - especially here where it is associated with Lake Lerna. There was a belief that lakes constituted entrances to the Under World.

A main element of the myth is, therefore, that the Hydra's extermination by Heracles is connected with his victory over death. Consequently, it is similar to the myth of Cerberus and belongs to the hero's struggle to gain immortality.

Heracles; detail from a metope of the Athenian Treasury at the Sanctuary of Apollo in Delphi (appr. 490 B.C.). Delphi, Archaeological Museum

THE ERYMANTHIAN BOAR

Eurystheus ordered Heracles to bring him the Erymanthian boar alive. The boar dwelled in Lambeia, on mountain Erymanthus in Arcadia, and ravaged the town Psophis. Due to the fact that the animal was really strong and there was the danger of gouging the hero with its sharp tasks, Heracles preferred to exhaust it so much that the boar became harmless. Heracles reached the boar's lair and, shouting as loud as he could, frightened the animal. It emerged and began to run round and round the snowy slopes of Erymanthus. When the boar, exhausted by the chase, could not run any more, Heracles approached carefully and, after tying up its legs, carried it to Mycenae.

Eurystheus was so frightened of its sight that ducked down in a big bronze pithos (jar). This picture is often seen in vase-painting. Then, Heracles killed the boar and wore its hide along with the lion's pelt or, in another version, gave it as a present to his companion Hylas. Another version of the myth has it that Heracles does not catch the boar; he kills it by dipping his sword in the animal's stomach.

THE CERYNITIS HIND

Once, Artemis was hunting on mountain Parrhassios when she saw five beautiful hinds with golden antlers. She was fascinated by their beauty and wanted to have them. She managed to catch and harness four of them on her chariot with a lot of difficulty.

The fifth hind escaped and found refuge on the mountain of Ceryneia, at the borders between Achaea and Argolis, and from then on it was considered the sacred hind of Artemis Orthosia.

This is the hind Eurystheus wanted to have and ordered Heracles to bring it to him alive

and unharmed. He, therefore, had to capture it from his golden antlers. The hind, however, besides golden antlers, also had hooves of bronze, which made it very fast.

For a whole year Heracles hunted the hind over all the mountains and the plains in the Peloponnese. In the end, the animal became weary but still Heracles could not keep up with it. The hind found refuge on mountain Artemisio where the hero followed it. It tried to

Heracle's struggle against the "Cerynitis Hind"; metope from the northern side of the Athenian Treasury at the Sanctuary of Apollo in Delphi (appr. 490 B.C.). Delphi, Archaeological Museum

escape crossing the river Ladon. There, Heracles had the chance to slightly injure it with his arrow, caught it, at last, and tied it up in order to carry it to Mycenae. On his way back he met with goddess Artemis and Apollo who were enraged to see the injured animal. When Heracles explained to them that Eurystheus was to blame for this, they calmed down and let him continue his way.

In another version, the hind was a noxious animal ravaging the fields and gardens of the villages. Heracles, after a long pursue, caught it using a trap net but was forced to kill it to relieve the people of this plague, and dedicated its head with the golden antlers to the sanctuary of Artemis Oenoatis, on mountain Artemisio. According to another version, Heracles captured the hind at Istria, in the land of the Hyperboreans, where Elysian Fields was said to be, and Artemis welcomed them.

THE STYMPHALIAN BIRDS

Along the densely vegetated banks of Lake Stymphalis in the northern Arcadia, there had migrated a flock of birds to escape from a pack of wolves roaming from the surrounding mountains.

These birds, though, were wild and cruel. They were vicious man-eaters bearing iron wings which could shoot their feathers like arrows. They ravaged the fields and the gardens and caused tremendous damage to both animals and people.

These birds, which when flying hid the sunlight, Heracles was ordered by Eurystheus to kill. Arriving at the banks of the lake, he armed his bow but found it was difficult to spot the birds nesting in the dense vegetation. Then, his patroness goddess Athena gave him a pair of bronze 'krotala', made by Hephaestus or, in another version, by her, which made a loud noise when clashed. With this weapon, Heracles approached the bank of the lake and began clashing them as loudly as he could. The birds were scared out of the trees and Heracles had the chance to shoot his arrows at them as they took flight and kill as many as he could.

The rest, according to a tradition, escaped on the island of Ares at Pondos where, later on, the Argonauts encountered them.

Metope from the back part of the nave of the temple of Zeus in Olympia with a representation of Heracles' labour against the Stymphalian Birds (470-456 B.C.). Paris, the Louvre

THE STABLES OF AUGEAS

Once, in the rich and fertile land of Heleia, there ruled king Augeas, a son of the Sun. His wealth was famed and it was so much that he summoned two prominent architects, Trophonius and Agamedes, to build an inviolate treasury.

Even more famous, however, were his countless herds of cattle and sheep; a single pasture offered not enough room for them. They had spread all over the land in Augeas' kingdom. Naturally, there came a time when the population was confronted with an enormous amount of dung and the unbearable stench emitting and making breathing impossible. There seemed to be no solution since the king's servants were not enough to clean it up and Augeas appeared not to have another way in mind to get rid of it.

Then Eurystheus, so as to humiliate Heracles, ordered him to clean up the dung in a single day, on his own, with his two bare hands. Heracles went to Elis, met Augeas and offered to clean up the dung for just one tenth of his herds as a reward. Although Augeas did not actually believe Heracles, he agreed but sent along his son, Phyleas, as a witness. Heracles did not, of course, start to carry the dung away with his own hands. He dug up a deep ditch through the king's stables and rerouted the river Alpheios flowing nearby. In a few hours the filth was washed away and the stables were clean. In the meantime, Augeas had found out about the task having been assigned by Eurystheus, therefore, when Heracles insisted on receiving his reward he refused to honour his agreement.

Judges were then appointed to settle the argument who summoned Augeas' son, Phyleas, as a witness. Phyleas acknowledged that Heracles was right and condemned his

father's bad behaviour. Yet, Augeas was still not convinced and exiled both of them.

Phyleas took refuge in Doulichio whereas Heracles, passing from Olenos, reached Mycenae where Eurystheus, having learnt the method the hero used to complete the task, refused to count the success of this labour.

Metope from the temple of Zeus in Olympia depicting Heracles washing away the dung from Augeas' stables, while Athena is supporting him (470-456 B.C.). Olympia, Archaeological Museum

THE CRETAN BULL

When Zeus carried Europa away from her homeland, Phoenice, he took her to Crete on the back of a taurus (bull), which is said to be Zeus himself in disguise. After his union with Europa, Zeus let the bull free, but it ravaged the island, especially the area of Knossos. This fierce bull, which emitted fire from its mouth, Eurystheus ordered Heracles to bring to Mycenae.

Heracles journeyed to Crete and asked Minos' permission to capture the bull. Minos agreed on condition that the hero had the ability to do so. Heracles, armed with his club and rope started to chase the bull. Eventually, he managed to catch it by the horns and tie up its legs using the rope. He carried it to Minos and afterwards drove it to Mycenae. In another version, along with the bull, Europa moved to the Peloponnese.

Eurystheus saw the bull, admired its beauty and wanted to dedicate it to Hera. The goddess, though, refused his gift and therefore Eurystheus let the bull go free, which, wandering from the Argolic plain to Marathon, caused tremendous damage. Theseus captured it there and, finally, he sacrificed it to Apollo Delphinus in Athens. According to other versions, this was the bull Pasiphae, the wife of Minos, fell in love with and gave birth to the Minotaur, or it was the one Poseidon had sent to Minos to sacrifice it. Minos, however, seeing the beauty of the bull, disobeyed the god's order, which enraged Poseidon who made the bull rampage all over Crete.

This myth and its versions constitute a posterior combination of local myths from Crete, Argos and Athens which must have been incorporated in the cycle of the labours Eurystheus had ordered later on.

Heracles is attempting to tame the wild bull of Cnossos; metope from the back part of the nave of the temple of Zeus in Olympia (470-456 B.C.). Olympia, Archaeological Museum

THE MARES OF DIOMEDES

Diomedes, a son of Ares and a brother of Cycnus, was the king of a war tribe, the Bistones, named after Lake Bistonis around which they lived. Diomedes kept four man-eating horses in his stable to which he sent every foreigner arriving in his land or every disobedient citizen. The horses were tied with heavy chains on their bronze manger and were watched over by numerous guards.

Eurystheus sent Heracles to bring him these horses and he, along with his companion Abderos, travelled to the land of the Bistones. After a short fight, Heracles and Abderos overpowered the guards and took the mares. On being informed of the incident, Diomedes asked the Bistones to pursue the invaders. Heracles entrusted the horses to Abderos and rushed to fight back Diomedes and his pursuers. After the horrible battle and the loss of a lot of men, the Bistones retreated. Heracles returned to the boat where he saw that the horses had slain Abderos. Burying his companion, he founded a city, Abdera, in honour of the slain Abderos. Heracles took the mares back to Mycenae and gave them to Eurystheus but he set them free. These horses, after wandering for a long time, reached Olympus where they were eaten by other wild beasts.

According to the main version of the myth, Heracles managed to capture the mares of Diomedes by throwing their master into the bronze manger. The horses ate Diomedes and calmed immediately. In another version, Heracles did not take the horses back to Eurystheus; instead, he killed them and their master with his club.

THE BELT OF HIPPOLYTE

The tribe of the Amazons lived in the city of Themiskyra on the mouth of the river Thermodon near the shore of the Euxine Sea (the Black Sea). The queen of this war nation, where women had the prominent role, was Hippolyte. a daughter of the god of war Ares and Otrere. Her father had offered Hippolyte a marvelous belt, a symbol of her high rank among the rest of the Amazons.

This famous belt Heracles was ordered by Eurystheus to bring him in his ninth labour. The hero, accompanied by select, brave, young men such as Telamon, Demolaeon, and Autolycus, set out for the land of the Amazons. After various adventures in Paros and Mysia, he finally arrived at the port of Themiskyra. Upon knowing about their arrival, Hippolyte and the other Amazons went to welcome them. Heracles revealed the purpose of his journey to Hippolyte straight away and she agreed to give him her belt. It was then that Hera, disguised as an Amazon, convinced them that the foreigner had come to overthrow their queen Hippolyte.

The Amazons put on their armour at once and attacked Heracles and his companions. This is how the battle started, during which the most competent Amazons as well as Hippolyte herself were killed. Heracles took the dead queen's belt and, with his companions, boarded the ships and sailed back home. After lots of adventures, eventually, he arrived at Mycenae and gave Eurystheus the belt.

According to certain versions of the myth, however, the land of the Amazons was not in the south of the Euxine Sea, it was in the north, at Lake Maeotis. Moreover, Eurystheus sent Heracles to bring the belt to give it to his daughter Admete as a present. In a later version, it is also claimed that Theseus participated in Heracles' expedition as well.

Bas-relief slab with Heracles, from the stage of the theatre in Ancient Corinth (Roman era). Corinth, the Corinth Museum

THE CATTLE OF GERYON

Geryon was a three-bodied and three-headed fearsome monster, a son of Chrysaor and Callirrhoe, daughter of Oceanus, which lived on Erytheia, an island in the far West beyond the Ocean. There grazed the herd of the famous red cattle. The shepherd was Eurytion, a son of Ares, along with his hound Orthus, which had two heads and a serpent's tail. This invincible hound was whelped by Echidna and Typhon and his siblings were Cerberus, the Lernaean Hydra and Chimaera.

Following Eurystheus' orders, Heracles set out from Mycenae for his distant destination. He passed through many countries and had adventures with various criminals. He crossed Europe, passed by Africa and reached the Iberic Peninsula, the town of Tartessos, located on a strait which was believed to separate Europe from Africa and be the end of the world. In commemoration of his journey Heracles erected two pillars there, one on the European side and the other on the African side, which later became known as the "Heraclean Pillars". Here now, the hero had to face the problem of reaching the island Erytheia since it was in the middle of the Ocean.

Then he asked Helios (the Sun) who granted him the golden cup, a piece of work by Hephaestus, which was the chariot drawn by Helios' mares. Heracles was also supplied with the horn of Amaltheia (of plenty), a present by Hermes, which was filled with food for the journey, and set out for the island. After he successfully confronted the rough sea of Oceanus he, eventually, arrived at Erytheia and immediately climbed up its mountain, Abas. However, the hound Orthus took notice of him and Heracles had to kill him with his club. He dealt the same way with the herdsman Eurytion who rushed to see what was happening. Heracles was now free to capture the cattle and begin his journey back home. He also killed Geryon, who rushed to take his cattle back, with his arrow. He drove the cattle into the golden cup and arrived at Tartessos where he returned Helios the chariot. On his way back, Heracles had

Heracle's struggle with giant Andaeus, a representation of a red-figured crater (510-500 B.C.).
Paris, the Louvre

numerous adventures such as in Italy with robber Cacus, in Sicily with Eryx, in Thrace, in Scythia with the woman-serpent whose union resulted in the birth of the father of the Scyths, Scythe, etc. In Epirus he was attacked by the Celts, the Chaons and the Thesprotians in order to steal the cattle from him but he eventually managed to herd them successfully to Eurystheus.

There are several versions to this myth. According to the main version, Geryon's cattle did not graze on Erytheia; they grazed the slopes of Iberia, from the side of the Ocean, where ruled the wealthy and powerful king Chrysaor. This is why Heracles had to recruit warriors from all over Greece. The expedition started on Crete, he travelled through Libya where he defeated Andaeus, went on to Egypt where he killed Busiris, returned to the west and, finally, reached Gadeira. There was the small strait separating Europe from Africa where the hero erected the "Pillars of Heracles". Then, he went to Iberia, crushed the sons of Chrysaor in a horrible battle and, eventually, captured Geryon's cattle.

CERBERUS

The Underworld was the dark, cold kingdom of god Hades and Persephone. Whoever reached this place on Charon's boat lost every hope of a return in the world of the living. To prevent the dead from escaping, Pluto had the gate guarded by a fearsome monster, an offspring of Echidna and Typhon, Cerberus. It had the body of a hound, fifty heads, the front ones of which were dog heads and the rest those of various other animals, and a snake's tail.

Heracles is delivering
Cerberus to Eurystheus
who, in panic, is jumping
into a large jar; a
representation of the labour
on a Caeretine urn
(appr. 520 B.C.).
Paris, the Louvre

In order to carry out Eurystheus' order who wanted this monster, Heracles had to accomplish the impossible. He had to descend the Underworld and fetch Cerberus before the king of Mycenae. Before he started this journey, Heracles visited Eleusis to be initiated in the Eleusinian Mysteries by Eumolpus, after having been purified by Musaeus, the son of Orpheus who then was the priest of the Mysteries.

The patron gods of the hero, Hermes and Athena, accompanied him to the gate of the Underworld. Heracles descended through a cave under one of Apollo's temples at cape Taenaron.

Several authors report that the gate to the Underworld was located in Lake Acherousia in Thesprote or in Hermione. Through the cave, the hero reached the sea separating him from the kingdom of the dead. He was taken across by Charon on his boat. There, he met the souls-shades of the dead who, frightened, fled away. After fighting with some of the shadows such as Menoetes, he met Meleagrus, Theseus, Peirethous and other heroes. Afterwards, he presented himself before Pluto and Persephone and asked their permission to bring Cerberus to Eurystheus. Pluto granted him the permission on condition that Heracles captured Cerberus with his own hands. When Heracles met Cerberus, so as not to disobey Pluto, left his weapons and took only some stones and his lion pelt as a shield with him.

Eventually, Heracles overpowered Cerberus after a horrible wrestle, as he had done with the Nemean lion. When the hero had tied the hound and made his way to the world of the living, Pluto broke his promise and did not allow him to go. Then Heracles shot an arrow and injured Pluto who was scared and let him go in the end. When Cerberus saw the sunlight for the first time at the exit of the Underworld in Troezen, it was so dazzled that its gull dropped from his mouth. At the place where its gull fell there grew a poisonous plant, *akonito*. On their way to Mycenae the people, horrified at the sight of the fearsome monster, fled away. So did Eurystheus who, once again, found shelter in his bronze jar. Having carried out yet another labour, Heracles brought Cerberus back to the Underworld, as he had promised Pluto.

THE APPLES OF THE HESPERIDES

Mother-Gaea's present for Zeus and Hera's wedding was some magnificent golden apples which gave eternity and immortality. They were so beautiful that Hera ordered to plant their seeds in her grove in the far West, beyond the Ocean (other versions place the garden in the land of the Hyperboreans). The seeds sprouted and grew the trees bearing the golden apples.

Near the orchard there was the place where Atlas, a son of Iapetus, was holding the pillars supporting the heavens on his shoulders. This is where lived the Hesperides, the daughters of Nyx (night), Aegle, Erytheia and Hesperethousa, "the Bright one", "the Red one" and "Arethousa of the West" respectively. The Hesperides, however, like others, occasionally picked golden apples from the orchard. This is why Hera placed Ladon, an enormous serpent, the offspring of Phorcys and Ceto, as a safeguard.

Eurystheus, having not counted the slaying of the Lernaean Hydra and the clean up of Augeas' Stables among the labours, assigned Heracles to bring him these magnificent apples. The hero, however, had to find out where the garden of the Hesperides was located. He set off for his long journey travelling first through the countries of the north, where he fought a duel and killed Cycnus, and reached Illyria on the river Heridanos. There he met the nymphs of the river and asked them how he could go to the garden of the Hesperides. They sent them to Nereus, the *sea-old man*, but warned him that it would be difficult to get the information he needed from him; therefore, he would have to use violence. Heracles found Nereus sleeping and tried to catch him. The old man escaped, though, and they started to

Heracles, with his supernatural power, is about to hurl one of the
Egyptians of king Bussiris; red-figured wide cup (appr. 470 B.C.).
Athens, National Archaeological Museum

wrestle but Nereus changed his shape all the time. Finally, Nereus gave in and told Heracles the location of the garden of the Hesperides. The hero travelled through Africa, where he killed Andaeus in Libya and Busiris in Egypt, and then he reached Arabia and Caucasus. There, he freed Prometheus, who was chained on the mountain having been punished by Zeus, after killing the eagle that had been eating on his liver. When Heracles finally reached the region of Atlas, he found the Titan holding the pillars of the world on his shoulders. The hero explained his mission to Atlas and he offered to go to the garden and bring him the apples himself, provided that Heracles would take his place and hold the pillars for a while. Having no other choice he agreed. Indeed, Atlas, in cooperation with the Hesperides, overpowered the guard Ladon and took the apples. However, Atlas wanted to deceive Heracles telling him that he, himself, would take the apples to Eurystheus. Despite the fact that Heracles found himself in a difficult position, he did not show. He pretended to agree with Atlas and asked him to hold the pillars of heaven for a little while in order to pad his shoulders and feel more comfortable.

Thus, he tricked Atlas and took the apples, bid him farewell and returned to Mycenae. Eurystheus offered Heracles the apples but he gave them to his patroness Athena, who sent them back where they belonged, the garden of the Hesperides.

Heracles is resting lying on a lion pelt on a rock;
marble dedicatory bas-relief (2nd c. B.C.).
Athens, National Archaeological Museum

AFTER THE LABOURS - HERACLES' OTHER DEEDS

The well known hero Heracles is credited with numerous accomplishments besides his famous labours.

After successfully completing these tasks and freeing himself of his commitment to Eurystheus and his sins, he returned to Thebes. He saw to marrying Megara to his friend Iolaos and began his quest for a new wife. Upon hearing that Eurytus, the king of Oechalia, would wed his daughter **Iole** with the most competent man in archery, he decided to participate in the contest and he won. The king, however, went back on his promise and Heracles' wrath fell upon the son of Eurytus, **Iphitus**, whom he threw over the walls of Tiryns, violating the laws of hospitality. When Heracles realised what he had done, he went again to Delphi to beg for mercy, but Pythia refused to consult him. This is why, being furious once again, he threatened to establish his own oracle stealing the Delphic tripod from the temple of Apollo. God Apollo fought with Heracles but after Zeus' intervention they reconciled. Then Pythia gave him directions advising him to serve the queen of Lydia **Ophale** for one year. In Lydia, he accomplished several other feats and soon was free again. Before leaving Asia

Heracles is attacking Centaur Nessus; black-figured urn (appr. 610 B.C.).
Athens, National Archaeological Museum

Minor, he helped Laomedon, the king of Troy, whose country was plagued by famine and a fearsome dragon.

According to an oracle, so as to save his country the king bound his daughter Hesione on a rock sacrificing her to the dragon. Heracles travelled to Troy, slew the dragon and freed Hesione after Laomedon had promised to give him the divine horses he had received from Zeus. The king broke his promise, therefore, Heracles returned to Argolis, recruited warriors and six ships, set off against Troy and besieging the city he destroyed it completely. This expedition took place prior to the one told by Homer in the "Iliad".

When he returned to Argolis, he launched more war expeditions. He conquered Helis and there he organised for the first time the Olympia, the first athletic contest in honour of his father Zeus. He went to Pylos, burnt down the town and killed all the sons of Neleus but Nestor. So he did in Sparta, where he slew the sons of Hippocoon who had fought him supporting Neleus. In Tegea, under the influence of alcohol, he raped Auge who gave birth to Telephus. She hid him in the forest where he was nursed by a hind, while later on she was sold to the king of Mysia, Teuthrus. Mother and son met again after a long time in Mysia and being unaware of each other's identity they wanted to become spouses. Fortunately, Heracles revealed the truth to them.

The last adventure Heracles was involved in would cost his very life. The hero asked for the hand of Deianira, the daughter of Oeneus the king of Aetolia. He had agreed upon this

Heracles with the tripod of god Apollo on his shoulder; red-figured urn (appr. 480 B.C.).
Würzburg, Martin von Wagner Museum

Dedicatory bas-relief in the shape of a small temple with Heracles resting and pilgrims with a bull to sacrifice (400 B.C.). Athens, National Archaeological Museum

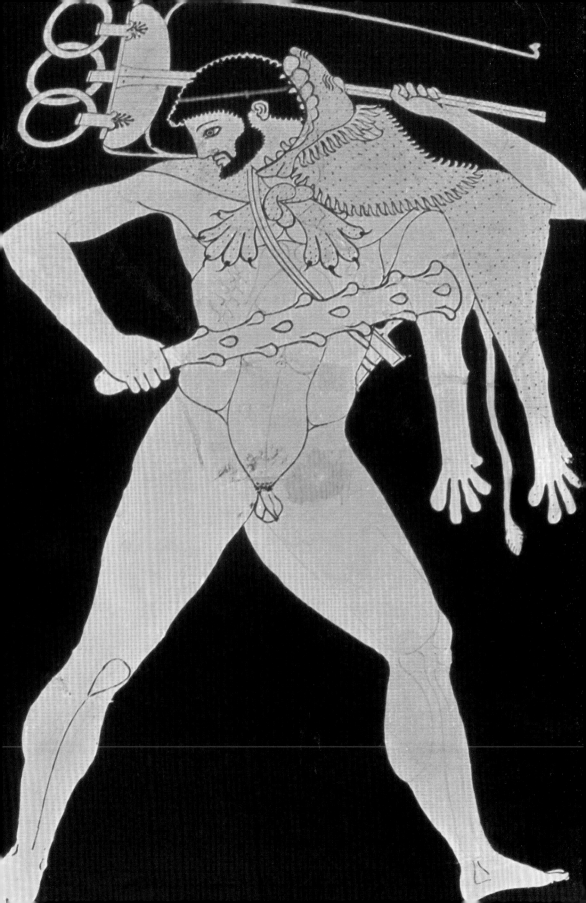

marriage with her brother Meleager when the hero met him in the Hades while carrying out the labour with Cerberus. In Aetolia, he had to face the river god Achelous; they fought because he, too, wanted to marry Deianira, and Heracles won. Achelous then gave him the horn of Amaltheia. After he wedded Deianira, Heracles left Aetolia and, exiled, he settled in Trachina because he had accidentally killed Eunomus, a relative of Oeneus.

On his way, he met the centaur Nessus who helped travellers cross the river Euenus. Nessus attempted to rape Deianira so Heracles killed him with his poisoned arrows. Before dying, Nessus advised Deianira to gather up his blood, already poisoned, and use it as a love potion if her husband ever desired another woman. Heracles left Trachina to take part in a series of war expeditions and find Eurytus to avenge his forbidding him to marry Iole who the hero always loved. Heracles destroyed Oechalia, killed Eurytus and his sons and abducted Iole.

Upon his return, he wanted to thank Zeus and sacrifice to him. Therefore he asked Deianira to send him his white robe with his comrade-in-arms and friend Lichas. Deianira soaked the garment with the blood of Nessus thinking that she would win him back with the magic potion. Heracles put on the robe the poison of which immediately entered his blood and caused the hero a horrible end. He himself asked to be burnt on the top of mount Oete. Philoctetes was courageous enough to grant him the favour and took his bow and arrows as a present. When the pyre lit, a cloud surrounded the hero and took him to mount Olympus. Despite Hera's objections, the hero was deified, became an immortal, married Hebe and found his place among the gods on Olympus.

HERACLES, THE ORIGINATOR OF OLYMPIA

The ancient authors hold divergent opinions as far as the originator of the Olympic Games is concerned. Some name Heracles from Thebes, the son of Zeus and Alcmene, as the first organiser of the Games in Olympia, and others Ideus Heracles, one of the Ideus Dactylus - Couretes, associating the games with the Cretan-Mycenaean cycle of myths.

The tradition which links Heracles from Thebes with Olympia is older and is found in Pindarus works, our earliest source. Although Pausanius praises Ideus Heracles for being the first organiser of the Games, when listing the names of the legendary rulers who associate with the establishment of the games, he also includes Heracles from Thebes.

What is certain is the existence of two myths, one earlier than the other; the latter supporting Ideus Heracles has become more popular. The fact that Ideus Heracles became the patron of the Gymnasium in historic times verifies the myth.

Generally speaking, you could ask yourself whether there was a primary religious connection between Heracles and Olympia, as, in essence, the hero plays a minor role in cult during the historic times.

There are only two altars mentioned in honour of Heracles in Olympia. One belongs to Ideus-Attendant to the Gymnasium and the second, found behind Herod Atticus Nymphaeon, is not known to even the traveller Pausanius, although it belonged to Ideus or Heracles from Thebes.

The only important element for the prevalence of Heracles from Thebes is the fact that, in the 5th c. BC, his labours will be depicted on the friezes of the narthex and the opisthodomus of the temple of Zeus, the great and main god of Olympia, along with the basic myth on the local hero Pelops.

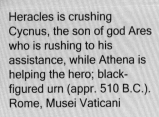

Heracles is crushing Cycnus, the son of god Ares who is rushing to his assistance, while Athena is helping the hero; black-figured urn (appr. 510 B.C.). Rome, Musei Vaticani

THE WANDERINGS

HADRIATIC SEA

TYRRHENIAN SEA

IONIAN SEA

22

23

24

27

39

43

41

42

19 20 21

33

29

28

25

26

11

8 9 10

48 46

49

34

NORTH AFRICA

1. THEBES
2. Thespies (Lion of the Mt. Cithaeron)
3. Orchomenos (Erginus)
4. Tiryns
5. MYCENAE
6. Nemea (Lion)
7. Lerna (Hydra)
8. Mt. Erymanthos (Boar)
9. Ceryneia (Hind)
10. Stymphalus (Birds)
11. Elis (Augeias' Stables)
12. Knossos (Bull) CRETE
13. Abdera (Horses of Diomedes) THRACE
14. Thasos
15. Paros
16. Themiscyra (The girdle of Hippolyta) AMAZONS
17. Heraclea (Mygdon - Vervykes) MYSIA
18. Troy (Hesione - Expedition - Capture of Troy)
19. EURYTHEIA (The cattles of Geryon)
20. Pillars of Hercules
21. Tartessus
22. LINGISTINE (Ialovion - Dercynes)
23. Rhône
24. Rome (Cacos) ROME
25. Regium
26. SICILY
27. Sire (Calchas)
28. Taras (Scylla)
29. AGRIGENTUM (Eryx - Lastrygones)
30. Eleusis (Mysteries)
31. Taenaron (Hades - Cerberus)
32. Troezen (Hades - Cerberus)
33. Hesperides (Apples - Atlas)
34. LIBYA (Antaios)
35. EGYPT (Vousiris)
36. ETHIOPIA (Emathion - Memno)
37. ARABIA
38. CAUCASUS (Prometheus)
39. THESSALY (Dryopes - Lapithes)
40. Pheres (Alcestes)
41. Thrachina
42. Calydon (Deianeira)
43. Oechalia (Iole)
44. AENUS (Sarpedon)
45. Torone (Polygonus - Telegonus)
46. Pholoe (Centaur Pholus)
47. Cos (Eurypylos)
48. OLYMPIA (OLYMPIC GAMES)
49. PYLOS (Neleus)
50. SPARTA (Hippokoontides)

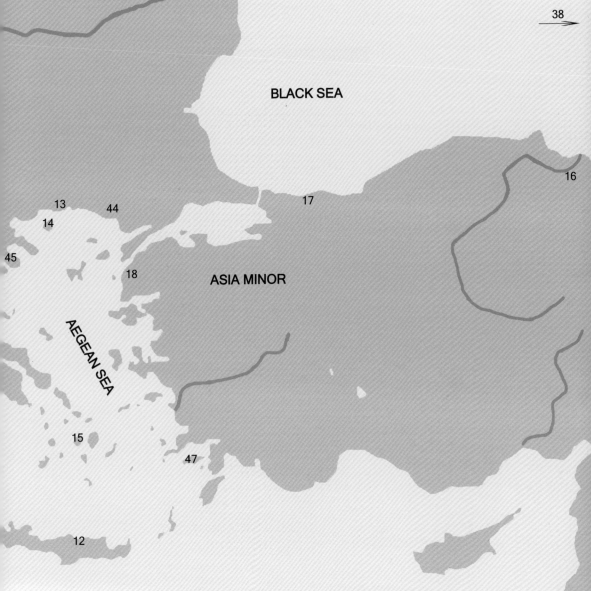

O F   H E R A C L E S

38 →

BLACK SEA

16

13   44
14

17

45

18

ASIA MINOR

AEGEAN SEA

15

47

12

MEDITERRANEAN SEA

37

36
↓

35

THESEUS

Theseus, the hero of the Athenian spirit and the city where democracy was born, is the only hero among all the rest of the Hellenic world who was able to compete with Heracles and, on certain occasions, completely overshadow his glory.

Still an unsolvable problem remains whether Theseus existed in reality or he was simply a purely legendary figure, a creation of the hegemonic politics of the Athenians. It is certain, though, that there existed a very old hero who stayed alive through the tradition, constantly being enriched even during the historic times, mainly for political reasons.

The glory of Theseus as a hero is comparable to the glory of Heracles. He is endowed with not only an ever victorious power but also with distinguished intelligence he offered in the service of the authorities of the Athenians. With this high intelligence and culture he completely defeats his enemies and, with his labours, he becomes the first finder of the wrestling and pankration techniques which he employs correspondingly when struggling with Skyron and the Minotaur.

Theseus, strongly bonded with Attica and Troezen since early times, is a purely Ion hero. This is why he relates to the Lapiths who are considered to be an Ionic tribe. With his double

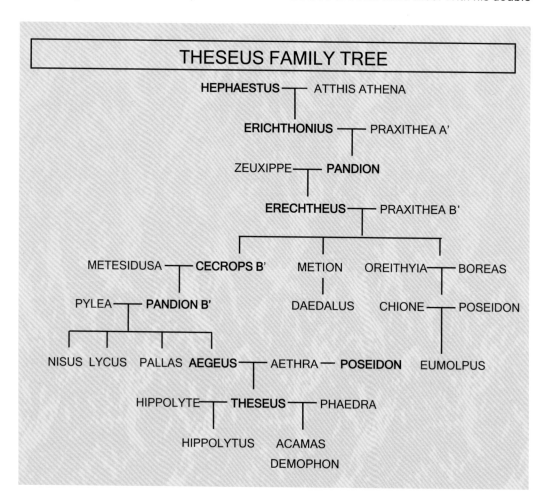

THESEUS FAMILY TREE

HEPHAESTUS — ATTHIS ATHENA

ERICHTHONIUS — PRAXITHEA A'

ZEUXIPPE — PANDION

ERECHTHEUS — PRAXITHEA B'

METESIDUSA — CECROPS B'   METION   OREITHYIA — BOREAS

PYLEA — PANDION B'   DAEDALUS   CHIONE — POSEIDON

NISUS LYCUS PALLAS AEGEUS — AETHRA — POSEIDON   EUMOLPUS

HIPPOLYTE — THESEUS — PHAEDRA

HIPPOLYTUS   ACAMAS

DEMOPHON

fatherhood - son of Poseidon and son of Aegeus - he becomes the founder of the Games in Isthmia, a fact which documents the involvement of the Athenians in these games.

Since the 5th c. BC, Theseus is not merely a legendary hero anymore; his glory grows and he plays an important part in the historic tradition of Athens. He becomes an Athenian par excellence, the very founder of the Athenian state, who unified politically (soenicise) the municipalities of Attica and supported the democratic institutions. As Potier writes "If we study Theseus a little closer, we shall discover some aspects of Solon and of Peisistratus as well as several aspects of Themistocles and even several of Alkiviades. However, in order for this full of life spirit to be created, the total of the Athenian people had to cooperate, the people who shouted *death to the tyrants* and *death to the Spartans*, the people who voted for the reform by Cleisthenes, who threw the ambassadors of the great King into the chasm and fought in Marathon".

Theseus is bidding farewell to his father Aegeus, while his mother is caressing his face and Poseidon is watching the scene; red-figured urn (appr. 470-460 B.C.). London, the British Museum

THE DIVINE AND THE HUMAN DESCENT OF THESEUS

When the legendary king of Athens Erechtheus passed away, his son, Pandion, succeeded him to the throne. Pandion and his wife, Pylia, had four sons, Aegeus, Pallas, Nyssus and Lycus. The authority of the four brothers extended from Megaris to Corinthia. Aegeus managed to take control and eventually become the king of Attica.

Although Aegeus had married twice to Meta and Chalchiope, he did not have an heir. Therefore he consulted the Oracle at Delphi which advised him not to open the longish neck of his skinbag before he arrived in Athens. Unable to explain the oracle, Aegeus began his journey back to Athens as his brothers were a threat to his throne.

On the way, he passed from Troezen where he was accommodated by king Pittheus. Aegeus asked Pittheus' opinion about the oracle. In the evening Pittheus got Aegeus drunk and had him spend the night with his daughter Aethra, who the same night had also slept with Poseidon. In spite of knowing that Aethra was pregnant to his child, Aegeus decided to return to Athens because he learnt about his brothers threats.

Before leaving, however, he guided Aethra to the temple of Sthenius Zeus where he hid his sandals and his sword under a rock. He told Aethra in case the child was a boy not to reveal the identity of his father and, when a teenager, take him to the rock, lift it and after he recovers the tokens bring them to Athens. Only then would Aegeus acknowledge him as his real child. Afterwards Aegeus left and passing from Corinth he met Medea and invited her to Athens.

The myth has it that Theseus had a double descent, human on the side of Aegeus and divine on the side of Poseidon. In antiquity already Aegeus was considered to be Poseidon's hypostasis. Well known is Poseidon's cult epithet *Aegeus*.

Aegeus organised the **Panathenaea** in Athens, and invited athletes from all over Greece to participate in the games. Androgeus, son of the king of Crete Minos, also took part in these games.

Following Aegeus' order, Androgeus fought with the Marathonian bull and lost his life. Minos blamed the Athenians for the death of his son. He sailed his fleet to the Saronic Gulf, seized Megara and besieged Athens for a long time which, surrounded, was affected by plague.

Then, the Oracle of Delphi consulted the Athenians to give in to Minos' demands. He required that every year (in another version every nine years) the city of Athens send seven selected young boys and girls to be devoured by the Minotaur. The Athenians could do nothing but accept Minos' conditions.

THE EARLY YEARS OF THESEUS

Aethra gave the son of Aegeus or Poseidon the name Theseus because his mortal father had 'defined' the tokens of recognition under the rock. The young man grew up in Troezen and demonstrated his great abilities and his bravery.

His grandfather Pittheus spread the word that his grandson was a son of Poseidon. When Theseus reached adolescence, he visited Delphi and dedicated a lock of his hair cut above the forehead to Apollo. This kind of haircut became later known as "coura Theseis" (Theseus haircut) and this is how he was depicted by artists. When time came, Aethra took him where Aegeus had hidden the tokens.

Theseus lifted the rock easily, recovered the tokens and headed off for Athens. Pittheus and Aethra advised the young man to go by sea, however, he preferred to go to Athens by land, although the route was very dangerous due to numerous outlaws who robbed and killed travellers.

Theseus' labours on the inner part of a red-figured wide cup; in
the centre, Theseus is dragging the about to die Minotaur out
of the Labyrinth (appr. 440-430 B.C.).
London, the British Museum

THE JOURNEY TO ATHENS – THE FIRST LABOURS

On his way to Athens there lurked numerous dangers.

At Epidaurus, Theseus killed the bandit Periphetes or Corynetes, son of Hephaestus, with his very iron club (*coryne*). From then on Theseus had the club with him and used it in the labours to follow.

At Cechreae, Theseus encountered Sinis, son of Poseidon. He had taken the name Pityokampes because he used to kill every foreigner he came across in the following way: he bent down the tops of two tall pine trees and tied his victim on them. Then, he let the two trees free and, as they took their original position, the poor victim was torn apart. Theseus killed Sinis by the same method. Sinis' beautiful daughter Perigounes gave birth to Theseus' son, Melanhippus.

When the hero reached Crommyon (modern Agioi Theodoroi) he killed **Phaea,** a wild sow, daughter of Typhon and Echidna, which ravaged the area. Next on his way, Theseus stopped at the Scironid Rocks, a place now known as "Evil Stairs", where was the lair of Sciron, son of Corinth and grandson of Pelops. When a traveller reached the place, **Sciron,** forced him to wash his knees for him. Then, as his victims knelt before him, Sciron kicked them into the sea where a giant turtle devoured them.

Theseus killed Sciron by the same method. A little later at Eleusis, he killed **Cercyon,** son of Poseidon, who used to challenge passers-by to a wrestling match with him. He lifted him up in the air and crushed him against the ground taking advantage of his intelligence rather

Theseus and Sinis are depicted in front of the pine tree on which the villain slew his victims; red-figured wide cup by the painter of Elpinicus (490-480 B.C.). Munchen, Staatliche Antikensammlungen

than his power. This is why it is said that wrestling was invented by Theseus.

On Hiera Odos (the Sacred Road), close to modern Daphni, Theseus killed the dangerous bandit Damastes or Polypoemon, our well known **Procrustes**. Procrustes had two beds, a short one and a long one. When he caught a passer-by, he measured him and, if he was tall he made him lie on the short bed and vice versa. Then he cut off their feet so as to fit the bed whereas he hammered the short ones in order to lengthen them to the size of the bed.

ARRIVAL IN ATHENS

When Theseus was close to Athens, near the river Kephissos, he was purified by the Phytalides at the altar of Zeus Meilichius. He entered Athens on the eighth day of the month Hecatombaeon.

His father had already heard about the young man and his deeds but didn't suspect of his being his own son. Medea, however, understood who he was and attempted to poison him. Theseus, then, presented Aegeus with his sword. Aegeus recognised his son and threw away the poisonous cup Medea had offered Theseus. He immediately introduced him to the citizens of Athens and exiled Medea and her son who found shelter in Asia Minor.

Afterwards, Theseus secured his father throne exterminating the pretenders, the Pallantides. Theseus underwent trial charged with the murder of his relatives but was acquitted. It is said that this was the first "not guilty" verdict by a court concerning the murder of relatives.

THE MARATHONIAN BULL

A little later, Theseus set off for Marathon to crush a wild bull roaming in the area. On his way, he was accommodated for the night by an elderly woman, Hecale, who, the next morning, bid him farewell and wished him luck with his catching the bull.

Indeed Theseus caught the bull which was considered to be the very same as the one Heracles had brought to Eurystheus from Crete or, in another version, the one which had carried Europe on its back. Theseus took this bull to Athens where, in his father's presence, he sacrificed it to Delphic Apollo.

Then, he instituted tributes in Hecale's commemoration and named a small town in Attica after her.

THE JOURNEY TO CRETE AND THE EXTERMINATION OF THE MINOTAUR

Theseus' most important labour which, according to the Athenian tradition, took place before he became the king of Athens was the extermination of the Minotaur.

According to ancient sources, because of the fact that Androgeus, son of the king of Crete Minos, was killed in Athens during an athletic contest, his father besieged and conquered the city blaming the Athenians for his death. He then imposed a cruel tribute on them, forcing them to send him every year seven young boys and seven young girls to be devoured by the Minotaur, a monster born after the union of Pasiphae with the bull ravaging Crete. Later on, the bull's capture became one of Heracle's labours and its extermination one of Theseus'.

Volunteering to free the Athenians of this tribute, Theseus set off for Crete along with the youngsters being sent to be devoured by the Minotaur. To prove Minos his divine descent from Poseidon, on the way he dived into the sea to look for the ring Minos had lost and visited the palaces of Amphitrite, Poseidon's wife. On his return, he brought the ring as well as plenty of gifts the goddess had given him.

Upon his arrival on Crete, Ariadne, daughter of Minos, fell in love with him and helped him carry out his labour. The Athenian technician Daedalus, who was in the service of Minos in Crete, advised her to give Theseus a ball of string one end of which he would tie at the entrance of the Labyrinth, where the Minotaur dwelled, so that he could find his way out, if he survived. This ball of string is the renowned **Ariadne's clue**.

Theseus fought the Minotaur; he overpowered it after a hard struggle and killed it. Following the string he reached the exit, took the youngsters and Ariadne with him and started his journey back home.

On the island of Naxos Theseus was made to abandon Ariadne advised by Athena and Dionysus who had fallen in love with her and took her for his wife. Continuing his return journey, Theseus landed on Delos where, along with the young Athenian boys and girls danced to the famous "*geranus*" around god Apollo's altar, which was made of horn. The hero, in order to honour Apollo, offered a sacrifice and Aphrodite's idol which Ariadne had given him.

Finally, he organised games in honour of the god and the winners were awarded palm tree branches for the first time.

Before Theseus left Athens for his mission on Crete, he had promised Aegeus to replace the black sails on his ship with white ones in case he had made it. Theseus forgot his promise and, when Aegeus, scanning the horizon at Sounion, saw the black sails on the ship he threw himself into the sea and drowned. Hence, the sea was named the Aegean Sea. According to an earlier tradition, Aegeus jumped off the Acropolis.

Mourning overshadowed the joy of the Athenians but Theseus instituted an annual festival, the *Pyanopsia*. The families of the youths who had escaped death were assigned to pay some tribute for the annual sacrifice, in charge of which were the Phytalides.

Since then the Athenians saw to the maintenance of the ship that carried home victorious Theseus and managed to keep it in good condition replacing the rotten pieces of wood. This was the renowned **Salaminian naus** (ship).

Statue of the Minotaur from a complex depicting him with Theseus; a Roman replica of a classical era complex by Myron set up on the Acropolis.
Athens, National Archaeological Museum

The Abduction of Helen
of Troy by Theseus;
red-figured Attic pitcher
by the painter
Polygnotes from
Marathon
(appr. 430-420 B.C.).
Athens, National
Archaeological Museum

PERSEUS

Perseus was the son of Zeus and gorgeous **Danae**, the daughter of **Acrisius**, king of Argos. Acrisius wanted to have a son therefore he consulted the oracle at Delphi to find out if his wish would be fulfilled. The answer he received was negative, but the oracle warned him that his daughter was to give birth to a son who would kill him.

Thus, Acrisius, for fear that the oracle would become true, confined **Danae** to an underground room and saw that no man approached her. However, Zeus had fallen in love with the gorgeous daughter of the king, came to her in the form of a shower of gold and impregnated her. Danae gave birth to Perseus, who she managed to hide from her father with the aid of her nurse. However, the cries and shouts of Acrisius' little grandson revealed him and he asked for the whole truth. Danae told him that the baby's father was Zeus but he did not believe her and cast her and Perseus into the sea in a wooden chest. The chest, drifted by the waves, washed ashore an island of the Cyclades, **Seriphos**. They were found by a fisherman, **Dictys**, who, according to certain myths, was a brother to the king of the island, **Polydectes**. Dictys freed Danae and her son, took them in and offered them shelter. The myth has it that Perseus reached manhood there on Seriphos until king Polydectes, desiring Danae for his wife against her will, found a way to remove him. He organised a banquet with his friends and invited Perseus as well. There, he announced that he wanted each of his guests to give him a horse for the wedding of Hippodamea, the daughter of Oenomaus, king of Pisa. When Perseus asked the occasion for the banquet he was given the reply "for Hippodamea's wedding". Other myths have it, though, that the king's answer was: "For horses!"

Then Perseus said that he had no objection to the offer to the king even if his demand was the head of **Gorgon - Medusa**. The next day the king accepted horses as gifts by his friends, but ordered Perseus to bring him the Head of Medusa he had boasted about. He also threatened him that in case he did not manage to do so, he would take his mother to be his wife against her will.

Gorgonion (5th c. B.C.).
Athens, National
Archaeological Museum

PERSEUS AND MEDUSA

Upset by the king's demand, Perseus sat on a rock at the far end cape of the island weeping over his bad luck. There, he was found by **Hermes** who told him that he and goddess Athena would aid him in getting the head of the Gorgon.

The **Gorgons** were the three daughters of **Phorcys** and **Keto** called **Stheno, Euryale** and **Medusa**. Of the three, only Medusa was mortal but even she was impossible to approach unless one had appropriate equipment: the **hood** making him invisible (i.e. "the **Cynen**"), the **winged sandals** and the **magic sachet** (i.e. the "**cybisin**"). All of these were kept by the **Nymphs** and only the **Graeae** (elderly women) could lead him to them.

The Graeae were elderly from birth and had only one eye and one tooth they all used in turns. Perseus, directed by **Athena**, snatched the eye and the tooth and would not return them until they gave him directions to the Nymphs. The Nymphs were willing to give him the three crucial for his mission tools. Thus, **Athena, Hermes** and **Perseus** crossed the **Ocean** to reach the Gorgons' dwelling.

When they arrived, they found them asleep. They had hair of living snakes, tusks of a boar, cupreous arms and bore golden wings. Perseus immediately put on the hood to become invisible and the sandals to walk in the air, took the sachet on his shoulder and, using the diamond scythe (**the harpen**) of Hermes, cut Medusa's head off without watching it directly; only its reflectin on the metal of his shield, as advised by Athena, so that he would not turn into stone.

From the wound on Medusa's neck sprang **Pegasus**, the winged horse, and **Chrysaor**, the father of three-bodied **Geryon** the Gordon had given birth to with Poseidon.

With Medusa's head in the sachet, Perseus fled pursued by the other two Gorgons but under the hood of invisibility (the cynen) they could not see him. It is said that flying over Africa, some drops of Medusa's blood fell on the earth and since then it was filled with wild beasts.

Three Nymphs; detail from a marble dedicatory bas-relief (2nd c. B.C.). Athens, National Archaeological Museum

PERSEUS AND ANDROMEDA

Corinthian coin depicting winged Pegasus (360 B.C.) Athens, the Monetary Museum

On his way back with Medusa's head, Perseus arrived in Ethiopia. He met a girl bound on a rock. She was fastened to a rock on the shore so as a sea monster to eat her.

She was the daughter of the king of the land, **Cepheus**, and was called **Andromeda**. Once, her mother **Cassiope** or **Cassiopeia** had boasted about her daughter being more beautiful that the **Nereids**.

Enraged they told **Poseidon** and asked him for revenge. The god sent an inundation on the land and a fearsome beast which destroyed everything. The people then consulted the oracle on how they would be saved and they were announced that they had to offer the king's daughter to the beast to devour.

When Perseus was told, he offered to slay the beast on condition that he would take beautiful Andromeda as his wife. The king agreed and, once the beast emerged from the sea, equipped with the weapons given to him by the Nymphs, attacked and slew the monster. He saved Andromeda and married her. It is also said that Perseus and Andromeda had **Perses**, whom they left to **Cepheus** to raise when they left for Argos. Perses was believed to be the ancestor of the **Perses**.

Another myth has it that once the danger was over, Cepheus went back on his promise to allow Andromeda to marry Perseus. Since **Phineus**, his brother, also wanted to marry Andromeda, he plotted a trick to take Perseus out of the way. However, Perseus realised what was being plotted against him, appeared before the king and his court, took the head of Medusa out of his sachet and, by the sight of it, everyone turned into stone.

THE RETURN OF PERSEUS TO ARGOS

After what had happened in **Ethiopia**, Perseus set off for his homeland along with Andromeda. On the way, he stopped at **Seriphos** where he found that his mother had to take refuge as a Hicetid to the altar of the god (Suppliant Maiden) because of the violent advances of **Polytectes**.

Then, Perseus appeared before Polytectes, opened his sachet and showed everyone the fearsome head of the Medusa declaring that he had accomplished his mission. Upon seeing the head, everyone was turned into stone and this is why the island is full of rocks.

Perseus made his protector **Dictys** king of Seriphos and continued his journey to **Argos** along with his wife and his mother. On arriving to Argos, he looked for his grandfather **Acrisius** who had moved to **Larissa** for fear that the oracle would come true and his grandson would kill him. Perseus went to Larissa, found his grandfather and talked him into returning to Argos together.

Before they set off, Perseus took part in **athletic games**, threw the discus which veered, struck Acrisius and killed him. Returning to Argos as his grandfather's heir he did not wish to succeed him to the throne and made an agreement with **Megapenthes**, king of Tiryns, to swap their realms. Thus, Megapenthes took over Argos and Perseus took over Tiryns. Later on, Perseus expanded his land by founding **Mycenae**.

According to the myth, Mycenae was named after Perseus himself because at the area it was founded, the "myces", i.e. his sword handle, had fallen, which was considered to be a good omen. In another version, he discovered a spring with plenty of water in the roots of a muces (mushroom), which grew in the area.

The spring was named "Persea" and supplied the Acropolis of Mycenae with water throughout its long lasting existence, whereas its water still flows nowadays.

The myths concerning the foundation of Mycenae also have it that Perseus used the Cyclops from Asia to construct the city, as well as the city of Tiryns.

THE PERSEIDES

Perseus was succeeded to the throne of Mycenae by his son **Electryon** who married to **Anaxo**, the daughter of his brother **Alcaeus**, and had nine sons and one daughter, **Alcmene**.

His nine sons were killed in a conflict with the **Teleboae**, the sons of **Pterelaus**, who also descended from Perseus and pursued power. Afterwards, to avenge his children's death, **Electryon** started a war against the Teleboae having entrusted power and his only daughter to **Amphitryon**, the brother of her mother. By bad fortune, Amphitryon unintentionally became the cause for Electryon's death just before he left for the war.

Then, another brother of Electryon, **Sthenelus**, seized the opportunity to take power and exile Amphitryon and Alcmene to Argolis. They arrived in **Thebes** where they got married after Amphitryon had won and the Teleboae had yielded. They had **Heracles**, who is considered to be a hero not only in Argolis, where he carried out accomplishments in the service of **Eurystheus**, but also a Panhellenic hero since his achievements and expeditions extended all over the then known world.

When Sthenelus seized the power in Mycenae, to enforce his authority, he summoned the sons of Pelops, his wife Nicippe's brothers, and offered them the power in the small town Midea.

The last king of the dynasty was **Eurystheus**, who imposed the twelve labours on Heracles and was killed in Attica before appointing a successor to his throne.

Panoramic view of the Acropolis of Mycenae.

PELOPS

Pelops was the son of **Tantalus**, king of Lydia, and **Dione** or **Euryanassa**. Being a fair king at first, Tantalus, a son of Zeus, was a favourite to the gods who loved him so much that they let him visit Olympus and taste nectar and ambrosia with them. Spoilt by his great wealth, Tantalus forgot that he was a mortal and did not respect the gods. He decided to also invite them to a banquet so as to test their omniscience. During the meal he offered them to eat his son **Pelops**. The gods, however, could not be deceived and after punishing Tantalus for his disrespect, brought young Pelops back to life requesting **Hermes** to reassemble his pieces and, using elephant bone, replace the only part missing from his shoulder as Demeter, preoccupied with Persephone's abduction by Hades had absentmindedly eaten it.

When revived, Pelops was even better than before and Poseidon, who the myth has it that he is either the father of the hero or his protector, gave him a wondrous winged chariot on which he could fly anywhere he wished.

At that time in Elis and in Pisa there ruled **Oenomaus (3)**, a son of **Ares**, who, according to an oracle delivered to him, would lose his life when his daughter **Hippodamea (5)** got married. Therefore, he announced that he would let Hippodameia marry to he who would beat him in a chariot race.

A strict prerequisite for the Race was that the suitors participating would have to have his daughter on the chariot with them, so that being engaged in her they would be easy opponents for him to defeat. Oenomaus had overpowering weapons at his disposal, his father's Ares presents, as well as two immortal horses which ran as fast as the wind. Moreover, he had a very competent charioteer, **Myrtilus (2)**, a son of Hermes, and due to all these, despite starting last, he managed to catch up with the suitors and kill them. The last suitor was **Pelops (4)**, the son of Tantalus; he had fallen in mutual love with the young girl who decided to do whatever within her power to win him for a husband. To succeed, the two sweethearts decided to use Myrtilus who also loved Hippodamea.

Pelops promised Myrtilus half the kingdom of Oenomaus and one night in bed with Hippodamea. Myrtilus agreed and during the chariot race he replaced the linchpins attaching the wheels to the axle of **Oenomaus' chariot (1)** with fake ones made of beewax. As the chariot raced, they melted and Oenomaus got killed tangled in his reins. Shortly before he died, he cursed Myrtilus to die by the hands of Pelops, too. His curse was soon to take effect.

The eastern pediment of the temple of Zeus in Olympia
which depicted the legendary chariot race between
Oenomaus and Pelops (470-456 B.C.).
Olympia, Archaeological Museum

1   2   3

After his victory, the hero left with Hippodamea on the chariot driven by Myrtilus. On the way, Hippodamea became thirsty therefore Pelops went to bring her some water. Then, Myrtilus attempted to rape her and Pelops took the opportunity to kill him by throwing him into the sea, which was named **Myrtoon Sea** after that. As Mirtylus died he cursed the whole family of Pelops and this curse fell heavily upon all the generations of the Pelopids.

After the murder, Pelops was expiated by god Hephaestus and became king of Pisa. Later on, he managed to dominate the entire Peloponnese, then called Apia, to which he gave his name.

THE DESCENDANTS - THE PELOPIDS

Pelops and Hippodamea had a lot of children: **Atreus, Thyestes, Alcathous, Pittheus, Nicippe** and **Lysidice**. With nymph **Axioche** he had one more son, **Crysippus**, who was his favourite. This particular love of his was the reason for Atreus and Thyestes killing Crysippus as they were jealous. Pelops cursed them and sent them away from his land. To escape his rage, they went to Argolis, to their sister **Nicippe** who had married Sthenelus, king of Mycenae.

When Eurystheus, Sthenelus' successor to the throne, was killed in Attica while fighting with the "Heracledae", the Pelopids seized the opportunity and enforced their power and influence in Mycenae, Argos, Tiryns and the rest of Argolis.

The sceptre of the Pelopids, "**fashioned by Hephaestus**", was the personal gift of Zeus to his beloved Pelops, who he particularly appreciated. He gave it to Atreus and Atreus, as he was dying, gave it to his brother Thyestes, since his children were still under age. Thyestes was an honest guardian to them and gave the sceptre to Atreus' legal heir **Agamemnon**, not to his own son, **Aegisthus**.

This is the most ancient tradition, known from the **Iliad**, concerning a rule in which prevailed trust between the brothers and lawful succession to the throne. It must connect with the original tradition of the Achaeans, who reached A. Minor after being driven away from Argolis by the Dorian domination and it is the only one in accordance with the prosperity and the glory that was the Mycenaean civilisation.

There also exists an opposing tradition and a second version concerning the Pelopids. It comes from a later tradition, perhaps meta-mycenaean, which has it that the renown generation of the Pelopids ended up cursed and wiped out after a series of murders, adultery and incests.

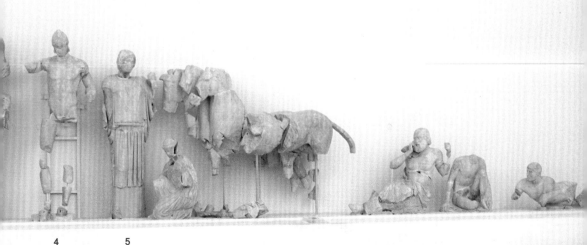

BELLEROPHON

Bellerophon, a hero of **Corinth** and **Lycia**, was a son of **Glaucus** and a grandson of **Sisyphus**. His divine father was **Poseidon** and his mother was **Eurynome** or **Eurymede**, a daughter of Nisus from Megara.

The hero bore a particular love for horses. One day, he saw **Pegasus**, the winged stallion that came from Poseidon's union with the Gorgon Medusa and was born from the blood that dropped after Perseus cut her head off.

As **Pegasus** was very fierce, nobody could capture him. Bellerophon, though, yearned to ride him so badly that he consulted diviner **Polyeidus**, who advised him to sleep close to Athena's altar and beg for her help. The hero spent the night by the goddess' altar and saw her give him a golden bridle advising him to show it to his father **Poseidon**, to whom he would have to sacrifice a white bull.

Bellerophon showed the bridle to the diviner and he suggested that he should sacrifice to Poseidon and create an altar to **Hippia Athena** before capturing the stallion. The hero honoured the gods and rushed to find Pegasus. He saw him drinking water at a spring close to Corinth. He approached, slipped the bridle over his head and the horse stood calm and ready for his tamer to mount him. Then, the horse and his rider flew in the sky and everyone watched in awe.

According to popular traditions, Bellerophon was a young man of exquisite beauty and bravery. He was exiled in Corinth owing to his accidentally murdering his brother, where, in expiation of his crime, he arrived as a suppliant to the king of Tiryns **Proetus**. However, Proetus' wife fell in love with him and, because he repulsed her advances, she told her husband that he had attempted to rape her. Proetus believed her and sent Bellerophon to **Iobates**, the king of Lycia his father-in-law, to deliver a letter which demanded the death of the bearer. Iobates accommodated his son's-in-law messenger for nine days holding feasts in his honour.

On the tenth day he asked him the purpose of his visit and Bellerophon handed him Proetus' letter. Once he had read it, he thought of sending him on three missions he deemed impossible to carry out, and as a result he would certainly lose his life. First, he asked him to kill the **Chimaera**, the daughter of Typhon and Echidna, a monster bearing a lion's head, a goat's body and a serpent's tail, which ravaged everything in the country with its hot breath.

The hero mounted Pegasus, flew in the sky and from high up he shot his arrows and slew the Chimaera. Next, Iobates asked him to fight the **Solymi**, a war-like people in **Lycia**, holding the belief that they would kill him.

However, Bellerophon slew them all and when he returned safe and sound, Iobates sent him to confront the **Amazons** on an expedition in their land. Needless to say, he won this battle, too, but he fell into an ambush by the bravest of the Lycians who carried out Iobates' orders. When he slew all the Lycians and returned victoriously, Iobates had to acknowledge Bellerephon's divine origin.

After the hero's consecutive accomplishments, Iobates kept him by his side in Lycia, offered him his second-born daughter **Cassandra** in marriage and shared his power with him. When he died, he left him his entire kingdom where Bellerophon ruled in justice and was praised with the glory of a hero. However, his end was far from good. He became very arrogant believing that he is perfect and wanted to go up to Olympus on Pegasus to be a table-mate of the gods.

The gods punished him for his arrogance by depriving him of his logic, throwing him off Olympus and letting him wander the **Aleion plain** in Lycia alone, forever away from the gods and the people.

Mosaic floor representing Medusa's head
(5th c. A.D.).
Sparta, Archaeological Museum

CADMUS

Mythologers refer to Cadmus as a hero of **Boeotia** and the founder of **Cadmea**, which comprised the core of subsequent **Thebes**. He was a son of the king of **Tyre** or **Sidon**, **Agenor** and **Telephassa** or **Argiope**. Agenor was of a divine origin from Zeus and Poseidon.

According to relevant myths, when **Zeus** fell in love with beautiful **Io**, a princess in Argos, Hera, well known for her jealousy, turned her into a cow and imposed tortures on her. As a cow, Io wandered on the mountains and the plains of Asia for a long time before she reached Egypt, where she took the human figure again and gave birth to the son of Zeus, **Epaphus**.

Epaphus became the king of Egypt and married **Memphis**, daughter of Neilus, with whom he had a daughter **Libya**, who paired off with Poseidon and had **Belus** and **Agenor**. The former son became king of Egypt and the latter became king of Tyre or Sidon. From his marriage to Telephassa or Argiope, Epaphus had **Cadmus**, **Phoenix**, **Cilix** and gorgeous **Europa**.

When Zeus fell in love with Europa and carried her off to Crete, Agenor sent his three sons to find her, ordering them not to return unless they bring her back. Then, Cilix went to an area in Asia Minor, named it Cilicia and stayed there, while his son **Thasos**, who accompanied him, reached Greece and settled down on the island of Thasos. Lastly, Phoenix stayed in Phoenicia.

Cadmus and his mother had to find shelter on the island of Rhodes due to a horrible sea storm. They offered sacrifices to Poseidon and Athena Lindia, dedicating, among other offerings, a metal pot with an inscription on it. It is said that Cadmus introduced the alphabet from Phoenice. After Rhodes, Crete, Thera and Samothrace, they reached Thrace, where his mother, who followed him, died. Then, Cadmus went to the Oracle at Delphi to ask about the right thing to do and was consulted to stop looking for Europa, follow a cow and wherever the cow stopped he would have to found a city and settle down there. Indeed, Cadmus and his companions, upon seeing a cow suiting the description given by the oracle, that is, having a circle like the full moon on each of her sides, they bought her and let her free to guide them. Once they arrived in Boeotia where modern **Thebes** is located, the cow being exhausted knelt down and Cadmus understood that he had to found his city right there. He decided, then, to sacrifice the cow to goddess Athena and sent some of his companions to fetch water from a spring. However, the spring was guarded by a huge **dragon**, a **son of Ares**, who slew Cadmus' companions. Cadmus got angry and confronted the dragon by himself, smashed his head with a rock, took water and offered the sacrifice.

Afterwards, under Athena's guidance, he sowed the beasts' teeth from which there sprouted armed men, who were called the **Spartoi** (Sown). The Spartoi killed each other after Cadmus had caused havoc among them by throwing a stone at them. They were all destroyed except for five of them, **Echion**, **Oudaeus**, **Chthonius**, **Hyperenor** and **Pelorus**, who became the founders of the families of the first noble class of Thebes. The first of them married to a daughter of Cadmus, **Agave**, who gave birth to **Pentheus**. For having slain the dragon, Cadmus had to serve Ares for a period of time.

When his punishment ended in the ninth year, the hero became the king of the city and married **Harmonia**, the daughter of Ares and Aphrodite. The wedding of Cadmus and Harmonia, renowned for its splendour, was attended by all the gods "leaving Heavens", as tradition has it. The Muses sang and the Charitae danced, while the couple received sumptuous gifts. Among them there stood out the groom's gift to his bride: an exquisite necklace, fashioned by Hephaestus, and a veil woven by the Charitae.

The city of Cadmus was founded atop a hill and was named **Cadmea**, while later on the descendants of its first residents, **Amphion** and **Zethus**, built a wall around Cadmea and created the Lower City named **Thebes** after the name of the wife of Zethus, Thebe. Amphion and Zethus were offspring of **Zeus** and **Antiope**, a daughter of **Nycteus** who pursued her for her misconduct, and so did her brother **Lycus**. Therefore, she had to have her two boys on mount Cithaeron and abandon them there.

The twin brothers grew up with a herdsman and when they found out who their mother was and what she had been through, mainly because of the wife of Lycus, **Dirke,** they killed her and had Lycus give them the power of Thebes.

Thus, they built the walls of Cadmea. It is said that Amphion was a brave warrior and

The abduction of Europa by Zeus-Bull; mosaic floor (3rd c. A.D.). Sparta, Archaeological Museum

hunter, while Zethus was such an excellent musician that, when they constructed the walls of the city, the rocks found their place on their own, bewitched by the exquisite sound of his music.

Cadmus and Harmonia had four daughters, **Semele**, **Ino**, **Agave** and **Autonome**, as well as an only son, **Polydorus**. **Semele**, their first-born daughter, paired off with Zeus who fell in love with her. From their union in love there was born god **Dionysus**, but unfortunate Semele had a tragic death before her delivery time due to Hera's jealousy.

Ino married **Athamas** and had two sons, **Learchus** and **Melicertes**. Hera was out of her senses from jealousy, because Ino had raised infant Dionysus, and sent them madness which made Athamas kill Learchus while hunting, mistaking him for a deer and Ino kill Melicertes leaping into the sea with him. However, Poseidon and the Nereids took pity on the mother and the child and made them aquatic deities taking the names **Leucothea** and **Palaemon**.

Agave became the wife of **Echion**, one of the Spartoi, and had **Pentheus**, who Cadmus, when he came of age, gave his kingdom to. Since Ino had spoken ill of Semele due to her affair with Zeus, Zeus avenged her. When the god reached Thebes in order to teach his cult, Pentheus did not respect him and sent him to prison. Being a god, though, he burst his fetters and took Pentheus outside the city, where the women along with Agave were in ecstacy holding rites in honour of god Dionysus. Pentheus fell in their hands; they mistook him for a wild animal and tore him apart. His mother, herself, entered the city holding her son's head as a trophy.

The youngest of Cadmus' daughters, **Autonoe**, was the wife of **Aristaeus**, a son of Apollo. They had a son, **Actaeon**, who bore a great love for hunting. He became so renowned that he accompanied goddess **Artemis** in the woods. Once, however, he accidentally saw the goddess bathing naked in some spring waters. She became furious, changed him into a hind and outraged his dogs which attacked him and tore him apart.

After Pentheus' death, Cadmus made his son Polydorus king of Thebes. **Polydorus** married **Nycteid**, daughter of Nycteus of the Spartoi family, and had a son, **Labdacus**, who became the founder of the family of the great Theban dynasty of the Labdacides, a descendant of whom was the tragic king of Thebes, **Oedipus**.

At an old age, Cadmus and Harmonia left Thebes. His end is associated with **Epirus** and **Illyria**. According to the relevant tradition, after they left Thebes, they ended in Epirus where they were changed into serpents and transferred to the Elysian Fields. In another version, Cadmus wanted to help the **Encheleis** against the **Illyrians** and this is why he was removed from Thebes. According to this version, after the Illyrians' subjugation to them, Cadmus and Harmonia ruled their country and had a son, **Illyrius**.

Their end is similar to the one accounted in the previous myth. As the hero believed that the serpent he had killed in his youth was of divine origin, he asked the gods to change him into a serpent, too. His request was granted and both Cadmus and Harmonia were changed into serpents and lived like this until Zeus sent them to dwell at the Elysian Fields.

Goddess Artemis; detail from the frieze of the eastern side of the Parthenon.
Athens, the Acropolis Museum

OEDIPUS

Oedipus, one of the most tragic heroes in Greek mythology, descended from the royal family of **Cadmus**. His father was **Laius**, son of **Labdacus**, the grandson of Cadmus and founder of the family of the Labdacides.

When Laius succeeded his father to the throne of Thebes, he married **Iocasta** or **Epicasta**, the daughter of **Menoeceus**, a descendant of the Spartoi. Since they had not had children for a long time, they consulted the oracle of Delphi.

Pythia, though, told them that they should never have children because the son they were to have was bound to kill his very father, marry his mother and bring tremendous disaster on the city. Laius avoided Iocasta out of fear but she managed to get him drunk and sleep with him.

When their son was born, Laius pierced his ankles with golden rings and gave him to a trustworthy herdsman ordering him to abandon the infant on mount Cithaeron. The herdsman took pity on the little baby, gave him to some horse-shepherds who were in the service of the king of Corinth **Polybus**. They took him to Polybus and his wife **Merope** who welcomed him as they had no children of their own. They kept him with pleasure and gave him the name **Oedipus** (swollen footed) because of an oedema he had on his legs. The king and the queen loved the little boy and raised him as if he were their own. He had a happy life until, during a fight with a drunkard, he told him that he was not a real son of the king.

Oedipus asked Polybus and Merope for the truth but he was given no answer. Therefore, he consulted the Delphic Oracle but, there too, the only thing Pythia told him was that he was destined to kill his father and marry his mother. Believing that the royal couple of Corinth was his parents, the proud young man did not return to his reputed parents.

On the way from Delphi to Phocis, at a place where three roads met, he encountered Laius who was going to Delphi and, having a fight over who had the right to go first, Oedipus killed him and his companions, being of course unaware of his identity.

At that time, Thebes was ravaged by a monster called **Sphinx**, who was the daughter of **Echidna** and **Typhon**.

She had the figure of a recumbent lion with a head and a bust of a woman and a bird's wings. She devoured the Thebans because they could not solve a riddle she asked them. The riddle was: **which animal walks first on four legs, then on two and finally on three.**

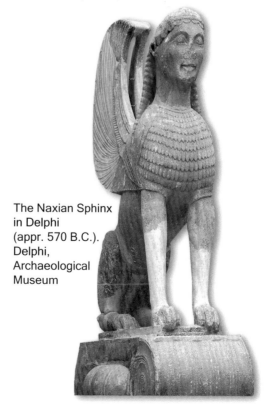

The Naxian Sphinx in Delphi (appr. 570 B.C.). Delphi, Archaeological Museum

Creon, Iocasta's brother, who acted as king after the death of Laius, promised to marry the widowed queen and give the throne to whoever would free Thebes from the monster. Oedipus is the one who will answer Sphinx **"man"** and she throws herself to abyss, while Oedipus, following his destiny, will become king of Thebes and marry Iocasta, that is, his mother, without knowing it.

OEDIPUS KING

From his marriage to Iocasta, Oedipus had four children: the sons, **Eteocles** and **Polynices**, and the daughters, **Antigone** and **Ismene**.

Life was peaceful in Thebes when, suddenly, a plague broke out and the citizens were decimated. In the quest for the truth, Oedipus sent Creon to Delphi to ask what it would take to end the suffering and Pythia replied that the plague would be lifted only when the murderer of old Laius was sent away from the city.

The king promised to allow the murderer to leave unharmed provided that he presented himself. Since nobody appeared, Oedipus called seer Tiresias who, at first, refused to reveal the truth. Oedipus insisted and accused him of being involved in the crime, therefore Tiresias revealed the terrible secret.

Still Oedipus is not convinced, suspecting that Creon was behind all these accusations. While Iocasta, though, mentions details of the murder, Oedipus realises he was guilty, having no idea whatsoever of the fact that Laius was his father. His identity will come to light when a messenger from Corinth arrives and announces the death of Polybus, adding that the people ask Oedipus to become their king. For fear that the second part of the oracle, prophesising that he was to marry his mother would come true, Oedipus refuses the throne of Corinth.

However, the messenger will tell him that Polybus is not his real father, since he knew that he, himself, had taken him as a baby to his reputed parents. Oedipus will ask for documentation from the herdsman of Laius, who will confirm that the child he had given was the son of Laius.

It was only then that king Oedipus does realise that his father was Laius and his wife was, in fact, his mother. After the horrible disclosure, Iocasta hanged herself and Oedipus blinded himself with his bare hands.

The, once, wise saviour of Thebes, a tragic figure now, decided to leave his city and asked Creon to protect his daughters. An earlier version of the myth has it that he remained in Thebes and, after he heroically died in the battlefield, he was buried in his land with honours. It is also mentioned that, after Iocasta's death, he marries **Eurygenea** or **Astymedusa** and then he has his four children.

The prevalent version, nevertheless, accounted by Sophocles in his "**Oedipus at Colonus**", has it that Oedipus was expelled by Creon for being a miasma, and after wandering for long, he arrived with his daughter Antigone at Colonus, a municipality in Attica, where he sought refuge in the **small wood** of the **Eumenides**.

These deities were also called the **Erinyes** (the Furies) when they punished criminals, whereas when a criminal was expiated, they became the deities of forgiveness. The citizens asked him to leave but he appealed to the Athenian hospitality and asked to talk to the king of the city **Theseus**, to whom he emphasised that the city will benefit from his presence.

Ismene also arrives at **Colonus**, having bad news from the palace in Thebes to announce. Since Oedipus had abandoned the city, his two sons had been fighting over the throne and power.

Eteocles, his younger son, eventually became the king and sent **Polynices** away giving him only Harmonia's jewel and veil. Polynices went to the king of Argos **Adrastus**, who married him to his daughter **Argeia**. Supported by Adrastus and his friend **Tydeus**, son of Aetolian Oeneus and Periboea, who had married the sister of Argeia **Deipyle**, Polynices organised the renowned expedition of the "**Seven against Thebes**", which was named after the fact that the army was led by seven leaders, who set off to occupy Thebes.

Creon had been informed of a prophesy delivered by the Delphic Oracle, according to which Oedipus had become a favourite of the gods after the hardships he had undergone, and could make the city he was found in either dead or alive unconquerable. Thus, he set off with his two sons to persuade him to either return to Thebes or aid one of his two sons. The miserable father decided to aid neither of the two.

When **Theseus** arrived, Oedipus asked him for hospitality for the rest of his life and permission to be buried at a place of his choice, stating that his presence and burial in the ground of Athens would bring prosperity to the Athenians. Theseus respected him and agreed to protect the powerless blind king. Eteocles' emissary Creon arrived first and asked Oedipus to return to Thebes and make it unconquerable. Since, however, he had murdered his father and was a miasma he would not be allowed to enter the city.

Oedipus refused and Creon, to convince him, ran off with his two daughters but Theseus freed them. After Creon, Polynices arrived but his father refused to talk to him. Antigone tried to talk him into seeing him and, eventually, he accepted to see Polynices, who tried to take him on his side so that he won, according to the oracle. Oedipus refused and, enraged with his two sons who cared only for power, cursed them to destroy each other.

After a while, he reached the end of his life. The gods notified him with thunder and Oedipus called Theseus to show him, and only him, the site of his burial. Each king would reveal the secret to his successor and, thus, Athens would be unconquerable. The elderly father bid his daughters farewell and was left alone with Theseus.

Amidst thunderbolts, Oedipus vanished miraculously passing in the Under World; nevertheless, he has remained in people's memory as their hero-protector.

Marble Attic sarcophagus depicting the expedition of the Seven leaders against Thebes (2nd c. A.D.). Corinth, Archaeological Museum

MELEAGER AND THE HUNT OF THE CALYDONIAN BOAR

Meleager was the son of the king of Aetolian **Calydon Oeneus** and **Althaea**, the daughter of the king of neighbouring **Pleuron Thestes** and **Eurytheme**. According to a version, he was of divine origin since he was considered to be a son of god Ares.

When Meleager was a seven-day-old infant, the **Moirae** (Fates) visited his house to predict his destiny. First **Clotho** said that he would become a great hero, and second, **Lachesis** enumerated the accomplishments he would perform. When **Atropos**' turn came, she looked at a log burning in the hearth and said that Meleager would die when that log was consumed by fire. Upon overhearing this, Althea took the log from the hearth and hid it to save her son's life.

Meleager grew into a brave young man. He took part in the Argonautic expedition and was glorified along with the rest of the Argonauts as a hero.

During a summer, while Oeneus was offering the first grains of that harvest to the gods, he forgot to offer to **Artemis** who happened to be the patroness of his country. The goddess became enraged and sent Calydon, a huge **wild boar** which ravaged the area and destroyed people and animals. Then, Meleager called many of the known heroes from all over Greece, as well as his relatives, Althea's brothers along with the **Couretes** who lived in neighbouring Pleuron, in order to hunt and kill the huge boar.

Among the heroes participating in the hunt of the Calydonian boar, the best known ones were:

Meleager, the leader of the venture; Althea's brothers who were single-sandaled warriors according to their tribe rank; **Laertes**, the father of Odysseus from Ithaca; a great number of the **Lapiths** from Thessaly, known as the Centaurmachoi or the Argonauts; **Caenen**; **Peirithus**; **Mopsus** and **Asclepius**; **Iphiclus** king of the Thessalian Phylace; **Admetus** king of Pherae; **Acastus** king of Iolcus and a son of Pelias; **Jason**, the leader of the Argonauts; **Peleus**, the father of Achilles, and **Phoenix**, his teacher; **Iolaus** from Thebes, a nephew of Heracles; **Iphicles**, the brother of Heracles; **Theseus** from Athens; **Telamon** from Salamis, the brother of Aeas and Teuctrus; **Amphiaraus** from Argos; **Angaeus** from Teges in Arcadia; the twins Apharetids **Idas** and **Lyngeus** from Messina; their cousins twins Dioscouri **Castor** and **Polydeuce (Pollux)** from Sparta; **Nestor**, king of Pylos, and from Crete, the son of Minos and Pasiphae, **Deucalion**. Among all these heroes, the only woman who participated was Atalanta, known from the myths as the unbroken young woman. When Atalanta was born, her father, who wanted a son, abandoned her on the mountains of Arcadia where she was nursed by a bear until some herdsmen found her and raised her. The girl grew to become unbeatable as far as racing, wrestling and arrow-shooting are concerned.

When all the heroes got together, they were accommodated by Oeneus for nine days. On the tenth, though, they had to set out for the hunt. Some of them, however, objected to a woman, Atalanta, participating with them. But Meleager, having fallen in love with her, imposed her participation on them. The struggle began but it was hard and a lot of the heroes were destroyed, for example, Angaeus and Hyleus who were killed from the tusks of the boar, whereas **Eurytion** was killed from the spear accidentally shot at him by Peleus. Finally, on the sixth day of the hunt, **Atalanta** first shot her arrows at the back of the animal. She was followed by **Amphiaraos** who targeted its eye and, finally, Meleager killed it by hitting it in the abdomen. The hunters shared the meat of the boar, but **Meleager**, being the victor, took its hide as a prize and offered it to Atalanta. His action was thought of as a great insult by his uncles. Thus, they took the hide from Atalanta, stating that it belonged to them since

Meleager did not want to keep it for himself. Meleager got really angry and there followed a fight during which, out of his mind, he killed his uncles. As soon as Althea found out about her brothers' murder from the hands of her son, in great grief, she remembered what the three Moirae had said and the log she had hidden. In an impulse, she threw the log in the hearth. No sooner had the log burnt completely than Meleager dropped dead.

After his death, his wife **Cleopatra** and his mother committed suicide. The women in the palace could not stop grieving and goddess Artemis, who took pity on them, changed them into birds, the **meleageres**, which have been crying for the unfair loss of the young man until today.

A version of the myth claims that goddess Artemis, who had sent the boar, provoked the argument over the prize which led two neighbouring cities, Calydon and Pleuron, to a war and the confrontation between two tribes, the **Aetolians** and the **Couretes**. During this fight, Meleager, either accidentally or in a duel, killed his mother's brothers and, when she found out she begged the gods of the Under World to take her son with them. In this war, Meleager, being the leader of the Calydonians, killed his relatives - opponents and his death occurred at the time when the brave man had forced his enemy to retreat, thus saving his city from definite destruction, whereas he was fully aware of the fact that his mother's curses would lead to his death.

Attic black-figured urn with a representation of Peleus fighting against invincible Atalanta; from Vulci (appr. 500 A.D.). Munchen, Staatliche Antikensammlungen

JASON

Jason, a son of **Aeson** and **Polymela** or **Alcimede** and a grandson of **Cretheus** and **Tyro**, descended from the generation of **Hellen**. Hellen had three sons, Dorus, Aeolus and Xuthus by nymph Orthreis or Orseis. **Dorus** was the **founder of the family of the Dorians, Xuthus** of the **Ionians** and the **Achaeans**, while Aeolus was the **founder of the family of** the Aeolians and ruled Magnesia, in Thessaly.

From his union with Enarete or Eurydice, he had five sons, Cretheus, Athamas, Sissyphus, Salmoneus and Perieres, as well as three daughters, Alcyon, Canace and Melanippe. From the **Aeolids**, i.e. the descendants of Aeolus, **Cretheus** and **Athamas** are closely connected with the myths of Thessaly, while the rest three, along with their sons and grandsons, reached every place in the Peloponnese.

Cretheus became the king of Iolcus and married his niece **Tyro**, the daughter of Salmoneus, who was the only survival after her family's destruction due to her arrogant father. Tyro fell in love with the river god **Enipeus** but he did not pay attention to her. On the contrary, Poseidon, who was in love with the young girl, approached her in the guise of the river god and united with her. Afterwards, he revealed himself and told her that she would have two boys and that she had to keep their relationship a secret. When time came for her to go into labour, Tyro gave birth to twins in the wilderness, put them in a tub and abandoned them to die.

However, the two boys, being the sons of a god, survived as a horse herdsman picked them up and named them **Pelias** and **Neleus**. Later on, they were acknowledged by their mother who, meanwhile, had married and given birth to three more sons, **Aeson, Amythaon**

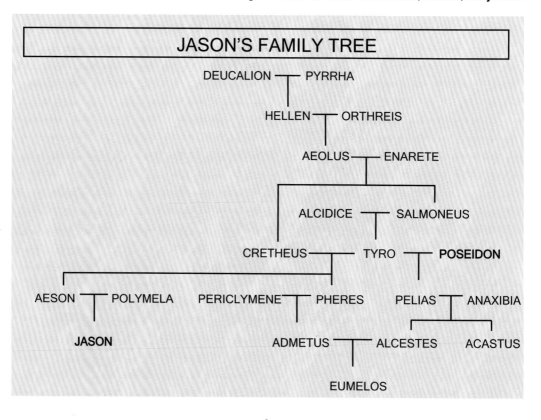

JASON'S FAMILY TREE

DEUCALION —┬— PYRRHA

HELLEN —┬— ORTHREIS

AEOLUS —┬— ENARETE

ALCIDICE —┬— SALMONEUS

CRETHEUS —┬— TYRO —┬— POSEIDON

AESON —┬— POLYMELA   PERICLYMENE —┬— PHERES   PELIAS —┬— ANAXIBIA

JASON   ADMETUS —┬— ALCESTES   ACASTUS

EUMELOS

and **Pheres**. As the legal heir, Aeson was to take the throne when his father died. However, Pelias became the king of Iolcus due to his divine origin. Since the two half-brothers were not in good terms, in an attempt to protect his only son **Jason**, Aeson said that his child had died during the night, whereas, in reality, he had sent him to the cave of the wise Centaur **Chiron**, who lived on Mount Pelion. There, living with the wise Centaur, Jason exercised his body and spirit and learnt a lot of important crafts.

At his twenty, he had already become a remarkable young man, possessing the necessary skills to deal with anything. He, then, set out to go to **Iolcus** and assert his right to power and the goods that belonged to his paternal allotment. On the way, the young man met **Hera**, disguised in an elderly woman, who asked him to help her cross the river Anaurus, in order to check how merciful he was. Without any hesitation, Jason helped her, but while crossing the river he lost one sandal. Thus, he arrived in Iolcus **single-sandaled**. Jason presented himself before Pelias and the people gathered around him admired the young man, who looked like a god. On the contrary, **Pelias** was petrified as he remembered an old oracle advising him to beware of a single-sandaled man. When Jason claimed the power of the city, Pelias pretended to have no objection on condition that he went to **Colchis** to fetch the **Golden Fleece**.

Poseidonian red-figured calyx-crater with a representation of Medea and Jason beside the sacred oak tree from which the Golden Fleece is hanging, guarded by the dragon-serpent which is coiled on the tree (appr. 310 B.C.). Napoli, National Archaeological Museum

He even claimed that **Phrixus** came in his dreams and urged him to go to **Aeetes'** palace to bring back home his ghost, which could not find peace in the foreign land, as well as the Golden Fleece from the ram that had saved him.

Phrixus was the son of the king of Boeotia **Athamas** and goddess **Nephele** (Cloud). He was the victim of his stepmother **Ino**. Athamas, a son of **Aeolus** and the brother of **Cretheus** who was Jason's grandfather, sent Nephele away and married Ino, who hated her husband's children and hatched a plan to get rid of them. She persuaded the women of the country to roast the crop seeds their husbands had to sow and, when they sowed them, no grain grew so that the following year there was no crop at all. Athamas sent men to the Oracle of Delphi to ask for advice. Ino, however, persuaded them to lie to Athamas and tell him that, in order for this misfortune to end, Phrixus should be sacrificed at the altar of Zeus. Under the farmers' pressure, Athamas guided his son to the altar. Nevertheless, Nephele, being a goddess, sent a golden wool ram Hermes had given her, which took **Phrixus** and **Helle** on its back and flew off. They flew over land and seas but, as they were over the strait separating the Thracian peninsula from Sygion, Helle fell off the ram and drowned in the waters of the Pontus which, since then, has been called the **Hellespont** (sea of Helle).

Phrixus continued his journey and arrived in **Colchis**. Alone amidst foreigners, he sacrificed the ram to **Phyxius Zeus**, who helped people in danger. Then, he asked and found out that the king of the land was **Aeetes**, a son of **Helios** and **Perseis** and a brother of **Circe**. He went to the king as a suppliant and asked for refuge; the king welcomed him and even gave him one of his two daughters, **Chalciope**, in marriage. Phrixus, then, gave him the **Golden Fleece** as a gift and he hung it in an oak tree in a grove, which was dedicated to **Ares**. In addition, he had it guarded by a serpent as long as a fifty-oared ship, which held it tightly between its teeth and stayed awake day and night.

Guarded like this, attempting to take the Golden Fleece was an impossible mission. Nevertheless, Jason undertook the mission and, immediately started the preparations for the journey, which has been known to humankind as the **argonautic expedition**.

THE ARGONAUTIC EXPEDITION

The ship Jason needed for his long journey was built by **Argus**, a son of Arestor, with the aid of goddess **Athena**. For her construction, they used pine trees from Mount Pelion, while goddess Athena fixed on her prow a special piece of timber from Dodona, which could speak and render prophecies. The ship had fifty oars and was very fast, this is why she was named **Argo** (argos = fast).

It is said that goddess Hera helped to gather up the most important heroes of Greece and venture this journey from **Iolcus** to distant **Colchis**. Among them there were Orpheus, Heracles, Peleus, Meleager, the Dioscouri, Amphiaraos, the seers Mopsus and Idmon, Tiphys, who became the captain of Argo, even the son of Pelias Adrastus and a lot more. When everything was ready, the **Argonauts** sacrificed to Apollo and chose Jason for their leader. They spent the whole night on the coast listening to **Orpheus** play his lyre and sing about the Beginning of the Cosmos, when the sky and the sea were united.

The next day, in the morning, they sailed and reached their first stop which was **Lemnos**, the island of **Hephaestus**. There lived only women whose queen was **Hypsipyle**. Due to the fact that for a long time the Lemnian women did not honour **Aphrodite**, to punish them, she made them so foul in stench that no man could bear sleep with them. They, then, became so angry that they killed all of them except for their king, **Thoas**, who they dropped into the sea sealed in a chest.

When the Argonauts reached Lemnos, for the sake of Hephaestus, Aphrodite made the women feel a sexual desire and they mingled with the men and had children again, a new

The inner part of a red-figured wide cup is depicting the dragon guarding the Golden Fleece with half-dead Jason in its mouth, while fully armed Athena is watching him in sorrow (480-470 B.C.). Rome, Musei Vaticani

generation for their island. Hypsipyle united with Jason and had two sons, **Euenus** and **Nebrophon**.

After leaving Lemnos, the Argonauts passed from the holy island of **Samothrace**, where they were initiated in the mysteries of the **Cabeiroi**, the "Great Gods", and learned ancient secrets so as to sail with safety.

Continuing their journey, the Argonauts sailed the Hellespont and landed among the **Doliones**, whose king, **Cizycos**, treated them graciously. However, when they left, they met with a horrible storm and rough sea and had to go back that night. The Doliones did not realise who they were and, mistaking them for enemies, attacked them. During the fight, a lot of men died and Jason, accidentally, killed their king Cizycos. When dawn came, the Doliones and the Argonauts realised their mistake, and, reconciled, buried their dead with great honours.

The Argonauts' next stop was the country **Kiane**, on the coast of **Mysia**, where the inhabitants welcomed them and provided food and wine for them. The heroes prepared their meal and **Hylas**, the companion of Heracles, went to a spring to fetch water. However, a

Nymph of the spring fell in love with the handsome young man and pulled him in the bottom. **Polyphemus** heard his screams and rushed to save him along with **Heracles**. They looked for Hylas all night and did not return.

In the morning the Argonauts set off, unaware of the fact that they had left their companions behind. When they realised, they wanted to go back but **god Glaucus** told them not to. Thus, Polyphemus remained in Mysia, whereas Heracles returned to Greece.

The journey went on and the Argonauts arrived in the land of the Bebryces whose king was Amycus, a son of Poseidon. Amicus used to challenge every foreigner arriving in his land to a wrestling contest and, because he was very strong, he killed them all. When the Argonauts arrived, he asked to wrestle with their best man and Polydeuce (Pollux), a son of Zeus, accepted his challenge. During the wrestling, though, Pollux killed him. Then, the Bebryces attacked the Argonauts but their heroes won and left their inhospitable land quickly.

Argo continued her journey to Bosporus amidst wild waves and strong winds and reached the coast of Thrace, where diviner **Phineus** lived. **Phineus** had been punished by Zeus because he revealed the gods' inmost deliberations to humans, withholding none. Zeus had blinded him and, every day, sent him the **Harpies** and snatched his food when preparing his meal. When the Argonauts arrived, poor Phineus asked their help. The Argonauts took pity on him, gave him food and, when the Harpies came, the two sons of **Boreus**, **Zetes** and **Calais**, chased them away. In return of this favour, Phineus revealed the Argonauts the way to escape the **Symplegades rocks** (Clashing rocks), the crossing of which was the most challenging part of their journey.

The Symplegades were two huge rocks which clashed continuously and crushed everything that travelled between them. The Argonauts arrived in front of them and saw them clash with a dreadful noise.

The heroes were frightened, but goddess **Athena**, invisible, supported them. Then,

Ivory bas-relief depicting the myth of Phineus (6th c. B.C.).
Delphi, Archaeological Museum

Euphemus, holding a dove in his hands, went to the prow of the ship and, the moment the rocks parted, he let it fly through. Diviner Phineus had told them that if the dove made it alive, they would manage to cross safely.

The dove flew swiftly through the rocks, which clashed swiftly, losing only a few tail feathers but, otherwise, safe. Rejoyced the Argonauts, once the rocks parted again, sailed on to cross the passage but the huge waves did not let the ship. She did not move and the Symplegades were about to clash again. Then, goddess Athena stopped one rock with one hand and pushed the ship ahead with the other so as to sail through. Immediately afterwards, the rocks clashed violently, hitting the extreme stern of the ship. From that time on, according to the gods' decision, the

Symplegades were joined forever, since someone had managed to cross them on his ship.

On their way to **Euxinus Pontos** (the Black Sea), the Argonauts came across an island of **Apollo**. In order to thank him, they built an altar in his honour and sacrificed to him. After that, they reached the land of the **Mariandynes**, where their king **Lycus** offered them hospitality and gave them his son **Dascylus** to join the crew. Afterwards, though, Argo's captain, **Tiphys**, died all of a sudden, whereas seer **Idmon** was killed by a wild boar. In despair, the Argonauts buried their companions with honours, while Hera supplied them with strength again to continue their journey with a new captain, **Angaeus**.

The next stop of the Argonauts was in the land of Assyria, where they were joined by three more companions. Then, they passed the land of the Amazons and reached the **island** of **Ares**. There, they were attacked by the birds but, once again, they managed to land. They met the four sons of Phrixus, who, after their father's death, had left Colchis and were on their way to **Orchomenus** to claim Athamas' property. The sons of Phrixus accompanied the Argonauts, who were approaching the wealthy land of **Aeetes**.

It was night when Jason and his companions arrived in Colchis and they hid their ship in the river **Phases**. Athena and Hera were awake, thinking of a way for Jason to get hold of the Golden Fleece. Eventually, they decided that **Aphrodite** and **Eros** would come up with a solution, once again.

JASON IN COLCHIS

As soon as Jason arrived at the port of **Colchis** (or **Aea**), he presented himself at the palace of king **Aeetes** with two Argonauts and the sons of Phrixus. Jason told the king about his origin and the purpose of his journey.

Aeetes remembered an old oracle his father **Helios** had given him, according to which he would die by the hand of an **Aeolid**. In parallel, he had had a dream in which dead **Phrixus** warned him that he would remain in power as long as the **Golden Fleece**, hung in the grove of Ares, was in his possession. For the above reasons, he decided to slay him. He told him he would give him the fleece on condition that he performed a task, holding the belief that he would get killed. He asked him to find a way to yoke two fire breathing **bulls**, which had bronze hooves, and, then, plough a fifty-plethron field (1 plethron=8,740m^2) opening up ditches one fathom (6ft) wide. Next he had to sow a **serpent's fungs** and kill the **armed giants** that would sprout from the earth. Jason accepted Aeetes' conditions.

Both goddesses, Hera and Athena, decided to aid him. They sent Jason's figure exquisitely beautified in the dreams of **Medea**, Aeetes' daughter. Then, they convinced Aphrodite to send Eros and make the princess fall in love with him. Seeing her sister in love, Chalciope, aided by her son **Argus**, managed to arrange that they meet secretly, behind Aeetes' back. As a real sorceress, Medea gave Jason an ointment whose effect lasted one day. Before applying it all over his body, he had to invoke **goddess Hecate**. The ointment was made of an herb grown from the blood of Prometheus and would protect him from the burning breaths and the bronze hooves of the bulls.

The bulls were in the grove of Ares but as they were veiled by a cloud, Jason had difficulty spotting them. When he went closer, though, they charged at him but he confronted them with his shield, grabbed them from their horns and harnessed them under an iron yoke, which was a gift to Aeetes by Hephaestus.

Afterwards, he ploughed the field and sowed the serpent's fungs Aeetes had given him. At once, the armed giants sprouted and surrounded him. Then, Jason threw a stone among them, following Medea's advice, and the giants started fighting each other until they were all slain. Realising how brave as well as dangerous for him Jason was, Aeetes summoned his consultants, and decided to assign him a new trial.

Guided by Hera, Medea understood that her father had new ordeals for Jason in mind and went to Argo to warn the Argonauts. She led them to the grove of Ares where the Golden Fleece hanged and, using a magic potion, made the huge serpent fall asleep. Then, they grabbed the Golden Fleece and, along with Medea, returned to the ship and left the land of Aeetes in the darkness of the night.

Argo and her crew, Jason and Medea, left her land as fast as they could. They sailed towards the northwest of Euxinus Pontus, reached **Paphlagonia** and the banks of the river **Haly** where Medea offered a sacrifice to goddess Hecate. Just then, they remembered that Phineus had advised them not to follow the same route back to Greece.

Argus, the son of Phrixus, suggested they sailed along the river Istrus (modern Danube) and Jason agreed. They bid farewell to Dascylus, the king of the Paphlagons, and started their journey along the river, which would lead them to the Adriatic Sea.

Meanwhile, **Apsyrtus**, Medea's elder halfbrother - they shared the same father - was ordered by Aeetes to chase them and bring back both Medea and the Golden Fleece. Apsyrtus recruited a team he sent to block Bosporus Strait and another one followed the flow of Istrus. It is said that Apsyrtus overtook Argo and blocked her way.

The Argonauts started to negotiate but Medea managed to carry her brother away to an island at the mouth of Istrus, which was dedicated to Artemis. There, Apsyrtus was entrapped by Jason and got killed. The Colchs, though, went on pursuing Argo. Goddess Hera sent them lightning and thunder to warn them and stop the pursuit. They were convinced to stop but did not return to Colchis. They stayed in the area and settled down either on the Illyrian coast or the islands **Apsyrides**.

THE RETURN OF ARGO HOME

After they managed to escape the Colchs sailing along the river Istrus (modern Danube), the Argonauts reached the **Hylles**, who inhabited the coast of Illyria.

Their King **Hyllus**, a son of **Heracles** and Nymph **Melite**, guided them through the libyrnic islands and supplied them with food and gifts so that Jason, delighted with him, gave him one of the two golden tripods he had taken with him, as he was consulted by the Oracle of Delphi.

They had nearly reached the island of **Kerkyra** (Corfu), when a strong wind, sent by goddess Hera, forced them to turn towards the north again.

Then Argo spoke and advised the Argonauts to seek purification for the murder of Apsyrtus, because Zeus was angry with them. She told them to go to the island of **Circe, Aeaee**, to expiate them. The Argonauts obeyed and arrived at the river **Heridanus** (modern Po). Then, they sailed along the river Rhodanus (modern Rhone) and reached the southern coast of France and the Tyrrhenian Sea.

According to another version of the myth, the Argonauts reached the western coast of Italy coming from Oceanus, which they had crossed, since from Colchis they sailed to Cimmerius Bosporus, Lake Maeotis and the rivers of the North.

While in Oceanus, they visited the **island** of **Circe**, who expiated them for the murder of Apsyrtus. The ancienmost myth has it that they reached the island of Circe when they came to the Tyrrhenian Sea.

After this visit, the heroes continued their journey southwards and reached the Sirens. The **Sirens** inhabited **Anthemoessa**, an island full of flowers in Tyrrhenia, close to modern Napoli. When the Sirens saw the ship approaching, they started to sing and the heroes were enticed.

Fortunately, however, **Orpheus**' lyre and songs drowned out the Sirens' bewitching voices and saved the Argonauts. Only **Butes** did fall into the sea, but goddess Aphrodite rescued him and took him to Lilybaeus in Sicily.

A little later, they encountered more dangers. In order to reach the Greek seas, they had to pass by the **Plangtae Rocks**. These were some floating rocks covered with fire and smoke, which drifted in the sea and caused shipwrecks.

Once again, with the help of Hera, who called Thetis and the Nereids to take care of Argo, as well as Aeolus to stop the winds, the Argonauts managed to overcome the danger and reach the island of the Phaeacians (Corfu).

First, though, they passed from **Thrinacia**, where the Cattle of Helios grazed, and then, free from misfortunes, landed the island of the **Phaeacians**. Aeetes had already sent some men to the island claiming Medea back from **Alcinous**. The king of the Phaeacians replied that he would send the young girl back to her father provided she were a virgin. Medea begged queen **Arete** and the Argonauts not to send her back and the queen, in sympathy, decided to organise her wedding immediately, after she had informed Jason on her husband's decision.

In a sacred cave, they made the bridal bed with the Golden Fleece, and the Nymphs, sent by Hera, decorated the cave with flowers. Jason and Medea united under the sacred vows of the wedding ceremony, while Orpheus played his lyre and the Argonauts chanted the wedding hymn. When the ceremony was over, Alcinous announced the Colchs his decision. They, then, asked permission to stay on his island, since they knew that Aeetes would punish them if they returned without Medea.

Seven days after the wedding, Argo sailed off the island of the Phaeacians carrying onboard plenty of gifts from the royal couple, as well as twelve young girls, who became Medea's attendants.

The weather was mild until, suddenly, a storm broke out and directed them towards the Libyan Sea. For nine days the heroes struggled in the storm and, eventually, the winds brought them to the coast of Libya, where their ship grounded. Surrounded by desert, there was no drop of water in sight. Convinced their end was close, there appeared three goddesses and told them what to do to escape.

They lifted Argo in their hands and walked twelve days and twelve nights until they reached Lake **Trichonis**. They sailed round the lake for days seeking a way out to the open sea. In the end, **Triton** helped them and they gave him a golden Tripod in return. He showed them the way to the sea and gave them a lump of earth that Euphemus took.

Sailing on, the Argonauts reached **Crete**, which they were not able to approach, because bronze Talos, assigned by Zeus to guard Europa, hurled rocks at them from the shore.

Talos belonged to the bronze race of humans and he was the only one left alive. This bronze man walked round the island three times a day and let no foreigner approach. His life depended on one blood vessel that ended in his ankle where it was bound shut by a metal nail. It is said that Medea hypnotised him and talked him into removing the nail so as to become immortal. Talos was convinced, but when he removed the

Child-Eros (of the Roman Empire era).
Athens, the Ancient Agora Museum

nail, he lost all his blood and dropped dead. Then, the Argonauts were able to get supplies for the last part of their journey. They spent the night on Crete and, in the morning, after they had built an altar in honour of Athena, sailed off.

On their way from the Cretan Sea to the Aegean Sea, they were surrounded by sudden darkness and were terrified. Jason begged god **Apollo**, who, holding his bow high, sent light everywhere. They saw, then, a small island nearby and named it **Anaphe** (anaphainomai = appear). They stayed there to rest and, before they left, they built a temple and an altar in honour of the god that had aided them. They set off afterwards and, during the journey, Euphemus told Jason about a dream he had seen at night.

Jason told him to drop the lump of earth Triton had given him into the sea. No sooner had he dropped it than a beautiful island appeared; Euphemus named it **Calliste** (the most beautiful) and stayed forever there.

Their last stop was **Aegina**, where they were supplied with water and participated in contests, and then the Argonauts, passing through Euboea strait, reached the port of Pagassae close to **Iolcus**, without adventures any more.

Jason was about to deliver the **Golden Fleece** but was informed that **Pelias** did not intend to keep his word and let him take the throne. On the contrary, during Jason's absence, Pelias had slain his parents and all his relatives so as not to claim the throne. Pelias' punishment would be decided by Medea, who had brought along many magic potions from her homeland and knew how to use them. Disguised into the figure of an elderly woman with white hair and a wrinkled face, she persuaded Pelias' daughters to help him by killing him and she would bring him back to life young and good-looking. However, first, they had to chop him up and boil his pieces in a cauldron full of magic herbs.

She demonstrated her abilities by doing an experiment with the pieces of a sheep she made the girls see intact with her magic. Pelias' daughters were convinced and stained their hands with their father's blood.

After the death of Pelias, his son **Acastus** succeeded him to the throne of Iolcus. Jason and Medea left this city forever, and went to live in **Corinth**. Before settling down, the hero and his companions boarded Argo, sailed to the Corinth Isthmus and dedicated their ship to **Poseidon**.

JASON AND MEDEA IN CORINTH

Jason and Medea, along with their two children, settled down in Corinth and led a happy life the first ten years of their living together. However, it seems that it was not meant to stay together till their old age.

The king of Corinth, **Creon**, had one daughter, **Glauce**, and suggested that Jason married her. Jason thought that with this marriage he would obtain power and accepted. Infuriated and feeling bitter with Jason for not having respected his love vows as well as the help she had given him, Medea decided to avenge him. However, Creon understood what she was up to and ordered her to leave Corinth with her children. Jason did not take her side and accused her of being selfish and causing trouble.

Then, Medea decided to avenge the hardest possible way. First, she sent Glauce a veil steeped in poison and a golden wreath as wedding presents. When Glauce had put the veil on, she was consumed with fire along with her father who rushed to her help. Medea's worst deed of revenge was her murdering her two children with a sword, knowing that she would hurt Jason. After the murder, Medea left in a chariot sent to her by Helios, and went to Athens where she got married to Aegeus. Because she attempted to murder Theseus, Aegeus sent her away from Athens and Medea returned to her homeland.

Jason was in great despair after the murder of his children and, while he was sleeping under the shade of Argo, he was killed by a beam from the ship that fell on him.

Another version of the myth has it that Medea did not murder her children to avenge Jason, but for fear that they would end up in Creon's hands. According to a yet another version, the children were not nurdered by Medea; the Corinthians killed them while she had entrusted them at the Sactuary of Hera Acraea in Perachora. The latest tradition but, at the same time, the most inaccurate, has it that Medea reconciled with Jason and left together for Colchis.

Once everything had reached an end, Argo, the ship of this renowned expedition, became a constellation in the Sky.

Talos, the bronze giant guarding Crete, was slain by the Argonauts with the help of Medea. The Dioscuri are supporting him here. Red-figured crater (400-390 B.C.).
Ruvo, Museo Jatta

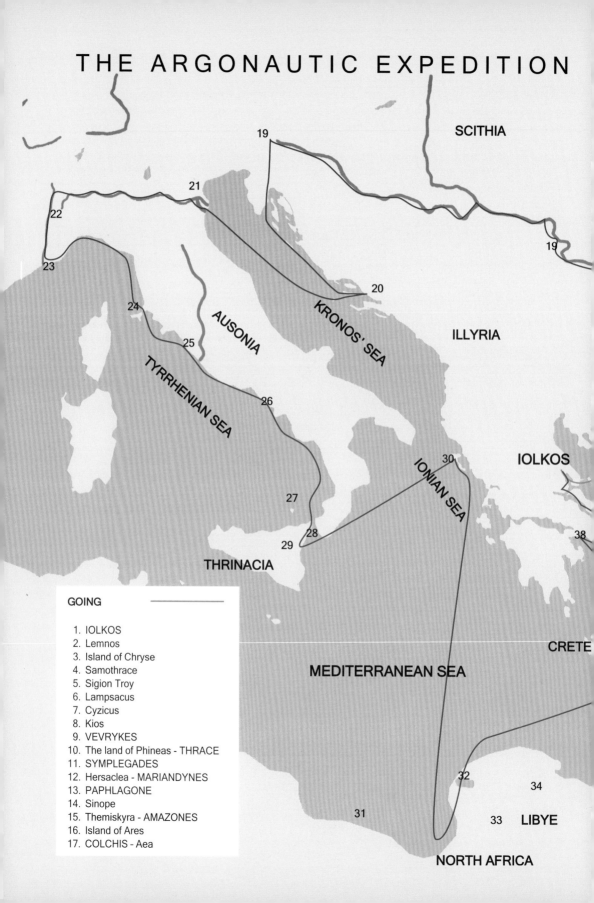

THE ARGONAUTIC EXPEDITION

SCITHIA

19

21

22

23

24

25

AUSONIA

KRONOS' SEA

20

ILLYRIA

TYRRHENIAN SEA

26

27

28

29

THRINACIA

30

IONIAN SEA

IOLKOS

38

CRETE

MEDITERRANEAN SEA

32

34

31

33 LIBYE

NORTH AFRICA

19

GOING ———————

1. IOLKOS
2. Lemnos
3. Island of Chryse
4. Samothrace
5. Sigion Troy
6. Lampsacus
7. Cyzicus
8. Kios
9. VEVRYKES
10. The land of Phineas - THRACE
11. SYMPLEGADES
12. Hersaclea - MARIANDYNES
13. PAPHLAGONE
14. Sinope
15. Themiskyra - AMAZONES
16. Island of Ares
17. COLCHIS - Aea

COLCHIS

18

BLACK SEA

TRACE

14

13

11   12   PAFLAGONES

10

VEVRYKES

9   15   16

7   8

AMAZONES

4

3 5 6

MYSIA

17

ÆGEAN SEA

36

CYPRUS

EGYPT

THE TROJAN WAR

CAUSES AND OCCASIONS

The Trojan War originated from a decision taken by the father of the gods **Zeus**, along with **Themis**, in the most ancient years, when the humans had become too many and burdened the earth, while, at the same time, they did not respect the gods at all. To relieve Gaea (the Earth), Zeus caused the **Theban war**, during which many people were killed.

After some time, the people increased again and Zeus asked the son of Nyx (Night), Momus, what to do and he advised him two things: to have a beautiful daughter and marry Nereid Thetis to a mortal man.

Then, **Zeus** united with **Leda**, the wife of **Tyndareu**s, king of Sparta, and brought **Helen** to life. At the same time, he prepared the wedding of **Thetis** and **Peleus**. These two events became the reason for the **Trojan War** to break out and the death of numerous mortals, so that the Earth was relieved.

THE APPLE OF DISCORD AND THE JUDGEMENT OF PARIS

Following the advice by Seer **Momus**, Zeus looked to the wedding of mortal **Peleus** to **Thetis**. The ceremony was held on Mount Pelion and all gods attended, bringing their presents. Only **Eris** (Discord) was missing because they did not want to invite her. To avenge them, she threw an apple in the middle of the gathering, saying that it was to be given to the most beautiful goddess.

Then, the three goddesses, **Hera**, **Athena** and **Aphrodite**, each one certain that she was the most beautiful, claimed the prize. Zeus sent them along with Hermes to Mount Ida, where **Paris**, the son of the king of Troy

Peleus and Thetis; inside of a red-figured wide cup (460 B.C.).
Athens, National Archaeological Museum

Priam, kept his father's cattle. It fell to his lot to decide which of the three was the most beautiful and deserved to win the prize. The goddesses appeared before startled Paris, each demonstrating her talents. According to their attributes, each one promised to bribe him with gifts. If he preferred Hera, she would offer him power and control of all of Asia and Europe. If he gave the prize to Athena, the goddess would make him a skilful warrior and, finally, if he chose Aphrodite, she would arrange for him to meet the most beautiful woman in the world. Paris awarded the prize to **Aphrodite**, displeasing the two other goddesses who, since then, became his enemies.

THE ABDUCTION OF BEAUTIFUL HELEN (HELEN OF TROY)

Aphrodite kept the promise she had given to Paris, the son of the king of Troy Priam and Hecuba, and told him that the most beautiful woman in the world was **Helen** of **Sparta**. Helen was the daughter of **Zeus** and **Leda**, daughter of Thestius, king of Pleuron, and the wife of **Tyndareus**, the king of Lacedaemon. One day, when Leda was bathing in the water of the river Eurotas, a swan, chased by an eagle, sought shelter in her bosom scared to death. The swan was **Zeus** and the eagle was **Hermes**, who employed this trick so that the father of gods united with her. It is said that the same night Leda also slept with her husband and, in a few months' time, there were born **Helen** and **Clytemnestra**, as well as the two **Dioscouri**. **Helen** and **Polydeuce** were the immortal children of Zeus, while **Clytemnestra** and **Castor** were the mortal children fathered by Tyndareus. When Helen was twelve years old, **Theseus** kidnapped her, being startled by her beauty, and confined her to fortified Aphidna, from

Zeus as a swan is having Leda in his arms (1st-2nd c. A.D.). Herakleion, Archaeological Museum

where she was rescued by the Dioscouri. Since, however, Helen became more and more beautiful as she grew up and her reputation had reached all corners of Greece, her father decided to marry her. There, then, appeared the most renowned leaders in Sparta, who competed for her and fought with each other all the time. For fear that if he chose one of the suitors to become Helen's husband, the rest would become his enemies, Tyndareus had an idea. Before choosing the husband-to-be, he thought of requiring the rest of them to promise that, if anyone ever dared offend or violently remove Helen from her husband, they would all together punish him. The suitors willingly swore the required oath, as each of them believed he would be the one to win Helen, having no idea then, of course, how much this oath would cost them.

After this agreement, Tyndareus decided to offer his daughter in marriage to **Menelaus**, a son of Atreus and a brother of Agamemnon, not only because of his wealth, but also because **Agamemnon**, who had already married his other daughter, Clytemnestra, was a supporter of his. Menelaus and Helen lived happily and had a daughter, **Hermione**. When Tyndareus lost his two sons, Castor and Polydeuce, he called Menelaus from Argos and offered him his kingdom in Sparta. Ten years after the marriage of beautiful Helen to Menelaus, **Paris** arrived in Sparta, driven by Aphrodite, to find the woman he had been promised by the goddess, the most beautiful woman of all. Before leaving Troy, his brother **Elenos** and his sister **Cassandra** had, in vain, prophesised the havoc that was bound to follow this journey of his.

Paris had been offered hospitality at Menelaus' palace for nine days when, on the tenth day, Menelaus had to leave for Crete, to bury the father of his mother, **Catreus**. His absence from the palace facilitated Aphrodite who, keeping her promise, brought Paris and Helen together. Immediately afterwards, the royal prince of Troy boarded his ship with Helen, some of Menelaus' treasure and some of Helen's maids, and left in the darkness of the night, leaving Helen's nine-year-old daughter, Hermione, alone in the palace. Their journey was not an easy one because the gods were alert. Hera sent them a storm which caused them to land in Sidon. They stayed in Phoenice and in Cyprus for a long time because Paris was afraid that they might be pursued. Then, they set out for **Troy** and, upon arriving, they celebrated their wedding.

Laconic marble pyramidal column with the figures of Menelaus and Helen in a private moment (appr. 580 B.C.).
Sparta, Archaeological Museum

Hector and Paris are bidding farewell to their wives before departing for the battle; from a bronze crater (530-520 B.C.). Würzburg, Martin von Wagner Museum

THE PREPARATIONS FOR THE WAR

After Helen's abduction by Paris and their elopement, Iris informed **Menelaus** on what had happened in his home. When he returned and found it empty, he left for Mycenae to meet his brother **Agamemnon** and require that he gathered up the leaders of Greece in order to march out with their army and their fleet and retrieve Helen. He sent emissaries all over Greece to tell about the misfortune, and the leaders accepted the call since they were bound by the oath they had given to Tyndareus, Helen's father, that they would avenge in such a case. And while the leaders were preparing, Menelaus went to Pylos to find **Nestor**, the eldest and wisest of all the leaders, to ask him to travel together and recruit **Odysseus** and **Achilles**, two of the heroes of the Trojan War. They were not bound by the oath, because the first had not asked for Helen's hand and the second was still a child at the time.

Along with Menelaus and Nestor, there travelled to Ithaca **Palamedes**, a son of **Nauplius**, another one of the wisest and most inventive heroes in the Greek mythology. However, Odysseus, having received an oracle telling him that if he took part in the war, it would take him twenty years to return home, had decided to pretend to be insane. When the three companions arrived in the island, they found Odysseus having yoked a horse and an ox and, wearing a hood on his head like Hephaestus, he was sowing salt in a field. Palamedes, who understood his trick, grabbed baby **Telemachus** from **Penelope's** arms and put him in front of the plough's path. Odysseus halted the animals at once and, having been unveiled, he had to promise to participate in the war.

Achilles was the only son of **Peleus** and **Thetis**, who, as a goddess, knew that if her son went to the war he wouldn't come back. When her son was nine years old, she sent him to Skyros, to king **Lycomedes**, so as to be raised with his daughters, wearing women's clothes.

There, he was given the name **Pyrrha** because he was fair-haired. As he grew up in the women's quarters, Achilles fell in love with one of the daughters of Lycomedes, **Deidamia**, and had a son, **Neoptolemus**. Seer **Calchas**, though, had prophesised that without Achilles the Achaeans would never conquer Troy. They searched for him everywhere, but when they asked Lycomedes for him, he denied that Achilles was in his palace. Wily Odysseus, disguised as a merchant, went to the women's quarters pretending to sell textiles to the daughters of the

Achilles; detail from the figure depicted on a red-figured urn (450 B.C.).
Rome, Musei Vaticani

Attic red-figured "epinetro" (weaver's ceramic knee protective) with scenes taking place in the palace of Admetus and Alcestes; piece of art by the painter of Eretria (appr. 425 B.C.). Athens, National Archaeological Museum

king. Among them he had hidden certain weapons which Achilles, upon seeing them, grabbed and, thus, he revealed his identity. After this, he also had to promise that he would lead the Myrmidons of Fthia to Troy.

The gathering site for all the leaders was Aulis in Boeotia, where their troops and fleet started to gather.

THE BEGINNING OF THE TROJAN WAR

Two years after Beautiful Helen's abduction, the Achaean army gathered in Aulis, in Boeotia, at the strait of Euripus. While they were sacrificing to the gods for the positive outcome of the expedition, there appeared a huge serpent, which sprang up from the altar and crawled up the branch of a plane tree. There was a nest with eight little sparrows, which it ate one after the other, while, in the end, it swallowed their mother. Immediately after, the serpent turned into a stone.

Then, the wise seer **Calchas** explained that the omen was sent by Zeus and stated the length of the Trojan War; in other words, the Achaeans would have to fight for nine years and in the tenth year of the war Troy would fall.

After they had offered sacrifices to the gods, the Achaeans sailed off, but reached **Mysia** by mistake and started a war, being unaware of the fact that they were in another land. In Mysia there ruled a son of Heracles, **Telephus**, who confronted the invaders immediately and killed quite many, such as Thersander, son of Polyneices.

Achilles along with Patroclus fought bravely and the first wounded Telephus in the thigh with his spear, which Centaur Chiron had given as a present. Despite his wound, Telephus went on chasing the Achaeans and made them leave. A strong storm scattered the ships and they returned to their homeland harassed.

Since the wound Achilles with his spear had caused to Telephus had festered, he asked the Oracle of Apollo, in Lycia, to find out how he could be cured. The answer was that he would be cured by the one who had wounded him, "he that wounded shall heal". Thus, he disguised as a beggar, because he was afraid of the Hellenes' enmity, and arrived in Argos to learn about the Achaeans' future plans.

At the time, the Greek leaders had assembled in Argos to decide whether they would repeat the expedition to Troy. Agamemnon was against a second attempt whereas Menelaus insisted on retrieving Helen, claiming that they could not allow the barbarians treat the Greeks as if they were slaves. The other commanders sided with either Agamemnon or Menelaus.

They all, though, hated Telephus for what he had caused to them in Mysia. Telephus approached them in Argos and only Odysseus did recognise him. Eventually, the Achaeans agreed to help him, after he had taken little Orestes, the son of Agamemnon, and sat on the altar of Zeus as a suppliant, in order to achieve his aim. However, Achilles, having arrived in Argos, refused to heal Telephus on the grounds that he was not a doctor. Then, Odysseus, who had understood the meaning of the oracle, scraped off a little rust from the tip of the hero's spear onto the wound in the thigh and it healed. To thank the Achaeans for their help, Telephus showed them the way to Troy, although he refused to fight on their side against the Trojans because he was a relative of theirs.

As they, now, knew the route to Troy, the Achaeans decided to set off to conquer it. Nevertheless, it took them eight years to prepare and gather in Aulis. At the time, because Agamemnon had entered a grove dedicated to Artemis and killed one of her sacred deer, the goddess had sent stillness so that the Achaean ships could not sail off. Then, seer Calchas revealed what the matter was and stated that, in order to appease the goddess, they had to sacrifice the daughter of Agamemnon, Iphigenia, on her altar. The commander of the expedition tried to avoid such a pain but, eventually, under tremendous pressure on the part of the other leaders, he sent a message to his wife Clytemnestra asking her to bring their daughter to Aulis on the grounds that Achilles wished to marry her. When the two women arrived at the encampment and found out that Achilles had no idea about the marriage, they made Agamemnon confess the real reason for their trip. In spite of his indignation because he had been used as bait, Achilles promised to stave off the sacrifice but the army disagreed. The decision concerning her sacrifice will be taken by Iphigenia, who will offer herself for the good of her country. At the very moment, however, seer Calchas had raised the knife Artemis took the girl and left a hind in her place for the sacrifice. She carried her off to the land of the Tauris (Bulls) and made her a maiden in her temple.

When fair wind blew, the Achaeans sailed off on board their ships heading for Troad. A popular myth among them had it that the first one to step on that land was to be killed. Therefore, no one made a move to disembark. Odysseus, then, dropped his shield on the ground and jumped off stepping on it and not on the land. He was followed by Protesilaus, a son of Iphicles and the king of Phylace, and he was the one to pay the cost of stepping first on the land.

The proud figure of Achilles; red-figured urn (450 B.C.).
Rome, Musei Vaticani

The Thessalian hero headed for Troy the day after he wedded **Laodamea**, a daughter of Acastus. However, he was destined to get killed upon stepping the land of Troy.

Protesilaus slew numerous Trojans when he jumped onto the land but, immediately afterwards, **Hector** killed him with his spear. His wife refused to believe what had happened, while Protesilaus was also tormented in the Under World. Thus, he asked **Pluto** to allow him to spend three hours with his wife. Pluto gave him permission but, when time came for him to return to Hades, he asked Laodamea to follow him and she grabbed his sword and killed herself.

Upon arriving in Troy, the commanders of the Achaean troops required a peaceful solution to their issue, i.e. retrieve Helen and the treasure Paris had stolen from the palace, and return home, but the Trojans refused.

Therefore, the war between the Hellenes and the Trojans started; a war that lasted ten years during which both sides suffered a lot of casualties.

THE COMMANDERS OF THE HELLENES

The massive army of the Greeks who set off to conquer Troy included warriors from all over Greece, as it is described by Homer, who calls the lot of the Hellenes the 'Achaeans', and sometimes the Argives and the Danaes.

Commander of the army was appointed **Agamemnon**, the son of Atreus and a descendant of Pelops. His wife was **Clytemnestra**, the eldest daughter of Tyndareus and Leda, the mother of **Orestes** and of four daughters, **Chrysothemis**, **Laodice**, **Iphianassa** and **Iphigenia**. In the tragedy, the name of Laodice is replaced by that of **Electra**.

Agamemnon was the king of Mycenae, the wealthiest and most renowned state in the Mycenaean World, which extended to numerous islands and the entire Argolis or, according to some historians, the entire Peloponnese.

Since he was ambitious, he agreed to become the Commander-in-Chief the others had requested on the grounds of not only the fact that he was the brother of offended by the Trojans **Menelaus**, but also because he had the biggest military force among the Hellenes and had prepared 100 ship fully manned for the expedition; moreover, he had given 60 more to the Arcadians as they had no fleet of their own. The Achaeans' Commander in the Iliad is depicted to surpass the rest as far as beauty and nobleness are concerned; and, whereas he does not stand out for bravery during the siege of Troy, his image is quite often described by the poet resembling Zeus in the head, Ares in the waist and Poseidon in the chest. Describing him Helen calls him a kind king and a brave warrior. His haughtiness makes him sometimes quarrel with the most glorious warrior of the Greeks, **Achilles**, which causes countless Achaeans to get killed and many of their ships to be lost. However, the poet depicts Agamemnon having not only a dark side, but a bright one as well.

Menelaus, a son of Atreus too, younger than his brother Agamemnon, was the king of Sparta and was renowned for his wealth. By beautiful **Helen**, he had a daughter, **Hermione**, who was 9 years old when her mother fled with Paris to Troy. Menelaus had a son with a slave, who he named **Megapenthes** (Great Mourning) so that he reminded him of his grief over the abduction of his wife.

When he and his brother Agamemnon agreed to undertake the expedition against Troy, he participated in the Greek army with 60 fully manned ships. In the Iliad, he is depicted as fair-haired, sturdily-built, reticent, prudent and kind-hearted. His kindness goes beyond normal, either when he pities his rivals, the Trojans, and spares their life like Trojan Adrastus, or even when he forgives those who scheme against him.

Before the start of the war, he asks the Trojans to give him Helen back, so as not to waste the lives of so many young men and avoid a bloody war. The hero is protected by **Hera** and **Athena**, who avert evil when he fights. He duels with **Paris** and defeats him, but when he wanted to duel with **Hector**, since no one else dared, Agamemnon stops him, telling him that his opponent was a lot stronger and that it would be plain insanity to fight with him.

During the war, the hero slays several Trojans: **Scamander**, the son of Strophius, **Pylamenes**, the king of the Paphlagons, **Peisander**, **Dolops**, **Thoos**, **Euphorbus** and **Podes**, who was the son of Hetion and Hector's favourite.

Nestor, a son of **Neleus** and king of Pylos, is considered to have been seventy-five years old, since he had lived through three generations of heroes, when he took part in the expedition of the Achaeans. While he was the oldest in the Greek army, he was the wisest of all, as much so as there was no Achaean who did not honour and respect him.

Achilles and Aeas, fully armoured, are playing with dice, a game with pieces (staves); black-figured urn (appr. 530 B.C.). Rome, Musei Vaticani

THE FORCES OF THE ACHAEANS	CITIES	COMMANDERS	SHIPS
BOEOTIANS	HYRIA, AULIS, SCHINOS, SCOLOS, ETEONOS, THESPIA, GRAIA, MIDEIA, MYCALESSOS, HARMA, EILESION, ERYTHRAE, ELEON, HYLE, PETEON, OCALEA, MEDEON, KOPAE, EUTRESIS, CORONEA, HALIARTOS, PLATAEA, GLISSAS, HYPOTHEBES, ONCHESTOS, HARNE, NISA, THISBE, ANTHEDON	PENELEUS, LEITUS, ARCESILAUS, PROTHOENOR, CLONIUS	50
MINYAE	MINYEOS, ORCHOMENUS, ASPLEDON	ASCALAPHUS, IALMENUS	30
PHOCAEANS	CYPARISSUS, PYTHON, CRISA, DAULIS, PANOPEUS, ANEMOREA, HYAMBOLIS, LILAEA	SCHEDIUS, EPISTROPHUS	40
LOCREANS	CYNOS, OPOES, CALLIAROS, BESSA, SCARPHE, AUGEAE, TARPHE, THRONION	AEAS (OELEUS)	40
ABANTES (EUBOEA)	CHALCIS, ERETRIA, HISTIAEA, DION, CERINTHUS, CARYSTOS, STYRA	ELEPHENOR	40
ATHENIANS	ATHENS	MENESTHEUS	50
SALAMINIANS	SALAMIS	AEAS (TELAMONIAN)	12
ARGIVES	ARGOS, TIRYNS, HERMIONE, ASINE, TROEZEN, EIONAE, EPIDAURUS, AEGINA, MASES	DIOMEDES, STHENELUS, EURYALUS	80
MYCENAEANS	MYCENAE, CORINTH, CLEONAE, ARAETHYREA, SICYON, HYPERESIA, GONOESSA, PELLENE, AEGION, AEGIALOS, HELICE, ORNEIAE	AGAMEMNON	100
LACEDAEMONIANS	PHARES, SPARTA, MESSE, BRYSIAE, AUGEIAE, AMYCLAE, HELOS, LAAS, OETYLOS	MENELAUS	60
PYLIANS	PYLOS, ARENE, THRYON, AEPY, CYPARISSEIS, AMPHIGENIA, PTELEON, HELOS, DORION	NESTOR	90
ARCADIANS	PHENEOS, ORCHOMENUS, RHIPE, STRATIA, ENISPE, TEGEA, MANTINEA, STYMPHELOS, PARRHASIA	AGAPENOR	60

ACHAEANS IN THE TROJAN WAR

THE FORCES OF THE ACHAEANS	CITIES	COMMANDERS	SHIPS
EPEIANS (ELIS)	BUPRASION, ELIS, HYRMINE, MYRSINOS, OLENIA ROCK, ALESION	AMPHIMACHUS, THALPIUS, DIORIUS, POLYXINUS	40
DULICHIANS	DULICHION, ECHINAE ISLANDS	MEGES	40
CEPHALLENES	ITHACA, NERITON, CROCYLIA, AEGILPS, ZACYNTHOS, SAMOS	ODYSSEUS	12
AETOLIANS	PLEURON, OLENOS, PYLENE, CHALCIS, CALYDON	THOAS	40
CRETANS	CNOSSOS, GORTYS, LYCTOS, MILETOS, LYCASTOS, PHAESTOS, RHYTION	IDOMENEUS, MERIONES	80
RHODIANS	RHODES, LINDOS, IALYSOS, CAMIROS	TLEPOLEMUS	9
THE KINGDOM OF NEREUS	SYME	NIREUS	3
DODECANESIANS	NISYROS, CARPATHOS, CASOS, COS, CALYDNAE ISLANDS	PHIDIPPUS, ANTIPHUS	30
MYRMIDONS-HELLENES-ACHAEANS	PELASGONIAN ARGOS, HALOS, HALOPE, TRECHIS, FTHIA, HELLAS	ACHILLES	50
THE KINGDOM OF PROTESILAUS	PHYLACE, PYRHASOS, ITON, ANDRON, PTELEOS	PROTESILAUS (PODARCES)	40
THE KINGDOM OF EUMELUS	PHERAE, BOEBE, GLAPHYRAE, IAOLCUS	EUMELUS	11
THE KINGDOM OF PHILOCTETES	METHONE, THAUMACIA, MELIBOEA, OLIZON	PHILOCTETES (MEDON)	7
ASCLEPIADAE	TRICCA, ITHOME, OECHALIA	MACHAON, PODALEIRIUS	30
THE KINGDOM OF EURYPYLOS	ORMENION, HYPERIA CRENE, ASTERION, TITANOS	EURYPYLOS	40
THE KINGDOM OF POLYPOETES	ARGISSA, GYRTONE, ORTHE, ELONE, OLOOSSON	POLYPOETES, LEONTEUS	40
ENIENAE-PERAEBI	CYPHOS, DODONA, AREA OF TITARHESUS	GOUNEUS	22
MAGNETES	PELION, AREA OF PINEIOS	PROTHOUS	40

He frequently referred to his accomplishments when he was young to boost the morale of the young men, who always consulted him.

His experience, his persuasive speaking abilities and guidance to the Achaeans are his main contributions during the Trojan War. He does not engage in combat himself, apart from once, when he risks to get killed by Hector and is rescued by Diomedes. Nestor's bravery is inherited to his two sons, **Antilochus** and **Thrasymedes**. It fell to his lot to inform **Achilles** on the death of **Patroclus**, and he will advise his son, who participates in the epitaph games Achilles organises in honour of the deceased Patroclus, on how to win.

Odysseus had been the king of Ithaca long before the war between the Greeks and the Trojans broke out. When the Trojan expedition started, Odysseus was aware of the oracle which stated that it would take him twenty years to return to his island all alone, without army and spoils. This is why he tried to avoid his involvement by pretending insanity, but once his plan failed, he committed to the war with all his abilities and contributed to every successful strategic plan of the Achaeans. Except for his bravery, he is particularly distinguished for his intelligence since he was a first-rate warrior and a convincing speaker. One could say that Odysseus was the ideal hero of the era, that is, a hero of both word and deeds. There are numerous epithets the poet attributes to the hero, who has been the model of the **Greek Warrior** since antiquity. In the Iliad, he is called **resourceful**, of cunning intelligence, enduring, of a persevering mind, characteristic traits that adorn no other hero, since no one demonstrated his versatility and endurance the way he did, during his return journey to Ithaca. He is the only one called "**ptoleporthos**" (he who seizes forts), because he will play a decisive role in the fall of Troy.

Aeas (Ajax) the **Telamonian**, a son of **Telamon** and **Eriboea** or Periboea, and the grandson of colonist of Salamis, **Aeacus**, was the king of Salamis and one of the major heroes of the Trojan War. He participated in the Trojan expedition with twelve ships from his island and, along with Achilles and Phoenix, commanded the Greek fleet. In the Iliad he is depicted as the bravest hero next to Achilles, equal to Hector, the first warrior of the Trojans. The epithets attributed to him in the epic are **great**, **colossal** and "**Achaeans' erkos**" (bulwark) referring to his stature and stamina. His shield, huge like a tower, could not be lifted by anyone else. It was fashioned for him of seven bull hides and a bronze outer coating by **Tychios** from Hyle, a renowned craftsman.

Despite his colossal frame, Aeas was good looking, mellow and kind-hearted, always the animating spirit of his co-warriors and willing to cooperate to settle disagreements between the commanders of the Hellenes. In the battlefield, Aeas is always found in the firing-line and, during Achilles' absence from the war, he was the only one who dared face Hector and not be defeated. Hector's admiration for him is expressed by giving him his sword as a present while Aeas offers him his girdle.

As the Trojans advance to break the wall of the Achaeans and burn their ships, Aeas organises the defence line and struggles all alone by the ships, slaying twelve Trojans; he had to yield only when Zeus intervenes for the Trojan advance. Moreover, he will, finally, win the body of dead Patroclus in the fight conducted over it and will confront Hector on his own.

One of the best fighters of the Achaeans was **Teuctrus**, also a **Telamon**, being the half brother of Aeas. He almost always fought with his bow and arrow from a distance but also knew how to fight with the spear neck to neck. However, he overpowered all the Achaeans with his talent in using the bow. Covered behind his brother's huge shield, he was able to kill countless Trojans with his arrows in a short time.

During the epitaph games held in honour of **Patroclus**, he is defeated in shooting by **Merione**, because Apollo did not allow him to win as he had not offered a sacrifice to him.

Aeas the **Locrus**, the son of Oileus and a Nymph, Eriopes, according to Homer, had taken

The encounter of
Achilles with
Penthesilea; inside
of a red-figured wide cup
(469 B.C.). Munchen, Staatliche
Antikensammlungen

part in the Trojan expedition with forty ships. Although he was of a considerably minor stature than his homonymous Salaminian Aeas and not being a relative of his, he always fights by his side. Together they array their troops next to each other and fight encouraging them, for instance, on the first and second days of the siege of Troy or during the defence of the **wall** and the **ships** of the Achaeans and the fight over the dead body of **Sarpedon** or **Patroclus**. In the Iliad, he is described as **tachys**, that is, swift, and a good spear fighter. His army consisted of soldiers armed with bows and catapults and this is why they did not follow him when he fought in the firing-line. In the epitaph games, being the fastest, he outwins everyone in the race contest, but goddess Athena promotes Odysseus to win and, at the last moment, she causes Aeas to slip and fall so that he finishes second.

Achilles, the son of Peleus and Nereid Thetis, is the most significant figure among the commanders of the expedition in Troy. He is the bravest of all, the most handsome and, in addition, the only son of a goddess among the commanders of the Achaeans.

He is the hero whose **Moira** (Fate) was written on the day he was born, that is, he was to die young below the walls of Troy. His goddess mother knew this, of course, but also Achilles himself was aware of it. Despite Thetis' attempts to keep him away from the war, which proved to be ineffective, Achilles took the decision to follow the rest of the Greeks on the

The birth of goddess Athena; detail from the representation on the pediment of the Parthenon. Athens, the Acropolis Museum

expedition by himself, when he found out that the fall of Troy would be impossible without him. This action of his -although he knew that he was not to return from the expedition alive- constitutes a heroic deed, which adorns and enhances the charismatic figure of this hero. Leaving for the war, he will take with him his father's weapons, given to him by the gods on his wedding day with Thetis, as well as a spear, a present from Centaur Chiron, which only Achilles could lift.

Also, he took with him his father's immortal horses, **Xanthus** and **Balius**, sons of Harpia Podarge and Zephyrus, which explains why they ran so fast. In Troy, he was accompanied by his inseparable friend **Patroclus**, a son of Menoetius and Sthenele. When Patroclus was a child, he accidentally killed his friend **Cleisonymus** as they were playing knuckle-bones, therefore, his father had sent him to Fthia where he grew up with Achilles.

On the day they both set out for the war in Troy with the Myrmidons and 50 ships, they promised their fathers to return safe and sound and with a lot of spoils after its fall. In the Homeric epic, Patroclus, being older than Achilles, had a milder personality, was smooth-tongued and compliant but was not deprived of bravery. Achilles was also accompanied on the expedition by his beloved tutor, **Phoenix**, who was always ready to consult and support him.

Diomedes, the son of Tydeus, belonged to the family of the Epigons who, after they sieged Thebes, also went to Troy. Along with **Sthenelus** and **Euryalos**, he arrives in Troy with 80 ships, leading his army from the state of **Argos**. Diomede's figure dominates the Achaean encampment from the first day. With the help of goddess Athena, who always stands by his side, manages to overshadow the rest of the Greeks who fought with him. The hero is renowned not only for his bravery but also for his excellent ethos, as becomes obvious from his various heroic deeds during the war as well as from the views he holds according to what happens during the war.

There were numerous brave men from all over Greece who reinforced the army of the Achaeans with their presence.

From Crete arrived **Idomeneus**, the son of Deucalion and a nephew of Minos, whereas the sons of Asclepius, **Machaon** and **Podaleirius** followed the expedition in order to offer their medical craft to the wounded heroes.

There also participated **Eumelos**, the son of Admetus, **Polypoetes**, the son of Peirethus, **Tleptolemus**, the son of Heracles, **Acamas** and **Demophon**, the sons of Theseus and Phaedra.

THE HEROES OF THE TROJANS

In the Iliad, the opponents of the Achaeans in the Trojan War are called the **Trojans** or the **Dardani**. The first had taken their name from **Troas**, the son of Erichthonius and the second from his grandfather, **Dardanus**. At the time of the Trojan War, their king was **Priam**, a son of Laomedon, who iniatially was named Podarces.

When **Heracles**, due to Laomedon's infidelity, besieged Troy and killed him, he gave the king's daughter Hesione to his companion **Telamon** with the right to buy out one of her brothers. And she offered her handkerchief and took the younger one **Podarces**, who was named Priam. **Priam** succeeded Laomedon to the throne, rebuilt the destroyed city of Ilion and married **Hecuba**, a daughter of Dymon, the king of Phrygia. By Hecuba he had 19 sons, while he also had thirty-one sons by various other women. In addition, he had twelve daughters. Priam and Hecuba with all their children and their grandchildren lived in the palace, in separate chambers each.

At the beginning of the tenth year of the Trojan War narrated in the Iliad, Priam is of a very elderly age and neither takes part in the battles nor consults with his experience. His son, **Hector**, is the commander of the Trojan army, while his cousin **Aeneias** commands the army of the Dardani with his sons **Antenor**, **Acamas** and **Archelochus**.

Hector, the eldest son of Priam and Hecuba, is the bravest warrior of the Trojans and the one who is in charge of the defence of the besieged; the corresponding heroic figure of the Trojans to the Greek heroic figure of Achilles. His wife is **Andromache**, the daughter of Hetyon, king of the Cilics, and their son is **Scamandrios**, whom the Trojans called **Astyanax** to honour his father because he protected their city bravely.

In the Iliad, Hector is the commander of the Trojan army and their bravest warrior. He plays the leading role while Achilles stays inactive because of his rage, and slays countless Achaeans in all the victorious battles of the Trojans. He rallies and leads his soldiers to the battle and struggles like the god of war Ares slaying countless anonymous and eponymous Achaeans. The Olympian gods aid him and mainly Zeus who admires him greatly and facilitates him in times of difficulty.

Even when he duels with **Aeas** and neither is able to obtain victory, he is supported by the gods, mainly Apollo, who guides him, protects him from dangers or saves him from certain death.

Homer in the Iliad depicts Hector not only as a fearsome warrior but he also complements his image with his presence in his family. He, consecutively, meets his mother, his siblings, Paris and Helen, and finally his wife Andromache and his child. When in a few days Achilles drops him dead and drags his naked corpse attached to his chariot around the walls of Troy, it is these women who mourn him on the walls and recollect with Helen the nobleness of his heart and the right way he treated each of them in. Only his younger brother does he treat cruelly and accuses him of the fact that he might be able to seduce women with his beauty however he is cowardly and shameless.

Paris (Alexander), who was already aware of the disaster Helen's abduction was to cause to his homeland, is the second son of Priam and Hecuba. A myth has it that when Hecuba was pregnant, she dreamt that she had given birth to a flaming torch dripping blood and setting Troy on fire.

Aeacus, an illegitimate son of Priam who could interpret dreams, advised his father to slay the infant upon his birth, otherwise Troy's days were numbered. Priam gave the infant to a slave with the order to take him to Mount Ida and kill him there. The slave, however, took pity on him and left the infant exposed in the mountain, where he was suckled by a bear.

Then, he was found by a herdsman, Archelaus, who raised him. His real parents,

Hector is preparing for the battle. On the right is Hecuba and on the left is Priam; detail from a red-figured urn (510-500 B.C.). Munchen, Staatliche Antikensammlungen

Hermes supervises the removal of dead Sarpedon. Detail from a red-figured crater by the painter of Euphronius (appr. 510 B.C.). New York, the Metropolitan Museum

believing that their little child was dead, every year held **games** to commemorate him and the victor was awarded a **bull**. Once, during the annual games, Priam's herdsmen chose from Archelaus' herd the best bull, Paris' favourite. He, therefore, decided to participate in the games and win the bull. So it happened.

Paris took part in the contest and was awarded the prize, but the princes, unaware of the fact that he was their brother, decided to entrap and kill him, feeling offended to have been outwon by a herdsman. Paris sought shelter at Zeus' altar as a suppliant and, there, he was recognised by **Cassandra**, who was a seer. However, knowing the disaster Paris would cause to the city, she, too, dashed at him to kill him.

This incident revealed the old story and his parents were so happy to have found their son again that they ignored the warnings first by Aeacus and then by Cassandra, and welcomed him with love.

An earlier myth Homer also uses as a source has it that Paris must have been one of the most important heroes of the Trojans. In the Iliad, he is mentioned as **Alexander** 46 times and only thirteen as **Paris**.

The first name denotes a warrior who confronts his enemies dynamically, whereas the second denotes an abductor lover, who, still, asserts himself and has the authority to persuade the Trojans to fight and perish for his sake. In the Iliad, the accomplishments of Paris are really few.

He usually fights with his bow and arrows shooting from afar so that he is out of the battlefield. On the whole, his image is that of a good-looking man but cowardly, shameless and boastful, without any sense of responsibility and shame for the disaster he has caused.

From Priam's offspring, who are called the **Priamids**, only twenty sons and three daughters are mentioned in the Iliad.

Apart from Hector and Paris, who are the main persons playing an essential role in the Iliad, the rest of Priam's sons are most mentioned merely by their names. **Deiphobus** is said to have been one of the brave Trojans and a very dear brother of Hector. He participates actively in the battle over the Achaean ships and slays Ipsenor, a son of Hippasus, and Ascalaphus, a son of god Ares, whereas he is wounded in the arm by Merione.

From the other Trojan families, **Aeneias**, a son of Anchisis and goddess Aphrodite and a second cousin of Hector, stands out. Aeneias along with Hector share the main responsibility of the war, since both distinguish for their bravery and intelligence.

Priam's nephew, the elderly at the time of the war Antenor, is perhaps the only one of the Trojans who acknowledges the fact that the Trojans are to blame for the war, because they accepted Paris with Helen in their city. He tries, at the right moment, to help the Trojans not to commit any worse violations or have conflicts, and sooths difficulties out. For this reason, he offers hospitality to Menelaus and Odysseus when, before the war, they went to claim Helen as well as Menelaus' treasure back and avoid the war.

In the Iliad, there are mentioned eleven legitimate sons and an illegitimate one of his. Among them, **Agenor** and **Acamas** stand out, fighting by the side of Hector while many times they save their compatriots from the fierceness of the Achaeans.

Panthous was one of the elders of the Trojans and belonged to a noble family. He is also referred to as a seer and a priest of Apollo. Homer mentions three sons of Panthous, **Polydamas**, who being a seer knows the forthcoming events and always consults Hector,as well as **Euphorbus** and **Hyperenor**, both of whom perished by the hand of Menelaus.

In addition, there were plenty the allies of the Trojans who came from distant countries, such as the **Paeonians** from Thrace, the **Ciconians**, the **Pelasgians**, the **Paphlagonians**, the **Mysians**, the **Phrygians**, the **Maeonians**, the **Carians**, the **Lycians**, the **Lelegians** and the **Cauconians** from Asia Minor, the most significant being the **Lycians** whose leaders were **Sarpedon** and **Glaucus**.

Sarpedon, king of Lycia, is considered to be a son of Zeus, either from his union with Laomadea, the daughter of Bellerophon, or with Europa in which case he is the brother to Minos and Rhadamanthys.

It is also said that, after a conflict he had with Minos, he abandoned Crete and settled down in **Lycia**. In the Iliad, he is the one who pulls down a rampart in the Acheans' wall and opens up the way for the Trojans to reach the ships of their enemies. Sarpedon, the only son of Zeus who fights in Troy, has the Moira (Fate) to perish by Patroclus, his divine father being unable to save him.

Around his dead body, the best warriors of the Trojans and the Achaeans engage in a terrible fight. His corpse, naked of his armoury, will be transferred to Lycia by Hypnos and Thanatos under the care of Apollo, who followed Zeus' order.

A hero of Lycia was also Glaucus, a grandson of Bellerophon and a nephew of Sarpedon, who always fights by his side leading the army of the Lycians together. His encounter with Diomedes at the battlefield and their acquaintance due to their ancestors' friendship are exquisitely accounted in the Iliad by Homer and is an evidence of the ethos of the two warriors as well as the value of friendship during the heroic era. Glaucus was slain by Telamonean Aeas in the fight around Achilles' corpse.

THE TENTH YEAR OF THE WAR

THE WRATH OF ACHILLES

The first nine years of the siege of Troy passed with no significant war events to mention. The tenth year of the war started upon the arrival of **Chryses**, a priest of Apollo, at the encampment of the Achaeans to ask for the release of his daughter **Chryseis**, who had been captured and kept in the Adrammytian gulf by Achilles during the conquer of Thebes and had been given to **Agamemnon** as a slave. Bringing along countless spoils, the priest presented his request at the assembly of the Achaeans and all of them appeared willing to return her, except for Agamemnon who sent her father away. Then, Chryses begged god Apollo to punish the Achaeans and the god, in anger, began to shoot and kill people and animals with his bow.

After a nine-day- havoc, prophet Calchas revealed that Apollo was angry because of Agamemnon's refusal. Apart from the sacrifice they offered the god to appease him they made Agamemnon give in and deliver Chryseis to her father. However, Agamemnon, being the commander of the troops, required that **Briseis**, Achilles' battle prize after conquering **Lyrnessus**, be brought to replace Chryseis.

The two leaders quarrelled, spoke harsh words against each other and their argument ended with Achilles' concession and consent to give Briseis, nevertheless stating that he withdraws from the war along with the army of the Myrmidons. At the same time, he asked Zeus for and was granted the intervention of Thetis so that Agamemnon and the Achaeans pay dearly for the offence they had inflicted upon him. Then, Zeus sent **Oneiros** (Dream) to Agamemnon to tell him that the time was right for him to conquer Troy.

Wishing to test the troops, Agamemnon summoned everyone to an assembly and suggested that they left for their homeland. And, while his suggestion almost disbanded the army, **Odysseus** gathered them again and convinced them to fight. The troops of the Achaeans and the Trojans were arrayed in the plain ready to fight. Then, **Paris** challenged whoever of the Achaeans wished to duel with him and **Menelaus** accepted. Both the Achaeans and the Trojans agreed to cease the war and, whoever of the two men of Helen won, he would keep Helen and the treasure which was stolen from the palace of Menelaus. The agreement was sealed under oath by both the kings, **Agamemnon** and **Priam**, and the duel started, while Helen watched her two men fight from the walls.

At the moment, however, when Menelaus dragged Paris from the crest of his helmet and was about to slay him, **Aphrodite**, his beloved goddess, intervened, snatched him and transferred him to his chamber in the palace while, at the same time, called Helen to go to him. She ran to Paris and scolded him for his behaviour, that is, his challenging Menelaus to a duel, since he was cowardly. Paris, though, made her go to bed with him, whereas Menelaus was looking for him among the Trojans.

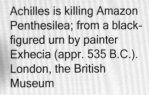

Achilles is killing Amazon Penthesilea; from a black-figured urn by painter Exhecia (appr. 535 B.C.). London, the British Museum

On Olympus, the gods decided for the war to continue. Athena then, disguised in the figure of a Trojan, persuaded **Pandarus** from Lycia to shoot his arrow at Menelaus while the truce was still in effect. The wound he caused was not a serious one and was easily healed by **Machaon**, the son of Asclepius, but after the incident there was no hope of maintaining peace.

The Achaean army prepared for war straight away, and the first day of the battle began. **Diomedes** excelled on that day by slaying numerous Trojans as well as Pandarus. When, however, he found himself face to face with **Glaucus** and learnt about their grandfathers' and their generation's friendship, he did not fight with him; on the contrary, they exchanged gifts.

As the battle turned against the Trojans, though, **Hector** returned to the city to beg his mother have the Trojan women beseech goddess Athena to protect them. Then, he urged Paris to take part in the battle and, finally, he met his wife, **Andromache** and his son, this being the last time they talked, for Hector was not to come back from the war alive.

While the fight was going on, Athena and Apollo agreed to postpone the confrontation till the next day, and incite **Hector** to duel with some Achaean. The lot fell upon **Aeas the Telamonian** but no one obtained victory because the heralds stepped in and stopped them before they got killed. According to the ritual, they exchanged gifts, with Hector giving Aeas a sword and Aeas offering Hector a girdle.

At the Achaean encampment, Agamemnon invited the leaders to a banquet during which Nestor persuaded them not to fight the following day so as to bury their dead. Moreover, he talked them into building a wall around their ships and tents, as well as digging a ditch to defend themselves against the attacks of the Trojans.

At the Trojan assembly inside the Castle, Paris did not agree to return Helen, but accepted to return the treasure. The Achaeans declined his offer, however, they agreed on a ceasefire so as to bury their dead.

The following day, at dawn, Zeus strictly forbade the gods to assist any of the opponent sides. He went to **Ida**, the mountain crowning Troy, to supervise the Struggle. Until midday, the fight was level.

Then the god cast thunder and lightning and the Achaeans withdrew, while Hector launched an attack. The Achaeans, however, did not stay still. **Teuctrus** killed nine Trojans with his bow and arrow while hidden next to Aeas, but he was wounded and retreated. Hera and Athena tried to help, Zeus, though, saw them and sent the word that he would strike them with his thunderbolt. He returned to Olympus and unveiled Moira's ((Fate's) will: Hector's brunt was not to be inhibited until **Patroclus** was perished and **Achilles** appeared at the battlefield again.

Night fell and Hector suggested the warriors stay awake outside the walls of their city, putting up fires all around so as to scare the Achaeans. The Achaeans, in great distress, sent a messenger to Achilles whose negative reply discouraged the Hellenes. Only Diomedes did have the courage to suggest continuing the war. At the same night, **Odysseus** and **Diomedes** scouted the enemy camp to find out their plans. They discovered and slew the Trojan spy **Dolon**, after they had found out that king **Rhesus** with his Thracian warriors had arrived in assistance of the Trojans. The two Achaeans sneaked into their camp when everyone was asleep, slew many of them along with Rhesus, stole his renowned horses and returned to their encampment.

On the morning of the third day, **Agamemnon** excelled killing numerous Trojans; he was wounded, though, and had to withdraw, while Hector was about to demonstrate his bravery. Diomedes and Odysseus withstood until the first was injured by Paris and the second by Socus and had to return to their tents.

Of the main warriors only **Aeas** did remain, but Zeus sent fright in him and started to retreat as did **Eurypylos**, who was hit by Paris. Machaon, also wounded by Paris, was taken

Achilles is tenderly taking care of Patroclus' wounded arm. From the inside of a red-figured wide cup (appr. 500 B.C.).
Berlin, Staatliche Museen

from the battlefield by Nestor in his chariot. Achilles, who was watching from a distance, sent Patroclus to learn who the wounded man was and, then, Nestor suggested that Patroclus fought with the Myrmidons so as the Achaeans to be assisted. On his way back, Patroclus encountered the wounded Eurypylos, healed his wound and stayed in his tent to keep him company while he was in pain. The battle, though, was going on and the Trojans had reached the wall, which they started to pull down.

At the same time, **Sarpedon** attacked a tower defended by **Idomeneus**. In his assistance rashed **Aeas** but the Lycians had already advanced, having broken the wall and making their way towards the ships of the Achaeans. The battle was equal until the moment when Hector smashed the gate with a rock and dashed into the encampment with his companions.

Zeus, who was watching the struggle, had already turned his eyes to other distant countries. Then, **Poseidon**, indignant, arrived at the battlefield to encourage the Achaeans. Their warriors, who were not wounded, lined up and stopped the charge of the Trojans. Deiphobus and Helenus were injured, while Paris, Aeneias and the rest of the Trojans tried to resist but in vain. Not even when Hector came did they manage to break the defence line.

Hera, not bearing to see Zeus supporting the Trojans, decided to employ her charms and lure him. She bathed, adorned herself, dressed in a seductive way after borrowing Aphrodite's bra, and, taking Hypnos with her, she arrived in Ida and appeared before Zeus. Upon seeing her, Zeus wished to make love to her and she, pretending not to want at first, accepted and a golden cloud covered them.

As soon as Zeus fell asleep, Hera notified Poseidon and he helped the Achaeans again to recover their courage. During the battle, Aeas threw a big rock at Hector and left him breathless. The Trojans retreated and, chased, they ran out of the ditch to the place where they had left their chariots.

When **Zeus** woke up and saw the outcome of the battle, he realised what had happened and became enraged with Hera who swore to him that she was not to blame for **Poseidon's** initiative to help the Achaeans. Then, the father of the gods sent Iris to tell the god of the sea to go away from the battle.

After that, he sent **Apollo** with the order to instil Hector breathing and give him back his robustness. With this divine intervention, once the Achaeans saw Hector before them, they ran away to their ships but for a few brave ones who stayed to confront the Trojans. When,

Hera is appearing in a seductive way before Zeus to distract him from the battles of the Hellenes and the Trojans he is watching from the top of Ida; metope from Temple E in Selinous (appr. 460 B.C.). Palermo, Museo Nazionale Archeologico

in fact, Apollo, carrying Zeus' aegis, stood in front of them, some Achaeans scattered and many of them perished. The god pulled the Achaeans' walls down and filled the ditch so that the Trojans could reach the ships of their opponents.

All by himself was left **Aeas** (Ajax) the Telamonian, the brave warrior, to save the ships from the fire and he ran from one ship to other defending them. Thus, only the ship of Protesilaus was set on fire.

THE DEATH OF PATROCLUS

At the very time of the rout of the Hellenes, **Patroclus**, urged by Nestor, asked Achilles to borrow his armour and fight leading the Myrmidons. Achilles agreed and ordered him, though, to return as soon as he had sent the enemy away. The sight of Patroclus in Achilles' armour on his chariot petrified the Trojans, because they thought that he was the first warrior of the Achaeans himself who had entered the battle.

They started to retreat, while Patroclus charged at the **Lycians** and their commander **Sarpedon.** Moira (Fate) had the time of the death of Zeus' son approach. Patroclus fought against Sarpedon and slew him, whereas a dreadful struggle began around his corpse. The Achaeans took his armour and left him naked and unrecognisable on the ground, until Hypnos and Thanatos picked him up, washed and dressed him, and carried him to his homeland, Lycia.

Having forgotten his friend's advice, though, Patroclus went on with the attack and was about to reach the fort of Troy, were it for the gods aiding the Trojans once again. Patroclus was hit in the back by Apollo who, taking advantage of him being dizzy, took every single weapon from him.

Euphorbus, a son of **Panthous**, continued by shooting his spear at him; he was followed by Hector, who finished him off and belted on Achilles' weapons. A fierce fight broke out around the dead body, which almost fell in the hands of the Trojans. While **Menelaus** and **Aeas** undertook to carry Patroclus' corpse to the Achaean camp, **Antilochus** went to break the news to Achilles. Upon hearing of the death of his companion, Achilles cried out so fiercely that the Trojans left scared to death.

The Achaeans carried Patroclus' lifeless body into Achilles' tent and his lament was so loud that **Thetis** heard it in the depths of the sea and rashed to her son. Determined to avenge his companion's death, the hero asked for new weapons and his mother ordered them from **Hephaestus**. The god spent the entire night in his workshop and fashioned the hero's armoury; the breastplate, the helmet and the shield, which he adorned with lands and seas, the sky and stars, the earth, fields and palaces, while, all around its frame, he depicted vast Oceanus.

THE DEATH OF HECTOR

The next morning, Thetis delivered the divine weapons to Achilles, while he was lamenting his dead companion. At the assembly of the Achaeans, **Achilles** reconciled with **Agamemnon** who, resentful, wanted to give him everything he had promised him. The hero, though, replied that the only thing he cared for was revenge and this is why he insisted on getting out to the battlefield immediately. The army, however, had to first eat and drink before they fought again, as, rightly so, Odysseus declared.

The only one abstaining from food was Achilles, who mourned beside dead Patroclus. And Zeus sent Iris to drop some nectar and ambrosia in his chest. Immediately after that, the hero belted on his weapons and dashed to the battlefield being aware of the fact that revenge was certain to drive him to his own death.

His **distinction** in the battle will overshadow that of all the other heroes. As the fight was about to begin, Zeus summoned the gods on Olympus and announced that his order not to intervene in the war was not in effect any more. Then, the patrons of the Achaeans, Hera, Athena, Poseidon, Hermes and Hephaestus on one hand, and the patrons of the Trojans, Ares, Aphrodite, Apollo and Artemis with their mother Leto on the other, set out for Troy and, at first, they did not participate in the struggle.

Aeneias started to fight with Achilles first. When he risked getting killed, though, Poseidon snatched him and carried him at the far end of the army, although the god had always assisted the Achaeans. Achilles began to slay the Trojans fiercely and, among them, he slew **Polydorus**, the youngest son of Priam. When Hector attempted to avenge his brother's murder, he was almost killed were he not rescued by Apollo. The Trojans entered the waters of the river Scamander to save themselves but Achilles followed them slaughtering mercilessly.

In parallel with the mortals, the gods also fought with each other. Athena hurled a rock against Ares and Aphrodite, Hera hit Artemis and Apollo got away to avoid fighting with Poseidon. Thus, the gods supporting the Greeks were the victors.

The Trojans, horrified by the rage of Achilles, ran to seek shelter inside the walls. Only **Agenor** did attempt to resist the hero but was rescued by Apollo, who snatched him and saved him. Then, the god, in the guise of Agenor, carried Achilles away from the Gate of the Wall, so that as many Achaeans as possible had time to protect themselves behind it.

Outside the walls, **Hector** was left alone, determined to face Achilles by himself. Nevertheless, when he saw Achilles dashing at him, he turned to flee and was chased three times around the castle. The time of the death of the Trojan hero had come, though, and his duel with Achilles started.

Athena, in the guise of Deiphobus, Hector's brother, approached him pretending to wish to support him and, when the spear of Achilles missed the target, she secretly sent it back, whereas, when Hector needed a second spear, Deiphobus was nowhere close to him. Being fully aware of the fact that the gods had decided on his death, the brave warrior and defender of Troy went on with his struggle. Achilles' spear hit him in the throat and, before dying, he begged him to give his body over to his own people for a proper burial.

However, Achilles treated the now dead hero in a fierce and particularly cruel way. After undressing him, he attached his naked corpse at his chariot and dragged him up to the Achaeans' encampment. From the towers of the walls of the castle of Troy, his parents and his wife Andromache watched the end of their hero.

When **Achilles** returned to his tent, he dropped Hector's corpse onto the ground, ordered his companions to have a meal, had a meal too, and went to sleep without having had a bath. In his dream there came the figure of **Patroclus** asking to bury him the soonest possible. At dawn, a big pyrhe (fire) was put up and his body was burnt with a great procession. The next day, they collected his remains and sealed them in an urn which was kept in the tent of Achilles. According to the last wish of the dead man, they would be buried along with his beloved companion later on. Next, Achilles organised athletic games to honour Patroclus.

For twelve days, **Hector** remained unburied. Then, Zeus sent Thetis to her son to tell him that the gods were angry with him for having mistreated the dead man and that he had to deliver his body to the Trojans. Zeus sent Iris to Troy to order **Priam** to go with a herald only to the enemy camp and claim Hector's body. **Hermes** himself drove Priam's chariot to Achilles tent, without anyone taking any notice. Achilles welcomed old Priam with due respect. They had a meal and drinks and spent the night there. The next dawn, the king of Troy left with his son's dead body and the promise that Achilles would cease fire until the funeral rites were over. Hector was buried amidst the lament of the Trojans, who knew that, after his loss, they had lost every hope to escape their fate.

Aeas is carrying the corpse of Achilles on his shoulders; from the handle of the crater Franc.ois
(appr. 470 B.C.). Florence, Museo Archeologico

THE DEATH OF ACHILLES

After Hector's death, there arose an immediate need for the Trojans to gain new allies, since Pandarus, Rhesus and Sarpedon, their main allies, were dead.

For the first time there appeared the queen of the Amazons **Penthesilea**, along with her all-women army to assist Priam, and, also, test herself in the battle. Penthesilea excelled at the fight and slew a lot of Achaeans, among which Machaon, the son of Asclepius. She also confronted **Achilles**, when he attempted to stop her. She did not hesitate to fight with him and he killed her. The hero, dazzled at her beauty, decided not to take her weapons and delivered her corpse to the Trojans for proper burial.

Immediately after the burial of Penthesilea, Troy welcomed its new ally, **Memnon**, the king of Ethiopia, a son of **Eos** and **Tithon**, the brother to Priam. The Trojans were encouraged by their brave ally who killed **Antilochus**, though, the son of Nestor and a close friend of Achilles. The murder caused the wrath of the invincible hero who, enraged, duelled with him. During their duel, their mothers, **Eos** and **Thetis**, turned to Zeus each one begging him to save her son.

Moira (Fate), however, had already decided upon Memnon to get killed first, and then, Achilles' death to follow. The only thing Eos managed to achieve was the fact that Zeus granted her son immortality.

Following the death of Memnon, Achilles rashed onto the battlefield to conquer the fort of the Trojans, who, petrified, rashed to hide behind its walls. Nevertheless, at the gates, there lurked god Apollo. He ordered Paris to shoot at the hero and the god himself directed the arrow so that it hit the vulnerable part in the hero's leg and he dropped lifeless onto the earth.

The son of Thetis, the bravest of all the Hellenes, died in this cowardly manner. There broke out a horrible fight over who was to claim his body.

Finally, **Aeas** the Telamonian managed to prevail and, carrying the lifeless warrior on his shoulders, took him to the encampment of the Achaeans, while Odysseus fought the enemy to provide cover for him. He delivered him to the Myrmidons. They washed the blood away, dressed him and lay him on his death bed. Around him Thetis, the Nereids and the Muses lamented with an endless bewailing, which made everyone's tears flow.

For seventeen days and nights mortals and goddesses mourned him and, on the eighteenth, they burnt his body,

"Achilles dying"; marble statue by Ernst Gustav Herter, 1884. Corfu, the Achilleion

collected his remains and put them, along with Patroclus' remains, in a golden urn, which Hephaestus himself had wrought. They, then, built a monument at the edge of the Hellespont, in Sigion, so that the passers-by see it and remind them of his heroic figure in eternity. Afterwards, to honour him they organised epitaph athletic games.

A Nereid.

After Achilles' burial, **Thetis** wished to give his armour to the bravest of the Hellenes. Only two of them decided to claim it: **Odysseus** and **Telamonian Aeas**. Since, however, none of them admitted the superiority of the other, wise Nestor suggested that the Trojans judged, as they would not be affected by likes or dislikes.

The Achaeans spied below the walls of Troy and found out, overhearing two women talking about the recent accomplishment of Odysseus and Aeas that is, snatching Achilles' corpse from the enemy hands, that, in their opinion, Odysseus demonstrated a braver behaviour. For this reason, Achilles' armour was given to Odysseus. When Aeas learnt about it, he felt insulted and, in the darkness of the night, he set off to kill the leaders of the Achaeans.

But Athena made him unable to think straight and the hero managed to slay their lambs and oxen. Once Aeas had recovered the next day, he felt ashamed of his behaviour and his ridicule before his companions and, grabbing a sword he fixed it in the ground and fell upon it ending his life. Later on, Odysseus met Achilles' son, Neoptolemus, and handed him over his father's weapons.

THE PROPHESIES OF HELENUS

Despite the death of Hector and that of the major ally commanders, Troy was still holding. One day, seer Calchas revealed Odysseus that he could not aid the Achaeans any more with his prophetic powers.

The only one who knew the oracles concerning the fall of Troy was **Helenus**, the prophet son of Priam. Odysseus, then, waited for him outside the walls and, at a night when Helenus was found all alone outside the fort of the Trojans, he captured him and drove him to the camp of the Achaeans. There, Helenus, under death threat, was made to reveal the oracles which protected Troy.

According to these oracles, Ilium would fall only when: the Achaeans obtained **Heracles' bow** and **arrows** kept by **Philoctetes**, a son of **Poeas** from Magnesia in Thessaly. Moreover, they would have to bring to Troy the bones of **Pelops**, as well as Achilles' son, **Neoptolemus**, and steal the Palladium that is, the wooden statue of Athena, from her temple on the acropolis of Troy; the **Skaiae Gates** in the wall of Troy should also be destroyed.

In order for all of the above to occur, the Achaeans sent first **Odysseus** and **Diomedes** or, in another version, Neoptolemus, to Lemnos where **Philoctetes** was. **Philoctetes** had sailed off along with the rest of the Achaeans on the expedition to Troy with seven ships.

When the Achaeans stopped over on the island of Chryse to offer sacrifices, he was bitten by a snake and his companions, who could not stand his cries from the pain and the horrible stench of the festered wound in his leg, abandoned him in Lemnos all by himself. Therefore, it would be difficult for the two emissaries to convince him. Employing mainly trickery rather than persuasion, they snatched the weapons from Philoctetes, who was forced to follow them so that he was not left deserted without arms and could not find food or be protected from wild animals.

As soon as they arrived at the Achaean encampment, Philoctetes was cured by Machaon. Immediately afterwards, he took part in the battle and slew many Trojans. Finally, he challenged **Paris** to a duel with their bows and wounded him fatally. His companions took his lifeless body from the hands of Menelaus, who saw to avenge him even if he were dead.

The next prophesy by Helenus the Achaeans fulfiled was to bring **Neoptolemus**, the son of Achilles and Deidamea, and fight with them below the walls of Troy so that the city fall. **Neoptolemus** was in Skyros, where he grew up with his mother and his elderly grandfather. Odysseus arrived and had no difficulty taking Neoptolemus to Troy with him. This hero, despite his young age, distinguished for his prudence and excellence at fighting. Once they had reached Troy, Odysseus handed his father's weapons to Neoptolemus. At night, he saw him in his dream and advised him not to shame his family in the war. He also informed him that he was to accomplish what he himself had not managed to despite his bravery, that is, to conquer the castle of the Trojans.

Neoptolemus' presence greatly encouraged the Achaeans, who singled him out at the assemblies of the leaders and, mainly, in the battlefield where he excelled like his father. His greatest moment of glory was his duel with **Eurypylos**, the son of Telephus and **Andioche**, sister to Priam.

Telephus was under oath to the Hellenes because, once, he had been healed by Achilles, therefore he did not participate in the Trojan War as an ally and a relative of Priam. However, Priam managed to talk his sister into sending her son to the Achaean encampment, giving her as a present a valuable piece of work created by Hephaestus, which had been donated to Laomedon by Zeus.

Eurypylos with a big military force consisting of Cetians (Mysians) and being delighted with his involvement in the war excelled at numerous battles and slew many Achaeans. He accepted the duel with **Neoptolemus** at once, but was doomed to perish from the spear of Achilles' son.

In fulfilment of the prophesies concerning the fall of Troy, another mission on the part of the Achaeans went to **Pissa** in Eleia, and brought **Pelops'** shoulder-blade to the Achaean camp, as accounted by Pausanius, documenting the fact that the hero's remains consisted an item of cult for the Hellenes.

THE TROJAN HORSE

After the death of **Eurypylos**, the Trojans locked themselves in the castle, while the Greeks went on with pincer movements around them. Helenus, however, had prophesised that Troy would not fall in its enemy's hands so long as the **Palladium** was in their city. Before the Achaeans ventured to snatch Athena's wooden statue, the goddess herself advised Odysseus to build a large wooden figure of a horse, the Dourios Hippos (dourios=wooden), known as the Trojan horse, and appointed **Epeios**, a son of Panopeus from Phocis, to construct it.

Indeed, within a few days, Epeios constructed a huge figure of a horse, having secret doors on its both sides, which could hide 3,000 warriors in its hollow insides and bore the inscription "**An Offering to Athena by the Hellenes**".

While the wooden horse was ready, it was time for the theft of the **Palladium**, which

The "Trojan Horse"; detail from an early depiction on an earthenware urn with bas-relief representations (appr. 670 B.C.). Myconos, Archaeological Museum

Odysseus ventured on his own. He entered Ilion (Troy) pretending to be a beggar asking alms of the Trojans.

Only Greek **Helen** did recognise him and tried to corner him. But, Odysseus managed to get away from her and convince the Trojans that he was a beggar. Helen asked and took him to her home so as to supposedly take care of him, and there, Odysseus unmasked and discussed the Achaeans' plans with her; she showed him the streets of the city and the guards at the gates. After Odysseus had found out everything he needed, he slew several Trojans and returned to the Achaean camp.

With the help of **Diomedes**, they will enter again Troy through a gallery under the walls during the night, snatch the wooden statue of the goddess from her temple and carry it out of the besieged city.

THE FALL OF ILION (TROY)

Once the Greeks had the Palladium in their hands, they prepared for the final fight.

They selected the bravest warriors and hid them in the hollow insides of the Trojan horse, their commander being **Odysseus**. When all the chosen ones had been locked in the horse, the rest set their tents on fire, boarded their ships and sailed off, pretending to have lost every hope of conquering Troy. Once they had sailed away enough, they hid at the island of Tenedus in the darkness of the night, choosing a bay that was not visible from Troy.

One man only was left behind, **Sinon**, a cousin of Odysseus who had directed him on what to do, when the Trojans would discover the wooden horse the following morning. Indeed, next dawn, the Trojans saw the encampment of the Achaeans deserted and no soul around.

Little by little they took heart and went to the plain, outside the walls, where they saw the horse and wondered what it was. Meanwhile, herdsmen found Sinon and brought him for questioning. He told them a story, though, made up by the ingenious king of Ithaca, so as to mislead them. He said he was a loyal friend to **Palamedes** who Odysseus had killed and, therefore, he hated him.

Since seer Calchas, after they had stolen the Palladium, had told them that due to their Sacrilege they would never conquer Troy, they decided to return to their homeland in order to expiate. And, because there was no wind, they wanted to sacrifice **Sinon**, like Iphigenia in Aulis some years ago. However, he managed to escape in the darkness of the night and hid in the forest, where he was found out by the herdsmen. Although a few of them doubted his honesty, the majority were convinced because the story had been well structured not to raise any questions about the Achaeans having left for Greece.

All together, they pulled the horse towards the walls and, at the **Skaiae** Gates, broke a part of them down so as to make room for the horse to enter. Then, they dragged it up to Pergama, their acropolis, and placed it next to Priam's palace. There, they were met by **Cassandra**, the insane seer, a daughter of the king, who anxiously told them that Achaeans were hiding in the horse, but no one believed her. Only **Laocoon,** seer and priest of Apollo and a brother to Anchisis, hurled his spear at the Horse while trying to persuade them not to give faith to the Greeks and fear them even when they bring gifts. The opinions of the Trojans were divided again but those insisting on dedicating it to Athena were more and prevailed.

A little later, while the tragic priest and his sons were offering a sacrifice to **Poseidon** at the seaside, two huge serpents sprang up from the waves, coiled themselves up the bodies of Laocoon and one of his sons and devoured them.

The Trojans were certain that the priest was punished due to the disrespect he had demonstrated when he aimed his spear at the **Horse** of the goddess, therefore, they returned home and held feasts all day long.

The Complex of Laocoon
(1st c. B.C.).
Rome, Musei Vaticani

Only **Aeneias** did understand the meaning of the gods' omen. Zeus may have hated Priam's family but he did not wish for Dardanus' family to vanish completely. Thus, Aeneias picked up his family and took refuge to Ida, leaving behind the Trojans to their fate.

While the Trojans, exhausted from the banquet and the drinks, had fallen asleep, at midnight, as Selene (the Moon) was rising, **Sinon** sent the predefined signal, fire lit on Achilles' tomb, so that the Achaeans see it and sail back to the coast of Troad.

At the same time, the brave leaders of the Hellenes, Odysseus, Neoptolemus, Diomedes, Menelaus, Philoctetes and many others, climbed off the secret doors of the **Trojan Horse** and opened the wall gates. The Achaeans were ready, flooded the city of Ilion and the slaughter of the Trojans began.

Assisted by Odysseus, **Menelaus** looked for the house of **Deiphobus** where **Helen** lived, having married him after the death of Paris. A great battle took place then, and Menelaus slew **Deiphobus**. After that, he found Helen and, while he was about to kill her too, she uncovered her chest and Menelaus forgave her and sent her to the ships of the Achaeans.

Right then, **Neoptolemus** burst into Priam's palace, slew first **Agenor**, the son of Antenor, then **Priam,** who had sought shelter at the altar of **Erkeios Zeus,** and threw Hector's son, **Astyanax**, down from the walls, while he took **Andromache**, the hero's wife, as a hostage. The one, though, who demonstrated the worst behaviour of all the Achaeans, was **Locrian Aeas**; he found **Cassandra**, the seer daughter of Priam, to have sought shelter as a suppliant at the statue of **Athena** in her temple and, after forcefully taking her away, he raped her inside the temple.

This sacrilege, which caused **Athena's wrath**, would cost his life later on as well as the life of his companions on their return journey to Greece. In addition, his compatriots "**the Locrians**" had to pay the tribute of sending two virgin girls to serve the temple of Athena in Troy for years.

Only **Aeneias** and his family did escape the slaughter which followed, along with **Antenor** and his people, because he had aided Menelaus and Odysseus when they had gone to Troy as ambassadors before the breakout of the war and the Trojans wanted to slay them. The rest of the Trojans were all perished and the city was set on fire.

THE RETURN OF THE HEROES HOME

THE DEPARTURE FROM TROY

After having conquered and burnt down Troy, the only thing the **Achaeans** wanted was to immediately return to Greece, to their families. Goddess **Athena**, however, who had always supported them, was very angry over the sack of the sacred temples of Troy and planned to destroy them. So did the father of the gods, **Zeus**, who was indignant at the disaster the Achaeans had caused during the fall of the city.

The first conflict, incited by Athena, broken out among the Atrids was the first bad sign. **Menelaus** quarrelled with his brother **Agamemnon** over the time of their return. The army divided in two and, at dawn, **Menelaus**, **Nestor**, **Odysseus** and **Diomedes** along with other leaders and their troops boarded their ships and sailed off, whereas Agamemnon remained in Troy.

Their first stop was in Tenedos. They kept on quarrelling, though, and Odysseus returned and joined Agamemnon's fleet. Menelaus, Nestor and Diomedes stopped in **Tenedos** and then sailed on to **Lesbos**, where they anchored and sought a divine sign on the route they had to follow back home.

Since these leaders' actions had not caused the wrath of the gods, they advised them to

The golden mask of an Achaean leader; from the Tomb Cycle A of Mycenae (16th c. B.C.). Athens, National Archaeological Museum

hurry and return via **Geraestos**, in the southeast of Euboea, so as to avoid the catastrophe that was to happen. Thus, with fair winds, they reached Geraestos and offered a sacrifice to Poseidon for saving them.

The same fair winds allowed Nestor to arrive in Pylos and Diomedes to arrive in Argos. As Menelaus, however, was approaching the coast of Attica with the other two commanders, he went through so many adventures and roamings that he reached Laconia after eight years.

THE WANDERINGS OF MENELAUS

As the ships of Menelaus reached Sounion in Attica, **Phrondes**, the son of Onetor, the competent captain of Menelaus' ship, suddenly passed away. Menelaus let the rest go on with their voyage and landed at Sounion, where he buried his companion. After a few days, they sailed off and met with a horribly bad weather.

The waves drifted them off course up to western **Crete**, at the port of Phaestos, where they were smashed onto the rocks. Menelaus and five ships, the only ones that had been left, reached **Egypt**, where he wandered for seven years.

In Egyptian **Thebes**, he met the king of **Polybus**, who gave him two silver basins, two tripods and gold worth ten talents (ancient currency), while queen **Alcandra** gave Helen a

Clytemnestra's murder by her son Orestes; bronze lamina (appr. 570 B.C.).
Olympia, Archaeological Museum

silver basket and a distaff of pure gold. Menelaus found himself in various other cities of the East, such as Sidon, Cyprus, Phoenice, Ethiopia, Erembia and Libya. Eventually, he set off from Egypt to return home, but, before leaving, he forgot to sacrifice to the gods.

When he, along with Helen, reached **Pharus**, the island located opposite **Alexandria**, the strong winds did not allow him to continue his journey. After days and nights of hardship, there appeared before him **Eidothea**, the daughter of **Proteus,** the old man of the sea, and, pitying him, she advised him to find her father and learn how and when he would return to Sparta from him. Menelaus, accompanied by three of his companions, went to the cave the girl had indicated, where she was waiting to give him sealskins so that they all covered themselves. Then, he waited for Proteus.

Proteus and a school of seals entered and filled the cave; Menelaus attacked Proteus, who, after a brave fight, was made to inform him that he had to return to the river Neilus (Nile) and offer a sacrifice to Zeus and the rest of the gods. Then, he told him about **Locrian**

Aeas' drowning and the death of his brother **Agamemnon** and, finally, added that, since he was the son-in-law of Zeus, after his death he was destined to the **Elysium Plains** (Heaven), where life rolled on carelessly and blissfully.

Having heard Proteus' prophesies, Menelaus had to return to Egypt to sacrifice to the gods. Before leaving, he established a cenotaph in honour of his brother Agamemnon, so that his name remained unforgettable in the foreign land as well. Then, he sailed off again with fair winds to return to his homeland, free of hardship, after an absence of eighteen years. Nevertheless, Menelaus was not to lead a happy life in Sparta.

Although he had beautiful Helen by his side and immense wealth, he lived engrossed in the memories of a long-lasting war, which had cost the life of so many of his beloved companions as well as that of his dear brother. Without an heir, having only a daughter, pretty **Hermione**, whom he had sent to Ftheia to become the wife of **Neoptolemus**, the son of Achilles, he waited for his end because he knew that, when he died, he would go to the Elysium Plains.

There is another version of this myth concerning the return of Helen from Troy, according to which Helen had never stepped on the land of Troy. The woman Paris had abducted was a replica of her which Hera had made in order to avenge him for having chosen Aphrodite as the most beautiful goddess. Real Helen had been carried to Egypt, where Proteus ruled, by Hermes and had settled there safe and sound, waiting for Menelaus to arrive and take her to Sparta.

THE RETURN OF AGAMEMNON

In Troy, **Agamemnon** with **Odysseus** and the rest of the leaders who had not already departed with the first group along with Menelaus, offered propriating sacrifices to the gods and, mainly, **Athena**, but did not manage to appease her.

Before sailing off, the shadow of Achilles appeared before Agamemnon foretelling him what would happen, but he ignored him and steered for Greece. Only **Neoptolemus**, advised by Thetis, did prefer to travel on foot through Thrace. The rest reached first **Tenedos** and then headed directly for cape **Caphereus**, in Euboea, modern Cavo-Doro.

There, they found a terrible storm, numerous ships wrecked and important heroes, such as **Meges** from the Echinades and **Prothous** from Magnesia, drowned. Goddess Athena, very angry particularly over the offences committed in her temple by **Locrian Aeas**, cast her thunder on his ship.

Although Poseidon tried to talk her out of it and helped him climb onto a rock, when Aeas boasted about his escaping and defeating the goddess, the god split the rock with his trident and Aeas fell into the chasm. His corpse was drifted to Myconos or Delos, where it was buried by Thetis.

Those having survived the fierce sea at **Caphereus** underwent another hardship. The father of **Palamedes**, **Nauplius**, having learnt that the ships were returning from Troy and wishing to avenge his son's, **Palamedes**, unfair death, went to Caphereus and put up fires at the most dangerous site for the ships. When they saw the fires, the Achaeans thought that shepherds had put them up to help them and, heading towards them, they crashed on the rocks. Only Agamemnon's ships did survive aided by Hera and, after they made it through the narrow passage between Kea and Attica, they reached the Argolic bay.

The commander of the expedition was destined to die a few days later, in his homeland, **Mycenae**. During the Trojan War, **Clytemnestra**, Agamemnon's wife, had an affair with **Aegisthus**, his nephew and a son of Thyestes. Once the return of the Achaeans' commander from Troy became known, the illegitimate couple decided to murder him. On the very day of his arrival at the palace in Mycenae, after a warm welcome, Clytemnestra murdered him in his bathroom; she also murdered Cassandra, the seer royal princess of Troy, who had accompanied him fully aware of her pitiful end. Another version of the myth has it that **Agamemnon** was killed by **Aegisthus** during the banquet held to honour his return, while **Cassandra** was stabbed by **Clytemnestra**.

Agamemnon's son, **Orestes**, was raised in Phocis with king Strophius, where he was sent by his mother so that he did not watch her disgrace or, in another version, his sister Electra had sent him there to protect him from the murderous couple. Orestes returned eight years after his father's murder to take revenge.

He arrived in **Argos** along with his friend **Pylades**, a son of Strophius, reunited with his beloved sister, **Electra**, and slew first his mother and then her lover. Pursued by the **Erinyes** (the Furies), the dark goddesses of the Under World, who implacably punished mainly matricides, he went at first to Delphi and god **Apollo**, and then to Athens requiring protection. Goddess **Athena** called the court at Arius Pagus, consisting of selected Athenian members and herself being the president, and Orestes was acquitted. The **Erinyes** were appeased by the goddess herself and were changed into good goddesses under the name **Eumenides** (the Gracious ones), settling down in Athens.

Some of them, however, did not agree with Athena's action and kept on pursuing Orestes. To escape them, according to Apollo's advice, he had to bring the most ancient wooden statue of **Artemis** from the **Land of the Tauris** (Scythia) to Attica. Orestes set out for this distant land along with his inseparable friend Pylades. Every foreigner arriving in this land used to be sacrificed in the sacred temple of the goddess where **Iphigenia**, the sister to Orestes, served as a priestess. Upon their arrival, the two friends were captured hostages and taken to the priestess for the sacrifice. When Iphigenia saw her two compatriots, she agreed to kill only one of them and let the other one free to go back home and notify her brother, Orestes, that she is alive so as to take her from the barbarians, who forced her to drive people to slaughter.

Then, Orestes, deeply touched, revealed his identity and his mission and decided for all three of them to leave, taking the wooden statue of the goddess as well. They risked greatly and achieved their goal; when they arrived in Attica, they established a sanctuary in honour of **Artemis** in **Brauron**, where they placed the statue of the goddess. **Orestes** was fortunate to succeed his father to the throne and died at an old age, bitten by a snake. His son, **Tisamenus**, whom he had from his marriage with **Hermione**, the daughter of Menelaus and Helen of Sparta (Helen of Troy), is considered to be the last ruler of the Mycenaeans. After him, the dynasty of the **Atrids** ends.

The Sanctuary of Artemis in Brauron.

THE ODYSSEY

The **Odyssey**, the second great epic by Homer, provides an account of the return journey of Odysseus to his homeland Ithaca, starting with the departure from Troy after its fall and concluding with his arrival in his land and the recovery of his kingdom. He was aware of an oracle stating that his return journey would last ten years and that during those years he was to experience dreadful and innumerable adventures, some of which he would go through successfully and some not.

If the **Iliad** is a heroic war epic, the **Odyssey** is the peaceful epic of the domination over the water element, of adventure and the exploration of everything the man of that era had managed to conquer during the journey of his life. Renowned is the verse of the Homeric Odyssey saying: "he saw the cities of many people and was acquainted with their spirit". The small world he had lived in until then was not sufficient for him and sought to see the world of other peoples and find out about their experiences as well their material and intellectual achievements. After the formation of the cities, there arose the need of communication with other peoples, of the quest for a better place of residence, as well as for the return of the traveller home, bringing along goods his land lacked.

The radical changes that had taken place in the society of the 8th c. B.C. are presented in a wonderful way in Homer's epics. In the Odyssey, the "sea-crossing" ships take him to unknown remote lands so as to acquire a broader knowledge of the world and satisfy his needs. A journey like this ventured Odysseus, this man of **cunning intelligence**, the wise and ingenious Greek of Homer, in order to struggle with the elements of nature, monsters, volcanoes, never seen before supernatural creatures and overpower them. Some of the lands he wandered in are real, some others are imaginary. However, since when the Odyssey was written, it has been considered to be the first written monument of the Greek Geographic science.

From antiquity until modern times, there have been numerous people who, following innumerable theories, have attempted to identify the route of Odysseus' journey and the lands he visited, which is not easy at all. Many cities in the world, being proudly named after him, claim that the hero arrived and lived there.

This journey of Odysseus, whose purpose was to return to his homeland, has become an **ideal** for those who make efforts to achieve similar goals in their life, struggling with the Cyclops and the Laestrygones. It has become a poem, a play and a song by top poets, literary men and musicians throughout the centuries until modern times.

Odysseus fastened on the ram's abdomen in order to get away from the cave of Cyclop Polyphemus; bronze bas-relief lamina from Delphi (605 B.C.). Delphi, Archaeological Museum

THE RETURN OF ODYSSEUS

AT THE LAND OF THE CICONES
AT THE LAND OF THE LOTOPHAGI
AT THE LAND OF THE CYCLOPS

When Odysseus, initially, left Troy on his ships with his companions, he followed Menelaus up to Tenedos. Then he returned and joined Agamemnon. Before long, however, their paths split, as the winds drove Odysseus' ships to the north and landed on the coast of the state of Ismarus, in Thrace, which belonged to the **Cicones**. Odysseus conquered the state, slaying all of its defenders except for the family of **Maron**, a son of Euanthes, who was a priest of Apollo. Maron, being grateful, gave him gold, silver and muscat wine.

The companions of Odysseus, though, fell to feasting and drinking, and the Cicones, assisted by their neighbours, set upon the Hellenes again, forcing Odysseus to leave, after having lost seventy of his companions on the battlefield. They sailed off but a tempest ensued and were carried away southwards by the waves for days until they reached the land of the **Lotophagi** (Lotus-eaters), far from Cythera, in seas unknown.

The Lotophagi were a hospitable race of men. The food, though, they lived on, lotus, made those who tasted it forget about their homeland and wish to stay there forever. Once again, Odysseus had to leave in a rush, not knowing where he was sailing for and, unfortunately, reached the land of the **Cyclops**. They landed on the coast of an isle opposite the harbour of the Cyclops and, the next morning, Odysseus sailed his ship with few of his companions to the coast opposite. There, he saw the cave of **Polyphemus**, a son of **Poseidon** and **Thoosa**, the daughter of Phorcys. Odysseus, with a chosen party of twelve followers, went to the giant's

The blinding of giant Polyphemus by Odysseus; detail from the decoration on the neck of a proto-Attic urn (appr. 670 B.C.). Eleusis, Archaeological Museum

cave who was away to feed his herd and, while his companions wanted to leave straight away, Odysseus preferred to wait for him. In the evening, the Cyclop returned to his cave, discovered them, devoured two of them, sealed the mouth of the cave and fell asleep. The following morning, he ate two more and left with his herd, after having secured the cave in any way possible, so that his hostages did not escape. Then, Odysseus decided to act making use of his cunning intelligence. He found an olive-tree trunk which he creared from its branches, sharpened it to a point, hardened its tip in the embers of a fire and hid it in the dung.

In the evening, when the Cyclop returned, he shut in his herd, milked the sheep and, then, devoured another two of Odysseus' companions. The hero offers him of the wine he was given by Maron to get him drunk. Polyphemus asked for more promising him a present in return. Then, he asked Odysseus for his name and he answered "**outis**", which means "no one". He kept on offering him wine until Polephemus got drunk and fell fast asleep. Wasting no time, Odysseus heated up the olive club in the fire and, along with four companions of his, drove it into the Cyclops single eye. Polyphemus started at the pain and yelled for the help of his fellow Cyclops.

When the others came, they asked him why he was crying out and Polyphemus told them that "no one" had blinded him. Thus, they left offering him no help. In the morning, the blind Cyclop opened his cave to let his herd out. However, Odysseus had tied his companions to the undersides of the strongest of the rams while he had got hold of the neck and the belly of one and, this way, the ones having survived managed to free themselves, board their ships and sail away.

Then Odysseus boasted to Polyphemus his real name "**Cyclop, if anyone asks you who blinded you, tell him: Odysseus, the son of Laertes from Ithaca, did**". Polyphemus, then, raised his arms towards the sky and begged his father, the god of the seas, to torment Odysseus as much as he could and if he was destined to return to his homeland, reach it all alone, after many years, on somebody else's ship and, also, have a lot of pains wait for him in his home. And god Poseidon heard his prayer.

Odysseus leaves the cave of Cyclop Polyphemus fastened on a ram's abdomen; from a black-figured pot of 500 B.C.

The renowned proto-Attic
urn on the neck of which is
depicted Odysseus blinding
Cyclop Polyphemus while
Perseus killing Medusa is
depicted on its body
(appr. 670 B.C.).
Eleusis, Archaeological
Museum

ON THE ISLAND OF AEOLUS

After the land of the Cyclops, Odysseus' fleet sailed in unknown seas and reached **Aeolis**, a floating island surrounded by bronze walls. There lived **Aeolus**, the son of Hippotes, with his wife and children, six sons and six daughters who he had married to each other so as to keep them close to him.

Aeolus, who ruled the winds at the command of Zeus, welcomed Odysseus and his companions and offered them hospitality for a month. When Odysseus wished to leave, he put all the winds apart from **Zephyrus**, the west wind, in a skinbag, tied it up tightly and gave it to Odysseus under the strict order not to open it during the journey. Zephyrus drove them very close to Ithaca after nine days and nights. However, when the hero exhausted from sleeplessness fell to sleep, his companions opened the skinbag thinking that it contained gold. Thus, all winds sprang out together and the storm brought them back to the island of Aeolus.

Being a suppliant, Odysseus will be sent away the worst possible way by Aeolus himself, who asked him to leave his island since the gods hated him so much.

IN THE LAND OF THE LAESTRYGONIANS

Odysseus had to leave the island of Aeolus and sail away in the sea without knowing where they were going. After seven days, they reached the land of the Laestrygonians, located higher above the harbour.

The inhabitants were fierce man-eating giants. Odysseus sent a herald and two of his companions to find out who were the people dwelling there. Upon seeing the foreigners, their king, Antiphanes, devoured one of them and, immediately summoned his people to send the foreigners away. Hurling huge rocks at the ships, which were moored in the harbour, they smashed them all and killed their crews.

Only Odysseus ship and his crew consisting of only forty-five Cephallenes escaped because he had anchored it out of the harbour. Thus, Odysseus loses his fleet and has been left with only one ship and forty-five companions.

ON THE ISLAND OF ENCHANTRESS CIRCE

Next, Odysseus reached **Aeaea**, the island of goddess **Circe** (falcon), a daughter of **Helios** and **Perse**, and a sister of Aeaetes, the king of Colchis, and of Pasiphae. On this island, there was located the palace of Eos (the Dawn), where Helios (the Sun) rose every morning. After three months, the Achaeans decided to walk inland to explore the island. Casting lots, they formed a group, consisting of half the crew with Eurylochus, a relative of Odysseus appointed as their leader, and started the exploration first.

When they reached a gorge, they saw the stone palace of Circe, who lived among various tame animals. **Circe** invited them to her mansion, offered them drinks laced with magic herbs and turned them into pigs.

Eurylochus had stayed behind and, seeing that his companions had not returned in time, he went back to the ships and begged Odysseus to leave. Odysseus, however, did not wish to sail off before he knew what had happened to his men. He took command and went to face the sorceress himself. Then, god Hermes appeared, warned him about had happened and gave him an herb, **moly**, to protect him from her witchery.

Upon meeting him, Circe tried to turn him into a pig, too, but, thanks to the moly, she failed. Recognising Odysseus, she invited him to her bed. He accepted on condition that she freed his shipmates from her spell and restored them to human form, this time younger and better-looking.

Apulian skinbag; its mouth is adorned with Scylla (3rd c. B.C.). Boston, the Museum of Fine Arts

Odysseus and his companions spent almost a year on the island of Circe and had a great time. When the hero told her they wanted to leave, Circe advised him to go to the Under World and ask seer Tiresias for an oracle regarding the way to return to Ithaca. She also guided him on how to treat the deceased he would encounter.

NEKYIA (Necromancy) – THE JOURNEY TO HADES

On the morning of their departure, one of Odysseus' shipmates, Elpenor, having woken up by the hustle and bustle of his companions who were preparing for the journey, was started up and losing his balance fell off the terrace he was sleeping at and got killed. In the fury of the preparations, no one took notice and, sailing off, they left him unburied. Circe sent them the wind Boreus (north) to ease their journey, the whole day in the sea and then in **Oceanus**. In the evening, they reached beyond Oceanus and landed in the land of the **Cimmerians**, where there was always night.

According to Circe's guidelines, Odysseus walked along the flow of the Oceanus, the long river girdling the earth, as the ancient Greeks believed, and reached the entrance to the Hades. There, he opened up a pit, made a libation to the dead, and killed a black ram and a black ewe, waiting for the soul of **Tiresias** to appear. Countless were the souls of the dead that gathered to drink blood from the pit, Odysseus, however, did not let them as he wanted to hear Tiresias first.

The soul of Elpenor, also, appeared and, as he had not been buried, he could speak without having drunk blood first; he asked not to forget to bury him when they returned to the island of Circe so that his soul rested.

A little later, Tiresias appeared, drank from the libation blood and prophesised what the hero had to expect and how he could protect himself until he arrived in Ithaca. He also revealed that Poseidon was enraged with him and would make his return difficult. He, and his companions, would return if, upon reaching **Thrinacia**, did not touch the cattle and the sheep of **Helios**. In case, nevertheless, they killed even one of the animals, they would all perish, whereas the hero, after many years and sufferings, he was to return all alone and on a foreign ship to his homeland, where more sufferings were in stock for him from the suitors of his wife, Penelope.

Tiresias added that, when he succeeded in destroying them, again, he would set out on his own with an oar on his shoulders to meet people who did not know the nature of what he was carrying. Then, he would have to stick the oar into the earth and sacrifice a bull and a boar to Poseidon. Afterwards, he would be able to return to his island, sacrifice to all the gods and live the rest of his long life in peace.

Tiresias spoke and left, and then Odysseus let the rest of the dead talk to him, after drinking the blood of the sacrifice. First spoke his mother, **Andiclea**, who had died during his absence. She told him everything about the situation with the suitors in his palace, the fact that Penelope was faithful to him, that his son Telemachus managed their property and that his father lived isolated, far from everyone, in the countryside.

Next he was spoken to by many women who belonged to the previous generation, such as **Alcmene**, the mother of Heracles, **Tyro**, the daughter of Salmoneus, **Iocasta**, the mother and wife of Oedipus, **Phaedra**, **Ariadne** and many others.

Afterwards, the soul of **Agamemnon** came and described the dreadful scene of his murder and asked him about his son, Orestes, but Odysseus did not know. There followed the soul

Pluto; detail from the fresco in the small tomb of
Vergina (4th c. B.C.).
Vergina, the Royal Tombs

of **Achilles**, along with the souls of his friends, **Patroclus**, **Antilochus** and Telamonian **Aeas**. Achilles asked him about his son, **Neoptolemus**, and his accomplishments during the Trojan War, and he left satisfied with what he had heard from Odysseus. Only Aeas did remain at a distance, still angry over not having been given Achilles' weapons. The hero also saw **Minos** making judgements among the deceased, **Orion** chasing **Tityos**, **Tantalus** and Sisyphus being eternally tortured. Odysseus was frightened by the great number of souls that had gathered around him and ran away to find his companions. They rushed to their ship and, with fair winds, they sailed along the flow of the Oceanus, out to the Sea and, before sunrise, they were back at the island of Circe.

Black-figured wide cup with a representation of the escape of Odysseus from the cave of Polyphemus (500 B.C.). Athens, the Cerameicos Museum

FROM THE SIRENS TO THE ISLAND OF CALYPSO

When the sun rose at the island of Circe, Odysseus saw to **Elpenor's** burial, who, after he was burnt along with his weapons on the beach, he was buried and put up a tomb. On top of it they fixed an oar so as to be seen by the travellers past the island. Circe gave them supplies for the voyage, as well as her last advice concerning the way to escape the dangers lurking during their journey.

At dawn the next day, they sailed off with a fair wind and, the first island they encountered was the island of the **Sirens**. The Sirens were two daemonic sisters whose sweet singing bewitched the travellers passing by. So much so, that they stayed there, forgetful of everything else, until they died.

Warned by Circe, Odysseus stopped his companions' ears with wax so that they could not hear, and he lashed himself on the mast so as to be able to listen to the song by the Sirens without risking his breaking loose and staying with them. He also ordered his shipmates to ignore his plead to untie him; instead, he told them to tie him even more tightly.

As they approached closer, Odysseus heard them call him by his name to stay with them. Their alluring song seduced his mind and the only thing he craved was to stay with them forever. However, no matter how much he begged his companions to untie him, they paid no

Odysseus' ship sailing past the rock of the Sirens; from the illustrations on a red-figured pitcher (appr. 475 B.C.). London, the British Museum

attention. More and more tightly lashed on the mast, Odysseus overcame the danger and left the island of the Sirens behind without any losses.

It is said that the Sirens threw themselves into the sea and drowned because, eventually, they failed to bewitch the hero.

On his way, Odysseus had to choose between two routes. The first was leading to the **Plangtae Rocks**, two huge rocks floating on the sea and regularly clinging to each other, thus smashing the ships attempting to sail through. Only **Argo** did escape on her way back from Colchis.

The second route led between two other rocks, in one of which there nested a horrible monster **Scylla** and in the opposite one **Charybdes** was hiding. Charybdes swallowed the sea in a whirpool three times during the day and then spat it up again. Woe in the ship sailing through the moment the whirpool was created by Charybdes swallowing the sea.

Circe's advice was to avoid the Plangtae Rocks and Charybdes as they would all, definitely, perish, and prefer the passage from the rock of Scylla where they would lose only six of their companions. Odysseus followed that route, hoping they would lose no one of his crew. However, they sailed very close to the rock the moment when Charybdes was swallowing the sea.

Then, Scylla leapt and grabbed six of the men devouring them with each of her six heads. This monster, having twelve legs, six heads and the voice of a barking puppy, used to stretch her long necks and feed on huge fish or some of the crew of ships sailing close to her rock. Having experienced so much slaying and suffering, even the Cyclop devouring his companions, Odysseus will remember Scylla's bad turn as long as he lives.

ON THRINACIA - THE ISLAND OF HELIOS

After the loss of their companions and the horrible sight of Scylla, rowing fast, they reached the island of **Thrinacia**, where the cattle of Helios grazed. Warned by Tiresias and Circe, Odysseus wanted to avoid landing there.

His shipmates, though, were so exhausted that he had to give in, after having them take

Gorgon (500 B.C.).
Athens, National Archaeological
Museum

an oath that they would not touch the sacred animals he gave in.

The bad weather conditions following their arrival maintained for a month and the supplies Circe had provided them with ran out, therefore, their hunger forced them to break their oath and slaughter the fattest of the cattle, while Odysseus was away in order to pray.

When **Helios** saw what had happened, he asked Zeus for their punishment. Under the threat that he would descend and shed light to the Under World, Zeus promised him to cast a thunderbolt onto the ship of Odysseus.

Seven days later, the wind calmed and the ship sailed away. Once the island was out of their sight, keeping his word Zeus caused heavy sea and, casting thunderbolts, split up the ship, killing those who had been disrespectful to Helios.

Only Odysseus did survive, as he had not taken part in the **"sin"** of his companions and had not eaten the meat from the sacred cattle. Holding on his ship's wreckage and struggling with the waves, he arrived back, at the rock of Charybdes.

There, hanging from a wild fig tree outside the monster's lair, he seized the opportunity when the water with the ship's wreckage began to rise and grabbed some of it; holding on to it, he escaped and had to struggle the fury of the sea and the gods for nine days until the wild waves washed him ashore on the island of Nymph **Calypso**, known as **Ogygia**.

God Hermes as a psycho pomp is leading a young woman, dead Myrine, across the river Acheron. Detail from a marble lecythus (appr. 430-420 B.C.).
Athens, National Archaeological Museum

ON THE ISLAND OF CALYPSO

Nymph **Calypso** (Veiled) was an immortal daughter of Atlas and dwelled in an exquisite cave, isolated from the rest of the gods, on a remote island, **Ogygia**. When Zeus sent Odysseus to her island, Calypso welcomed the shipwrecked hero, helped him recover and loved him so much that she kept him with her for seven years.

The beauty and the kindness of the Nymph, initially, charmed Odysseus, but, after a few years, he began to feel nolstagic for **Ithaca** and **Penelope**. Calypso begged him to stay with her promising him immortality, but, in vain. Eventually, there came the time the gods had defined for the hero to return to Ithaca.

On a morning when **Poseidon**, the hero's worst enemy, was away in the land of the **Ethiops**, urged by Athena and with the consent of the rest of the gods, Zeus sent **Hermes** to Calypso to order her to release Odysseus, as he was destined to see his homeland again. The Nymph was upset and, although she complained to Hermes, she agreed to help him leave. Then, Odysseus built a raft with her help and, in four days, he sailed off bidding her farewell forever.

For seventeen days and nights, Odysseus sailed and, on the eighteenth, he saw the mountains of **Scheria**, the island of the **Phaeacians** (Corfu), ahead in the horizon. However, his sufferings would not end there. As soon as Poseidon returned from Ethiopa, he saw him all alone on the raft in the vast sea and decided to punish him once again for what he had caused to Polyphemus. Stirring the sea with his trident, he smashed the hero's raft and threw him off into the wild sea. Fortunately, a sea deity, Leucothea, took pity on him and gave him her hangkerchief to wind around his chest so as not to drown.

Odysseus struggled with the waves for two more days and nights until, in the end, aided by Athena, who calmed down the winds when Poseidon had gone back to his palace in Aegae, he managed to swim, reach the coast of Scheria and step on dry land.

ON THE ISLAND OF THE PHAEACIANS

The **Phaeacians** inhabiting **Scheria**, that is modern Corfu, was a peaceful people, particularly loved by the gods. They also were brilliant seamen and used to help the shipwrecked return home.

Their first king was **Nausithous**, a son of Poseidon and Periboea, a daughter of **Eurymedon**, the king of the Giants. At first, the Phaeacians lived in **Hyperia**, close to the Cyclops. As they could not stand them as neighbours, they moved to **Scheria** and built a wonderful city there.

When Odysseus was washed ashore on their island, there ruled **Alcinous**, the son of Nausithous, who had married **Arete**, the daughter of **Rhexenor**, the second son of Nausithous. They had five children, four sons and one daughter, **Nausicaa**.

Zeus had assigned Athena to aid Odysseus. Thus, the goddess came to Nausicaa's dream and exhorted her to go to the river and wash her clothes. The young woman and her girlfriends met Odysseus there and, after giving him food and clothes, Nausicaa urged him to present himself as a suppliant to her mother and ask for her help telling her his story. Following her advice, Odysseus presented himself in the palace, where he impressed everyone.

Alcinous promised him to equip a ship and send him to his homeland. To honour him, he organised a great banquet, during which singer **Demodicus** sang an episode of the Trojan War, which deeply moved Odysseus. Tears also filled his eyes at the farewell dinner, when the singer chanted the story of the **Trojan horse**. Seeing his guest so moved, Alcinous asked to tell him who he was. Odysseus revealed his identity and narrated his adventures in detail.

The next day, the Phaeacians offered him many gifts and saw him to the ship that would take him home, and then he fell asleep. While still sleeping, they laid him, along with the gifts, down on the shore of Ithaca, and left.

ODYSSEUS IN ITHACA

When Odysseus woke up, he did not realise he was in Ithaca at first. Goddess Athena appeared before him, though, calmed him down and helped him hide the gifts he had been given by the Phaeacians in a cave belonging to the Nymphs.

Afterwards, she guised him as an old beggar and advised him to go and stay in the pigsty of his loyal swineherd Eumaeus, to avoid being recognised. The goddess told him about what had been going on in his palace, that is, the disgraceful conduct of the suitors and Penelope's struggle to remain faithful to him. There had been a long time since everyone on Ithaca had started to believe that Odysseus would never return to his homeland, as many years had gone by since the war was over.

The palace was crowded with young men of noble origin, who pushed Penelope to become

The fair punishment of the suitors by Odysseus, who is about to shoot his arrow at them, while they are trying to defend themselves from their settees of the banquet; from the decoration of a red-figured vessel (appr. 450 B.C.). New York, the Metropolitan Museum

Odysseus as a humble beggar is approaching Penelope sitting in deep sorrow. Behind her, there stands a young man, probably Telemachus, as well as two elderly men, perhaps Laertes and his swineherd Eumaeus, who are watching them; earthenware Melian bas-relief (appr. 460-450 B.C.).

their wife. To gain time, she declared that she would choose a husband after she had finished weaving a burial shroud for her father-in-law, elderly Laertes.

However, for three years, she wove during the day and undid part of the shroud at night, until one of her maidens revealed what was going on to the suitors. From then on, all the suitors gathered in the palace to press her to decide and, there, they ate and drank and feasted spending Odysseus property, whose legal heir was his son **Telemachus**.

Intending to devise a plot to perish the suitors, the goddess sent Odysseus first to Eumaeos, who had remained loyal to his master. Unaware of the foreigner's identity, Eumaeus talked to the old beggar and accused the suitors of spending the royal property and pushing Penelope to remarry. Telemachus also arrived at Eumaeus' hut, having just returned from Pylos. Then, Athena changed Odysseus into his noble figure; father and son acknowledged each other and assisted by Eumaeus and Philoetius, another loyal herdsman, they devised the plan of the suitors' destruction.

According to the plan, Odysseus went to the palace as a beggar. No one recognised him but for his dog, **Argus**, which died right afterwards. The suitors, unaware, unwelcomed the beggar and they treated him in an insulting and humiliating way. On the contrary, Penelope invited him to tell her whether he had heard of her husband and asked her maidens to attend on the stranger. Then, **Euryclea**, the elderly and loyal housekeeper in the palace, recognised Odysseus, because she saw an old scar, caused by a boar on Parnassus, while she was washing his feet. Odysseus persuaded her not to tell anyone and keep his arrival a secret.

At night, father and son, aided by Athena, collected all the weapons found in the palace. The goddess herself infused Penelope the idea of organising an arrow shooting contest with the promise to marry whoever could bend her husband's rigid bow and shoot an arrow through twelve shafts fixed in a row. All the suitors tried but they failed to merely hook the string of the bow. Due to Telemachus insisting on the stranger having a shot, the bow came to Odysseus' hands, much to the suitors' objections. Meanwhile, Penelope had withdrawn and the palace doors were shut. Odysseus checked the bow and after a thunder, signalling the consent of Zeus, he easily achieved the goal and, afterwards, he revealed his identity.

Before the suitors realised what was happening, they dropped dead by Odysseus who, with the help of Telemachus and the two herdsmen as well as with Athena's support, cleared the profane situation they had settled in his house. As well as them, the servants and the maidens who had supported the suitors will also be punished.

Loyal Euryclea broke the news of Odysseus' return to Penelope, but she was cautious and asked him to tell her the secret of their wedding- chamber. Reassured by his reply, united after twenty years, they spent the night, which lasted longer than usual, as Athena did not allow Eos to bring out the light of the day.

The next morning, Odysseus looked for his father, who lived isolated in his estate with his tender **Dolius** and his family. Laertes recognised him since Odysseus named every single tree he had given him when he was young.

However, the news of the suitors' murder had spread in the city and their relatives gathered to take revenge. Fortunately, due to Athena's intervention, they reconciled and took an oath of loyalty to Odysseus.

In the Homeric Odyssey, the long voyage of Odysseus ends upon his return to Ithaca. The hero everyone believed perished in foreign lands, after plenty of sufferings as well as numerous accomplishments, returns to his homeland; in other words, he materialises his major aspiration, even if this happens twenty years after his departure for Troy.

Ithaca.

THE RETURN OF ODYSSEUS IN ITHACA

10

HADRIATIC SEA

8   9

TYRRHENIAN SEA

11

16

IONIAN SEA

7 12

13

6

14

17

15

4

5

MEDITERRANEAN SEA

N
W ← → E
S

NORTH AFRICA

BLACK SEA

ASIA MINOR

AEGEAN SEA

2 1

1. TROY
2. TENEDOS
3. ISMAROS - LAND OF CICONES
4. MALEAS
5. THE LAND OF LOTUS-EATERS
6. THE LAND OF CYCLOPES
7. THE ISLAND OF AEOLUS
8. THE LAND OF LAESTRYGONES
9. AEAEA - CIRCE'S ISLAND
10. LAND OF THE DEAD
11. THE ISLAND OF THE SIRENS
12. SKYLLA AND CHARYBDIS
13. «PLANGTES» STONES
14. THRINACIA - THE ISLAND OF HELIOS
15. OGYGIA - THE ISLAND OF CALYPSO
16. SCHERIA - THE ISLAND
      OF THE PHAIACIANS
17. ITHACA

Publication editor: Evangelia Chyti

Translation: Eleni Petropoulou

Creative - Image processing: Ledy Griva

Photos: Studio Kontos-Photostock

CTP - Printing - Binding: EM-ES PRESS S.A.

© copyright 2018 worldwide:
DIM. PAPADIMAS Reg't Co.
56-58 Char. Trikoupi St., Athens 106 80 Tel.: (++30) 210 3640235, 210 3645830
Fax: (++30) 210 3636001
e-mail: papa-ekd@otenet.gr

ISBN 978-960-6791-72-7